D1562895

Black Liberation in Kentucky

Black Liberation in Kentucky

EMANCIPATION AND
FREEDOM, 1862-1884

Victor B. Howard

THE UNIVERSITY PRESS OF KENTUCKY

Copyright © 1983 by The University Press of Kentucky

Scholarly publisher for the Commonwealth,
serving Bellarmine College, Berea College, Centre
College of Kentucky, Eastern Kentucky University
The Filson Club, Georgetown College, Kentucky
Historical Society, Kentucky State University,
Morehead State University, Murray State University,
Northern Kentucky University, Transylvania University,
University of Kentucky, University of Louisville,
and Western Kentucky University.

Editorial and Sales Offices: Lexington, Kentucky 40506-0024

Library of Congress Cataloging in Publication Data
Howard, Victor B.
  Black liberation in Kentucky.

  Bibliography: p.
  Includes index.
  1. Afro-Americans—Kentucky—History—19th century.
2. Reconstruction—Kentucky. 3. Kentucky—History—
Civil War, 1861–1865. 4 Kentucky—Race relations.
I. Title.
E185.93.K3H68   1983   976.9′00496073   82-40461
ISBN 0-8131-1433-0

Contents

To my mother and father

Preface

ELEVEN YEARS AGO I began research on the material that has been incorporated in this book. The quest for source material led me to many libraries. I am indebted to so many people for their help that it is impossible to name all of them.

I express my gratitude to the staff of the Camden-Carroll Library, Morehead State University, particularly to the interlibrary loan librarians, LeMerle Bentley and Carol Nutter. I owe a debt of gratitude to the Margaret I. King Library of the University of Kentucky, the Filson Club Library, the Public Library of Lexington, Kentucky, the Kentucky Historical Society Library, the Cincinnati Historical Society, the libraries of the historical societies of Illinois, Indiana, Wisconsin, Western Reserve, and the University of Michigan. The librarians of the Kentucky Library of Western Kentucky University, the Berea College Library, and the Louisville Public Library rendered useful assistance. Elaine Everly of the National Archives was particularly helpful, and Richard Sommers of the U.S. Army Historical Collection helped me trace down many leads.

I am indebted to James A. Rawley, who read the book at an early stage, and to Stanley Engerman; both offered helpful suggestions. August Meier's perceptive comments led to significant changes in the manuscript. I am also indebted to Eric Christianson, Paul Oberst, Lawrence Knowles, and Stuart Sprague, who gave me the benefit of their expert knowledge on specific questions and problems with which I had to deal. They bear no responsibility for any shortcoming in the book.

The Morehead State University Faculty Research Committee was generous in making grants that helped finance the travel necessary for my research. I thank Dean Alban Wheeler and Sherman Arnett, who made typing assistance available, and Kitty Wilson, Carolyn Hamilton, and Debbie Fouch, who typed the manuscript. Through many years and drafts, Wilma B. Howard read all that was written and offered frank and critical suggestions on revision.

The substance of chapters 9, 10, and 11 has been published previously.

The chapter on black testimony was published in the *Journal of Negro History* in April 1973; the chapter on Negro politics was published in the *Register of the Kentucky Historical Society,* April 1974; and the chapter on black education was published in an earlier form in the *Journal of Negro Education,* summer 1977. They are included here by permission of the original publishers.

Introduction

NO HISTORIAN to date has attempted to record the experience of blacks in Kentucky during the Civil War and Reconstruction, with the result that society has never been depicted as it really existed in the state at that time. In trying to correct this flaw, I have sought to write not an exclusively black chronicle, because such a work would distort the past as much as a book concerned solely with white people, but rather an integrated history. I have, in other words, tried to tell the story of *all* the people of Kentucky during the Civil War and Readjustment.

Throughout most of the antebellum period, the antislavery advocates in the North openly predicted that if slavery were abolished in the South, Kentucky would lead the way by taking legislative action. The states of the lower South were uneasy because they feared that Kentucky was not loyal to the Southern institution. In 1833 the Kentucky legislature passed the Non-Importation Act, which prohibited the importation of slaves into Kentucky by purchase. Kentucky and Arkansas were the only states that did not prohibit slaves from being taught to read, and Kentucky differed from the states farther south by requiring a jury trial for blacks. The Kentucky churches took the lead in the South by keeping the problem of slavery before the people,[1] and various antislavery groups, although their numbers were few, continuously addressed the question. Discussion of the institution, both in the press and in public, was freer in Kentucky than in any other slave state.

When a constitutional convention was called in 1849, the small group of abolitionists made the question of gradual emancipation the chief issue before the delegates.[2] Fearful that popular opposition to slavery would grow, the proslavery forces decided to write into the constitution of 1850 provisions that would place elimination of the institution beyond the reach of a majority.[3] They incorporated in the bill of rights the following statement: "The right of property is before and higher than any constitutional sanction, and the right of the owner of a slave to his property is the same and as inviolate as the right of the owner of any property whatsoever."[4] It was also provided that before a convention could be called to change the constitution, a referendum must be carried in two consecutive elections. Thus a period of four years could be required to change the organic laws of the state. This stricture hindered the more liberal citizens of Kentucky in their efforts to abolish slavery, and individuals who looked to the federal government for relief were opposed by others who were jealous of state sovereignty.[5] Many liberal leaders, disillusioned, left the state;[6] Silas Woodson, who had been the most outspoken opponent of slavery at the constitutional convention of 1849, migrated to Missouri and became its governor in 1872. In 1860, while Maryland had only 87,189 slaves and Missouri 114,931, Kentucky's slaves numbered 225,483. Only Virginia and Georgia had more slaveholders than Kentucky.[7] When the Thirteenth Amendment was adopted by Congress, legal slavery existed only in Kentucky and Delaware.

Still, by the end of 1863, slavery in the state had been considerably undermined. Its disintegration started shortly after massive troop movements began across Kentucky; with or without the army's consent, slaves rushed to join the Union ranks in large numbers. Soldiers, disregarding military orders that slavery should be left alone, aided the runaways. Although the blacks acted with restraint and fought bondage chiefly by passive resistance, their disruptions forced Lincoln to change his border-state policy. It was no longer possible to support the antebellum order in Kentucky, as the president had sought to do, and the effort to secure gradual emancipation with compensation had proved unsuccessful. Lincoln felt compelled to issue the Emancipation Proclamation.

The initiative taken by large numbers of blacks thus lay at the heart of slavery's decline in Kentucky; blacks recognized in the war an opportunity to lessen their burdens, and they began to take advantage of the situation almost as soon as the conflict started. As slavery collapsed, the blacks moved to the cities or created communities on the outskirts of county seats. Wages earned by labor or from army service during the Civil War were translated in time into institutionalized wealth in the form of schools, churches, fraternities, and small businesses such as boardinghouses and barber shops. The developing middle class supplied leadership in the struggle for equal rights and suffrage.[8]

When W. E. Woodward published his biography *Meet General Grant* in 1928, he observed that "the American Negroes are the only people in the history of the world . . . [who] ever became free without any effort of their own."[9] The statement went unchallenged at the time, as it probably would not today, but in any case it is certainly not true of the blacks of Kentucky. As the following pages show, Kentucky's slaves participated in the drama from the beginning, refusing to continue in bondage and proving themselves accomplished actors destined to play a critical role in the Civil War.

CHAPTER ONE

Kentucky Responds to War

JOHN BROWN'S RAID on Harpers Ferry in 1859 called into question the ability of the South to prevent a slave revolt and so helped push the region into civil war. Many Southerners believed they were "living above a loaded mine in which the negro slaves were the powder, the abolitionists the spark, and the free negroes the fuse."[1] As a border state, Kentucky was even more agitated by the fear of abolitionist-led slave uprisings than were the Gulf states, and the Republican victory in the national election of 1860 aroused new anxieties. Regardless of the state's ultimate position in the division of the Union, the distrust of the North in connection with the institution of slavery created problems that eventually distorted Kentucky's natural inclinations.[2]

In the early months of the crisis and war, the drama in Kentucky was shaped by three groups: the federal administration and Abraham Lincoln, the white community, and the slaves. When the lower South began to secede, local statesmen made frantic efforts to settle the sectional controversy by compromise, but their most ingenious and well-conceived plans failed.[3] They then turned their efforts toward keeping their own state in the Union. John Brown's Raid had strengthened pro-Southern sympathy in Kentucky, but Lincoln acted promptly to check such sentiment. Securing the border states became a major objective of the federal administration during the first year of the war, and Kentucky remained the keystone of Lincoln's policy of continuous appeasement.[4] In his inaugural address in March 1861, the president assured the South that he did not aim, "directly or indirectly, to interfere with the institutions of slavery."[5] Since Kentucky's governor was a Confederate sympathizer, the Union supporters agreed that the state should be neutral in order to maintain unity—but neutrality proved impractical and did not last the year.

Kentucky masters made concerted efforts to withhold from the slaves information about the issues dividing the nation, but the blacks inevitably gleaned news and spent hours discussing the war's effect on the institution of slavery. They eavesdropped when whites held council, and they sometimes induced literate yeomen to read to them about the war. In Simpsonville, for example, Elijah Marrs had the task of going to town to pick up the mail for his master. As he could read newspapers addressed to his owner, he kept the other slaves in the neighborhood informed.[6] During his tour through Kentucky in the summer of 1861, Allan Pinkerton conversed with a Bowling Green slaveholder about the knowlege blacks had acquired concerning the war. "There has been so much talk about the matter all through the State that the niggers know as much about it as we do . . . and too much for our safety and peace of mind," concluded the master. A Crittenden County slaveholder wrote a friend that the blacks were "so free" and considered slavery "such a sin" that owners would be better off if the slaves were all sold to the South.[7]

From April to September the secessionists in Kentucky argued publicly that the North was making war on the South to abolish slavery. If they failed to convince the Unionists in Kentucky, they made ready converts of their unobserved audience among the slaves. Although the Kentucky Unionists in public insisted that the war was being fought to preserve the Union, in private conversation at the supper table and with visitors during the evening, they confessed that slavery would surely be destroyed if the war continued for any length of time. Their domestic servants viewed their private pronouncements as proof that, as the blacks had hoped, the conflict was a war of liberation.

After Kentucky entered the war on the side of the Union, slaves began to express themselves openly. When the Fourteenth Ohio Infantry Regiment moved into Frankfort late in September, the blacks turned out en masse.[8] One night in New Castle during the winter of 1861, a group of forty to sixty blacks was engaged in killing hogs. After completing their chores they paraded through the streets for approximately two hours singing political songs and shouting for Lincoln. Particularly unusual and disorderly demonstrations took place in front of the dwellings of one or two citizens who were prominent advocates of states' rights.[9]

Before the war some slaves had developed a strong sense of self-esteem and had rejected the concept of slavery but concealed their views to avoid trouble. A large number believed that God had foreordained a millennial destruction of servitude during their lifetime, and the Civil War seemed to be the time and the Union army the instrument for the providential deliverance. As the soldiers of the Eighth Infantry Regiment of Kentucky steamed up the Cumberland River early in 1862, they observed approximately fifty slaves dancing on the shore as their leader sang:

O, praise and tanks! de Lord he come
To set de people free
An' massa tink it day of doom,
An' we of jubilee.[10]

The chaplain of the Third Minnesota Regiment found the slaves at Fort Heiman full of hope and anticipation for their deliverance from slavery by God. As they sang in their religious meetings he scribbled down parts of their hymns: "Oh Cannan Sweet Cannan, I boun for de lan' of Cannan" and "Dah's a better day commin in de army of de Lord."[11]

The progress of events so loosened the bonds of servitude that large numbers of slaves sought freedom north of the Ohio River. A soldier of the Seventy-second Indiana Infantry Regiment stationed in Southern Kentucky in 1861 asked a slave why he did not run away. The black explained that it was a thousand miles to the Ohio River, that the stream was ten miles wide, that there were terrible men with vicious dogs to catch or shoot every slave who crossed, and that Canada was twenty thousand miles from the Ohio. The soldier encouraged the black by informing him that the Ohio River could be reached on foot in two nights' travel. An informed observer in Owensboro believed that the number of slaves crossing the Ohio in a four-month period in 1861 was as great as the number making the journey during the first half of the century.[12]

The chief attraction for the slave, however, seemed to be the Union army camps. The nucleus of a black community existed in the army from the beginning. Many Union officers from Kentucky took their personal servants with them when they entered service, and a considerable number of officers from the Midwest, particularly from Illinois, hired free blacks as servants when they enlisted.[13] At first the slaves who sought out Union camps came singly from adjoining farms after striking up an acquaintance with the soldiers. By the end of 1861, however, they had begun to enter the Union lines in large groups. A correspondent from the camp at Paducah asserted that each company in the regiment employed five or six blacks, and the number was growing by night and day. The slaves soon learned that they would be more readily received if they reported that they were free blacks or that their masters were Confederates. To the slave it really did not matter whether or not his master was a Union sympathizer; the slave's freedom was just as precious in either case, after all.[14]

Most of the blacks who arrived in the camps early in the war worked as cooks and personal servants, but as the war continued they turned more and more to military labor. Many had a strong desire to be soldiers and lost no opportunity to practice military arts. A correspondent from a camp near Smithland concluded his dispatch with the following statement: "In the rear of our quarters, 'Big Nigger Bill' is drilling the sooty cooks in the school of the soldiery." When a regiment moved farther south, the blacks who had attached themselves to it also marched in formation, often joined by other slaves as the units crossed the countryside.[15]

Although from the beginning all Northern soldiers who came into the state were suspected of being abolitionists, during the first year of the war the Union generals went to considerable lengths to avoid offending the slaveholders of Kentucky. The view of the military administration harmonized with Lincoln's position on Kentucky, but it often varied widely from the army's policy for most other fields of operation. And it also often conflicted with the war measures passed by Congress.[16]

On August 30 Gen. John Frémont, commander of the Department of the West, issued a proclamation freeing all the slaves in Missouri who were owned by persons resisting the United States. The gains the Unionists had made in keeping Kentucky from seceding seemed doomed. Kentuckians feared that the order would have a wider application if it were sustained by Lincoln; the war for the preservation of the Union might now become a war for the extermination of slavery.[17] All of the Kentucky press denounced Frémont's proclamation, and a petition before the state legislature inquired as to the measure's lawfulness and appropriate action that could be taken against it.[18]

Garret Davis, a powerful force among conservative Unionists, wrote Secretary of the Treasury Salmon Chase that the proclamation had had the effect of a "bombshell." It "has greatly disconcerted and I fear scattered us," he lamented.[19] On September 1, Joshua Speed, who had once shared a room with Lincoln in Springfield, Illinois, wrote the president from Louisville: "Our constitution and laws prohibit the emancipation of slaves among us—even in small numbers—it will be a most difficult matter to get our people to submit to it." He reported that there were fears that Frémont's proclamation might cause the slaves in Kentucky to claim their freedom. Two days later Speed wrote Lincoln another letter and informed him that the majority of the Kentucky Unionists would leave the Union party if the proclamation stood. "So fixed is public sentiment in this state against freeing negroes . . . that you had as well attack the freedom of worship in the North or the right of a parent to teach his child to read, as to wage war in a slave state on such a principle," he warned.[20]

Speed next wrote Joseph Holt, a fellow Kentuckian serving as judge advocate general, that several defeats "like that of Bull Run" could be stood better by Kentucky Unionists than Frémont's proclamation "if endorsed by the administration." Speed reported on a meeting of Union leaders with Col. Robert Anderson, commander of the Department of Kentucky, during which all present expressed fears that the Union cause had been seriously weakened. He pleaded with Holt to use whatever influence he had to have the proclamation withdrawn.[21] For his part, Anderson reported to Lincoln that a company of Union volunteers in Kentucky had thrown down their arms and disbanded when they heard of the measure. If Frémont's proclamation was "not immediately disowned and annulled," he warned, Kentucky would be "lost to the Union."[22]

Lincoln did not need to wait to test the response from the border states. Frémont had exceeded his military authority in dealing with far-reaching matters of policy belonging to the federal government. The president asked the general, "in a spirit of caution and not of censure," to revise his proclamation in relation to the liberation of slaves so that it conformed to the congressional act of August 6, 1861, confiscating property used for insurrectionary purposes. Frémont was informed that his action would turn Southern friends against the Union. It would "perhaps ruin our fair prospect for Kentucky," Lincoln added.[23]

Strong-minded and stubborn, Frémont would not budge. In the meantime the strength of the Unionists in Kentucky deteriorated. The states' rights Democrats, meeting in Frankfort on September 10, denounced the proclamation as "a manifest violation of the constitution" and called for "the unqualified condemnation of every citizen."[24] The next day Lincoln ordered Frémont "to change the clause to conform with and not transcend" the action of Congress.[25] A series of letters written on September 12 by Lincoln and Holt, together with Lincoln's order of the previous day, was forwarded to James Speed, the brother of Joshua, for immediate publication to inform Kentuckians that Lincoln had rejected Frémont's proclamation.[26] Several days later, Lincoln confessed that intelligence from Kentucky had convinced him that the very arms he had furnished the state would be turned against the Union government. "I think to lose Kentucky is nearly to lose the whole game," he wrote an Illinois senator. "Kentucky gone, we cannot hold Missouri, nor as I think, Maryland. These all against us, the job on our hands is too large for us. The Kentucky legislature would not budge," Lincoln added, "till that proclamation was modified."[27] The legislators of course appreciated Lincoln's resolution of the Frémont matter, and Dr. T. S. Bell of Louisville, one of the state's most thoroughgoing Unionists, declared: "The President handled that matter with an honesty of purpose, and a good sense that I have never seen surpassed."[28]

Yet Lincoln did not come out of the crisis unscathed. His order caused an uproar among antislavery forces and seriously damaged his standing with the evangelical religious groups.[29] Throughout the North a considerable number of the press had been quick to commend Frémont's measure. James Russell Lowell asked, "How many times are we to save Kentucky and lose our self-respect?"[30] George Hoadley, a future governor of Ohio, privately warned a member of Lincoln's cabinet: "Let Mr. Lincoln, while he is conciliating the contemptible state of Kentucky, a state which ought to have been coerced long ago, bear in mind that they are not wasting their substance to secure the niggers of traitors, but are in war, red-handed war."[31]

Despite all of the criticism from a mounting opposition to slavery in the North, Lincoln had acted correctly. Perhaps nowhere did he display greater tact than in his handling of the situation in Kentucky.[32] Had the presidency been held by a man with less understanding, this pivotal state might have been lost, and the Ohio River might have become the battle line.[33] Nevertheless, the hostility resulting from the suppression of Fremont's proclamation was directed primarily against Kentucky rather than against Lincoln. When this antislavery sentiment became dominant in the government, the consequences for the state would be dire. Slavery was a vital ingredient in the contest: the slaves sensed where their interest lay and would react accordingly.[34] From a military point of view, the quicker the slavery issue was resolved, the sooner it would cease to distract attention from the real question of the war. Since the Confederacy was moving to profit from Frémont's political mistake, Lincoln acted correctly by choosing an immediate political victory instead of a remote military advantage that would come from abolishing slavery and recruiting blacks.

In November, Don Carlos Buell was put in command of the Department of the Ohio, and George McClellan became commander in chief of all Union forces. Two days after his appointment, the latter instructed Buell on the slavery question in Kentucky. McClellan thought that political affairs in the state were probably more important than military matters. "I know that I express the feelings and opinions of the President," he wrote, "when I say that we are fighting only to preserve the integrity of the union and the constitutional authority of the general government. The inhabitants of Kentucky may rely upon it that their domestic institutions will in no manner be interfered with." Buell zealously obeyed McClellan's instructions and faithfully followed Lincoln's program.[35]

Frémont was removed November 2, 1861, but the controversy over the emancipation of slaves had not been resolved. Before the end of November, a new conflict centered on Simon Cameron, secretary of war. On November 13, Col. John Cochrane, a nephew of the abolitionist Gerrit Smith, in a speech to his regiment stationed near Washington took a stand in favor of "the military necessity of unconditional emancipation." Cameron was present and was said to have spoken approvingly of Cochrane's doctrine, which included the arming of slaves against the masters. The event caused great excitement in Kentucky.[36]

On December 1, Cameron issued the annual report of the War Department, and copies were mailed to some of the press before it was sent to the president. The document urged the emancipation and arming of slaves. When Lincoln learned of Cameron's recommendation, he asked the secretary to recall and revise the report, but some of the copies were not returned, and the unrevised recommendations began to appear in the press. Kentucky was again shaken by an outpouring of emotion and inflammatory speeches.[37] A resolution was introduced in the Kentucky legislature calling for an expression of that body on Cameron's proposal, and on December 7, the General Assembly formally approved Lincoln's action in requiring a revision of the report and urging the dismissal of the secretary of war.[38]

Many Northern journals condemned the Kentucky legislature for trying to exercise sovereignty over the federal government, and a correspondent for the *Cincinnati Gazette* expressed the belief that Cameron's removal was engineered by the "neutrality kitchen cabinet" in Kentucky, which "caught the conscience of the king." The path to Washington, he wrote, was "kept warm with the feet of the kitchen cabinet officers."[39]

Until the last half of 1862, Congress rather than the executive took the lead in evolving a program to deal with slavery as a problem relative to the war. The First Confiscation Act, which provided for seizure of all property used for "insurrectionary purposes," was vague as to the manner of forfeiture and never took effect as a general policy of the army, but its adoption was vigorously opposed by the congressmen from Kentucky. After its passage on August 6, 1861, three representatives from Kentucky called on Lincoln to urge him to veto the act. They left in the mistaken belief that the president would do so, but Lincoln knew that a veto would appear to sanction the Confederacy's use of its slaves for military purposes.[40]

In December 1861 a stronger confiscation act was brought before Congress for consideration. The Kentucky delegation led the opposition to this bill, but it passed on July 17, 1862. The act authorized the president "to employ as many persons of African descent as he may deem necessary and proper for the suppression of the rebellion." On the same day that the Second Confiscation Act passed, Congress approved the Militia Act, which authorized the president to employ black soldiers and to emancipate their families.[41] The acts of July 17 gave Lincoln the initiative in liberating slaves, because the new laws had no effect until they were implemented by the president. As the sole architect of the policy of nonintervention in slavery, he did not immediately make use of the provision in the Militia Act to use blacks in military service. On April 15, 1861, when he had called for troops to suppress the rebellion, he had promised "to avoid any . . . interference with property," that is, slavery. Lincoln renewed his pledge in a July 4 message to Congress, but by the end of 1861, he was already in the process of changing his policy and was moving to take the initiative. As early as December 3, 1861, in his annual message to Congress, while discussing the First Confiscation Act of August 6, 1861, he declared: "The Union must be preserved, and hence, all indispensable means must be employed. We should not be in haste to determine that radical and extreme measures, which may reach the loyal as well as the disloyal, are indispensable." Lincoln indicated that if a new confiscation act were proposed, "its propriety would be duly considered."[42]

The president meanwhile adjusted to the quickened pace of congressional antislavery action. Within the framework of border-state strategy, he formulated a policy of compensated emancipation. In his message of March 6, 1862, Lincoln reiterated his caution about radical measures but hinted that they might be indispensable if the war continued. For the time being he asked Congress to pass a joint resolution offering the cooperation of the United States to any state which adopted gradual emancipation of slavery.[43] The resolution was brought directly before the House by a suspension of the rules. "But the Kentucky delegation desired time for consultation" and concluded that it would oppose the resolution. John Crittenden spoke the sentiments of all when he asked why Kentucky should be asked to surrender its "domestic institution" after having given up so much for the Union. The measure passed the House but was put aside for future consideration and adoption in the Senate because the hostility from the border states was so great.[44]

The Kentucky press denounced Lincoln for agitating the question of emancipation, and in the U.S. Senate Garret Davis insisted that Lincoln's proposal was an invitation to a race war. He presented petitions from citizens of Kentucky asking Congress to disregard all schemes for emancipation and to attend to the business of saving the country. A Kentucky correspondent wrote Crittenden that emotions had reached boiling point in the state. "For goodness sake keep those critters off of the niggers—if they go ahead, we shall have trouble in Kentucky," he warned.[45]

On March 11, Lincoln called the border-state delegations to the White House. J. W. Menzies, John Crittenden, and Robert Mallory were among those representing Kentucky. Lincoln disclaimed any intention of injuring the interests of the slave states but noted that the conflict concerning slavery in the border states "was a serious annoyance to him and embarrassing to the progress of the war." The conflict over slavery "kept alive a spirit hostile to the government" and strengthened the hopes of the Confederacy that the border states would eventually unite with them. Lincoln believed that the resolution of the conflict concerning slavery in this part of the Union would shorten the war.[46] The Kentucky delegation went away unconvinced.

Although Lincoln had doubts about the constitutionality of the measure, on April 16 he signed the act abolishing slavery in the District of Columbia.[47] Lincoln believed it unfortunate that the bill did not provide for gradual emancipation and expressed regret that "families would at once be deprived of cooks, stable boys, etc." Showing a callousness curious in someone capable of remarkable humanity, he delayed signing the bill until Charles A. Wickliffe of Kentucky could remove two families of slaves from

Washington so that the law would not apply to them. Then, despite his reservations, the president deliberately moved to more radical measures. A Lexington correspondent for the *Cincinnati Gazette* thought Kentucky Unionists might possibly survive the abolition of slavery in the District of Columbia, but if "the everlasting tinkering of congress upon the slavery question" did not stop, Kentucky would be lost.[48]

On May 9, 1862, Gen. David Hunter of the Department of the South issued a proclamation arming slaves, but the president nullified Hunter's measure before the public was fully aware of it, and there was very little excitement in Kentucky. The border states, however, failed to notice the first signs of a change that indicated an erosion of Lincoln's slave policy and that forecast the program he would adopt in September. In the same document in which he nullified Hunter's proclamation, Lincoln urged the border states to undertake gradual emancipation. "You cannot, if you would, be blind to the signs of the times," he urged.[49]

The border states failed to respond, and on July 12, with more radical measures pending before Congress, Lincoln summoned the border-state congressmen to the White House again. He repeated that in his belief the war would have been substantially shortened if the border states had voted for the resolution in the March message on gradual emancipation. "If the war continues long, as it must . . . , the institution in your states will be extinguished by mere friction and abrasion," he warned.[50] The president reiterated that compensated emancipation would be voluntary and gradual. When a deputation from the western states urged him on August 4 to enlist blacks as soldiers, he refused. The president argued that the nation could not afford to lose Kentucky and that to arm blacks "would turn 50,000 bayonets from the loyal border states against us that were for us."[51] But Lincoln had been moving toward emancipation since July 13.

The progress of the war inevitably focused attention on slavery as the central issue. During the first year of the conflict, Kentuckians had stubbornly refused to see that the Union must embrace antislavery as a war aim. Lincoln was not initially ready to antagonize the border states and tried to check the momentum toward the inevitable by his conservative proposal of gradual, compensated emancipation, but Kentucky's intransigence accelerated the impulse toward a more radical solution of the race question. The president's incremental departure from his original policy of leaving slavery alone, thereby avoiding any alienation of the border states, resulted from the growing antislavery sentiment in the North and the impossibility of barring slaves from the military lines.

CHAPTER TWO

The Army and the Slave

AS THE REGIMENTS from the Midwest moved into Kentucky in the autumn of 1861, the army had little contact with the institution of slavery. Under the threat of severe punishment the men and officers were instructed not to tamper with the slaves.[1] The owners frowned on any effort of the soldiers to converse with the slaves, and the masters warned their slaves to stay away from the army camp. The Thirty-fifth Ohio Infantry had hardly settled into the first camp in Kentucky in September 1861 when orders went out to the officers to send their free black servants back to Ohio.[2]

The Kentucky slaveholders saw the blacks in the army camps as a threat to their control over their slaves. The Confederate sympathizers in Kentucky insisted that the war was being fought to abolish slavery and warned their neighbors that an alliance with the North would ultimately be fatal to the institution. The army went out of its way to prevent any incident that would give the secessionists ammunition for propaganda against the government. Although the Southern sympathizers sometimes made up false accounts of seizure of slaves by soldiers and persisted in stereotyping all soldiers as abolitionists, the army did everything possible to avoid alienating slaveholders and even on occasion guarded the property of secessionists.[3]

The issue was forced, however, by the blacks. News gleaned by eaves-dropping became more exciting during the political campaign of 1860, and the appearance of soldiers in 1861 convinced the slaves that the day of jubilee had arrived.[4] On the first Sunday after the arrival of the troops, the blacks from the whole region usually moved on the army camp. If the officers were determined to conform to orders, the picket lines remained secure for a time, but the blacks persisted. The slaves were motivated not only by the belief in their ultimate deliverance but also by an insatiable curiosity, by an urge to escape the monotony of their daily life, and by the promise of adventure. Under the circumstances a massive influx of blacks was all but inevitable.[5]

The Kentucky slaveholders were their own worst enemy. As a steady chain of soldiers streamed through the countryside, even loyal Kentuckians expressed reservations about having Northern troops on Kentucky soil. On the streetcorners, in the stables, upon the public highways, at the table, and in the public press, citizens daily labored the point that the war was being conducted by abolitionists solely for the purpose of freeing the blacks. The slaves accepted these teachings and believed that their day of redemption would come as soon as the Union army was victorious. Many of them hastened to gain their freedom, as they supposed, by forcing themselves into the army camps.[6]

The standard procedure of the army was to return a slave upon the owner's request. In practice, however, slaves often remained in camp. As late as March 1, 1862, the Louisville correspondent for the *New York Evening Post* lamented "the lack of a great moral principle" in the army. Yet he admitted that Lincoln was "never so universally popular in Illinois" as he was at that time in Kentucky.[7] It might be said that the army never did develop a "moral principle," but a change effected by the slaves and the soldiers had already taken place in the field by March 1862. It was true that few of the soldiers were abolitionists, and many of the Northern troops had no love for the Negroes, but the rank and file of the soldiers, often with the assistance of the lower echelon of officers, greatly damaged slavery in Kentucky and significantly influenced administration policy in the state.[8]

By 1861 opposition to the South had become more widespread in the North, and hostility was directed as much at Kentucky as at the Confederate states. A private in an Ohio regiment stationed at Camp Robinson probably best expressed the feelings of the average soldier in Kentucky. "As for interfering with slavery," Mingo Murray wrote to his parents, "I will not, unless its abolition becomes necessary to purchase victory and peace." Many soldiers believed that the opposition of the border states prevented the use of slaves in all capacities in military service and that success could not be achieved until this obstacle was removed. Others saw slavery as the Achilles' heel of the Confederacy and thought the war could not be brought to an end until the protection of rebel property ended. "Since I have become a soldier I have grown stronger in patriotism," Murray continued, "and if it became necessary for victory, slavery must go."[9]

Patriotic feelings were reinforced by the humanitarianism of the soldiers. The men of the Thirty-fifth Ohio Infantry Regiment faithfully obeyed the regulations in the early days of their sojourn in Kentucky, but when an old, "worn out . . . , and severely crippled" slave entered the lines, the rules went by the board, and he found an attentive audience which the officers did not challenge.[10] After John Beatty had served in Tennessee, his unit returned to Louisville. As he marched through the city on November 30, 1861, Beatty saw a sign inscribed in large black letters: "NEGROES BOUGHT AND SOLD." The novelty of his first trip through Kentucky vanished as Beatty thought, "These signs must come down."[11]

Practical considerations were far more weighty in shaping the soldiers' feelings concerning slavery than philosophical reflections. The troops resented standing guard to keep the slaves out of their lines and protecting slave property while the owner was in the field against them. They equated all slaveholders with secessionists, and so they were convinced that Kentuckians who owned slaves could not be sound Union men. Judson L. Austin of the Nineteenth Michigan Infantry Regiment described a case which seemed to verify the Northern soldiers' feelings. While stationed in the vicinity of Lexington, the men of his outfit were required to secure the farm property and slaves of a rich slaveowner. After they had stood several days of guard duty, the son of the farmer "had the impudence" to tell them that his father was a colonel in the Confederate army. Thomas M. Stevenson, chaplain of the Seventy-eighth Ohio Infantry stationed in Kentucky, was sensitive to the soldiers' complaints. "This thing of guarding rebel property when the owner is in the field fighting us is playing out. That is the sentiment of every private soldier in the army." A soldier of the Twenty-third Wisconsin confirmed the general accuracy of Chaplain Stevenson's conclusions. On October 12, 1862, the Wisconsin soldier wrote his wife: "There is no more protecting of rebel property. . . . that thing has been played out." But in some commands in Kentucky the practice continued until the end of 1862.[12]

Since the assistance of a servant made army life more comfortable and easy, many officers hired a fugitive slave and passed him off as a free black after leaving the vicinity of the owner's residence. The enlisted men found the slaves even more useful and often enticed them with rations, clothing, and a camp life with much leisure. Some of the early blacks taken into the Union regiments with the consent of the commanders had left Confederate units. The first slave hired by the soldiers of the First Ohio Light Artillery was a Confederate general's servant who had come into the Union lines in the autumn of 1861. As the demand for slaves spread through the ranks, niceties of prior ownership were overlooked.[13]

Some Kentuckians who came into the camps looking for their slaves faced a rough reception. At the end of March 1862 a soldier of the First Wisconsin Infantry at Camp Munfordville wrote in his diary: "Mr. Man got drilled thro' camp by Adjt. with big stick." On the march from Lexington to Frankfort in November 1862, the Twenty-third Wisconsin Infantry took a slave into the ranks. His master immediately appeared and, placing a pistol against the slave's head, threatened to blow his brains out unless he returned home. The black agreed to obey the slaveholder, but the colonel of the regiment rode up, took custody of the slave, and informed the master that he would need an order from the general before he could recover his property.[14] During the summer of 1862, while he was in Kentucky, the policy of Col. Hans Christian Heg, commander of the Fifteenth Wisconsin

Infantry Regiment, was to permit the return of a slave to his master only if the black was willing. Perhaps as a consequence, the colonel could write his family: "I have got a good house to live in and plenty of Negroes to wait on me."[15]

In almost all cases in 1861 and early in 1862, the blacks who came into the camps were Kentucky slaves seeking freedom. Fugitives were usually asked about the status of their master. Almost always, often in response to leading questions, the answer was an admission that the master was a Confederate or a Southern sympathizer. Convinced that Kentuckians were secessionists if they were slaveholders, many soldiers placed the stamp of disloyalty on the whole state. A second lieutenant of the Twenty-first Indiana Battery wrote his father from a camp near Paris in October 1862: "In my opinion, Kentucky is a secession state." Another soldier from Indiana wrote his father: "This finds me in the Southern part of Kentucky—Calloway County, in an enemy's land."[16]

The slaves did not always take the initiative by coming into the army camps. Sometimes they were sought out by the soldiers. In October 1861, three soldires of the Forty-ninth Ohio Infantry Regiment were detailed to take prisoners about thirteen miles from the camp on the Bowling Green road. The chaplain went along with them and tried to persuade some blacks to return to the camp with them. During the winter of 1861–1862, it became obvious that the army's policy of keeping the slaves out of the lines had failed in Kentucky. While the soldiers and many officers in the field had earlier pretended to cooperate with the slaveholder or had limited their obstruction, for example requiring deeds of ownership or orders from the provost marshal or commander, by the early months of 1862 they often openly resisted the recovery of slaves. A surgeon attached to the Forty-fourth Indiana Infantry Regiment in Kentucky who had earlier favored returning fugitive slaves to their masters became a kind-hearted humanitarian when a slave pleaded with him for aid in escaping from slavery. The doctor, who had just finished emptying a large box of hospital underwear, ordered the runaway to jump in the box. Then he laid the boards back on the box, and he was busy packing the clothing on top when the master rushed in the room. In May 1862 a conductor at the Louisville railroad depot became suspicious when a Union officer attempted to convince him that three black men who wanted to buy tickets to the North were freedmen from Illinois who had been with the army. The trainman summoned a policeman, who discovered that one of the blacks was a woman disguised as a man. The Louisville authorities made arrangements to return her and another slave to their owner, but a group of soldiers thwarted the attempt. An investigation revealed that Col. J. B. Turchin's adjutant had signed the passes as a favor for a friend.[17]

A slave girl about eighteen years old who had fled into the lines of the

Twenty-second Wisconsin Infantry Regiment stationed in Central Kentucky reported that she had been sold for use in a house of prostitution in Lexington. When the new owner came to the camp, she was hidden by the troops. Later she was dressed in soldier's clothing and was taken out of the state in a wagon loaded with hay. Her passage was paid to Racine, Wisconsin, to prevent her recovery by the owner. After it was learned that three lieutenants of the Forty-first Illinois Regiment in Paducah had, at different times, given up slaves to masters who had reportedly paid them for their service, the members of the regiment addressed to the general a paper expressing their unwillingness to serve with these officers. The colonel of the regiment, however, although voicing sympathy with the feelings of the signers, would not forward the document to the commander. All the officers of the unit were said to have been willing to sign the paper if the lieutenant colonel and the colonel had approved of it.[18]

By the middle of August 1862 most of the Union regiments openly flouted the regulation against interfering with slavery. The exclusive authority of the master over the slave had broken down, and the army was recognized as the only reservoir of power. As an established institution, slavery in Kentucky had ceased to exist and could not be reconstituted with its antebellum vitality, for the blacks would have resisted. Lincoln probably was largely relying on his familiarity with the Kentucky theater of war when he acknowledged on July 1, 1862, "I believe there would be physical resistance" to the reenslavement that could "neither be turned aside by argument, nor driven away by force."[19]

The diaries and letters of the soldiers and the regimental histories and records of the troops from the Midwest who served in Kentucky illustrate the degree to which the orders to keep slaves out of the camps were defied and Kentucky's Fugitive Slave Law was violated. (The 1830 act made it a felony to aid or assist a fugitive, to entice the slave to leave his master, or to conceal him from his owner.) Of the regiments from the Midwest in Kentucky for which there is a record, 93.06 percent violated the order and Kentucky's Fugitive Slave Law (see table on pages 18–19). Only Kentucky's own regiments showed any degree of consistency in adhering to the state law.

In the autumn of 1862 the problem of slaves escaping to the army camps in Kentucky intensified. On August 13, 1862, Kirby Smith's army invaded the state. After the Battle of Richmond, he moved to Lexington and occupied Frankfort two days later, on September 3. By the thirtieth, Braxton Bragg was moving on Bardstown. To counter these actions, Federal forces moved into Kentucky from Middle Tennessee and from north of the Ohio River. Bragg's invasion set the slaves in motion, because they feared they would be carried off to the South. The mass movements of Union troops across the state during and after the invasion provided the opportunity for large numbers of blacks to rush into the Northern lines. The Union troops had seen the extensive use of slaves by the Confederacy in Tennessee and in Kentucky, and the time seemed right for any policy that would weaken the allegiance of the servants to their masters or would induce them to favor the Federal cause and thus to cripple the Confederate armies. With the sentiment of the soldiers now crystallized against servitude, a crisis for the institution of slavery developed in Kentucky.[20]

Both the troops that had returned from Tennessee to engage Bragg and the regiments newly arriving from the Midwest destroyed slavery. The Seventy-seventh Illinois Infantry, which had only recently entered Kentucky, caused a general "exodus of slaves from bondage as they marched from Richmond to Louisville" in November 1862. Wherever blacks appeared along the line of the regiment's march, the soldiers called out an order from the ranks to "fall in," and the slaves in most instances obeyed without reluctance. To such an extent were servants enticed from their legal owners that Gen. S. G. Burbridge was reported to have said that the Seventy-seventh "was an abolitionist regiment and would steal all the niggers in Kentucky if they had a chance to do so."[21] Most regiments were not so aggressive. The action of the 105th Illinois Infantry Regiment on the march from Louisville to Shelbyville was more typical. The troops permitted several slaves to fall into their ranks when the blacks took the initiative, and they were not hindered later in the day when they backed out and left the regiment. On the march from Bowling Green to Nashville, the 127th Indiana Regiment found a multitude of blacks along the way who would eagerly have joined if the officers and men had wanted them. The Kentucky slaveholders blamed the Union soldiers for the damage done to the institution of slavery in Kentucky during the last half of 1862 and the winter of 1862–1863, but Gen. John Logan was closer to the truth when he said: "It is not done by the army, but they [the slaves] are freeing themselves."[22]

Some of the army units in Kentucky were easily aroused by attempts of civilians to seize blacks who were marching with the regiments. As the Eighty-third Kentucky Infantry Regiment moved through Versailles, two townsmen seized at gunpoint a black cook owned by the colonel in the belief that the man was a fugitive. The soldiers fixed bayonets at the order of the major, who told the whites that if they stopped a slave belonging to the regiment "we will destroy your whole town."[23] A handbill inserted in the *Frankfort Yeoman* calling for recruits for a new company of cavalry which would subsist upon the rebels of Kentucky by confiscating, appropriating, and emancipating according to their needs perhaps best indicates the extent to which the army policy in Kentucky had deteriorated by the end of the summer of 1862.[24] Certainly that policy no longer commanded respect.

After President Lincoln issued the preliminary emancipation proclamation in September, there was widespread open resistance to the army's

Regimental Compliance with the Kentucky Slave Law
August 1861 to March 1863

ILLINOIS
Violated
  9th Inf.[a]
  10th Inf.[a]
  19th Inf.[c]
  24th Inf.[c]
  27th Inf.[a]
  34th Inf.[a]
  41st Inf.[a]
  63rd Inf.[a]
  77th Inf.[ab]
  78th Inf.[a]
  79th Inf.[a]
  92nd Inf.[a]
  93rd Inf.[a]
  95th Inf.[a]
  96th Inf.[a]
  97th Inf.[a]
  104th Inf.[ab]
  105th Inf.[c]
  108th Inf.[a]
  112th Inf.[a]
  129th Inf.[c]
Henshaw's Batt.[a]
De Kalb's Horse Art.[a]

INDIANA
Violated
  10th Inf.[bc]
  11th Inf.[c]
  33rd Inf.[b]
  39th Inf.[c]
  44th Inf.[abc]
  70th Inf.[c]
  72nd Inf.[c]
  74th Inf.[ac]
  77th Inf.[b]
  79th Inf.[b]
  84th Inf.[a]
  87th Inf.[a]

INDIANA, (cont'd)
  99th Inf.[a]
  100th Inf.[a]
  127th Inf.[c]
  2nd Cav.[a]
  4th Batt.[c]

KANSAS
Violated
Brown's Sharp-shooters[a]

KENTUCKY
Violated
  83rd Inf.[bc]
Obeyed
  8th Inf.[b]
  16th Inf.[c]
  20th Inf.[c]
  23rd Inf.[bc]
  7th Cav.[c]
  9th Cav.[c]
  10th Inf.[ac]

MICHIGAN
Violated
  1st Inf.[ac]
  9th Inf.[ab]
  18th Inf.[ac]
  19th Inf.[abc]
  22nd Inf.[ac]
  23rd Inf.[ac]
  25th Inf.[ac]
  1st Eng.[a]
Obeyed
  11th Inf.[a]

MINNESOTA
Violated
  3rd Inf.[a]

NEW HAMPSHIRE
Violated
  11th Inf.[c]

OHIO
Violated
  3rd Inf.[b]
  9th Inf.[a]
  14th Inf.[a]
  18th Inf.[a]
  19th Inf.[a]
  21st Inf.[c]
  35th Inf.[b]
  38th Inf.[a]
  41st Inf.[a]
  42nd Inf.[a]
  44th Inf.[a]
  49th Inf.[ac]
  53rd Inf.[a]
  93rd Inf.[a]
  100th Inf.[abc]
  101st Inf.[a]
  102nd Inf.[c]
  103rd Inf.[a]
  104th Inf.[abc]
  105th Inf.[ab]
  111th Inf.[c]
    1st Batt.[b]
    4th Batt.[a]
  Kronkles's Batt[a]
  100th Squirrel Hunters[a]
  1st Lt. Art.[bc]

OHIO, (cont'd)
Obeyed
  2nd Inf.[a]
  19th Inf.[a]
  21st Inf.[b]
  22nd Inf.[a]
  83rd Inf.[a]
  118th Inf.[a]

PENNSYLVANIA
Violated
  79th Inf.[ac]

WISCONSIN
Violated
  1st Inf.[ac]
  6th Inf.[a]
  10th Inf.[c]
  13th Inf.[a]
  14th Inf.[a]
  15th Inf.[c]
  19th Inf.[b]
  21st Inf.[a]
  22nd Inf.[abc]
  23rd Inf.[ac]
  25th Inf.[a]
  27th Inf.[a]
  33rd Inf.[a]
  Foster's Batt.[a]
  Loomis's Batt.[a]

Sources: [a] Newspaper letters. [b] Regimental manuscripts. [c] Manuscript letters and diaries.

Tabulations were based on an examination of the following archives: the National Archives, War College Library, Indiana State Historical Library, Indiana Historical Society Library, University of Illinois Library, Illinois State Historical Library, Chicago Historical Society Library, University of Chicago Library, Wisconsin State Historical Library, University of Michigan Historical Collection, Ohio State Historical Library, Western Reserve Historical Society Library, Rutherford Hayes Library. All the regimental histories in these libraries were examined, and all of the extant newspapers published in Illinois and Wisconsin and most newspapers in Michigan, Indiana, and Ohio. The newspapers were examined for a period from August, 1861 to March, 1863. Approximately 331 Union regiments served in Kentucky.

regulations in the ranks of the regiments from the North that were stationed in Kentucky. The slave problem became an intolerable distraction to the army in the state. Gens. Gordon Granger and Q. A. Gillmore went out of their way to conciliate the people by issuing orders to appease them. The generals listened respectfully and patiently to all sorts of city and village committees and tried unsuccessfully to satisfy them. Explosive tensions developed between the army and citizens in several centers in Kentucky. Lexington, Georgetown, Munfordville, and Lebanon were ripe for violence. In a letter to his wife dated October 24, 1862, Maj. James A. Connolly of the 123rd Illinois Infantry, stationed at Lebanon, expressed the sentiments of a growing number of line officers: "Oh! for an active earnest leader from the free states! One who sees nothing sacred in Negro slavery— one who can say to neutral Kentuckians, 'Get thee behind me, Satan.' One who will . . . drive every cowardly sympathizer out of the state and confiscate his property.[25]

In October 1862, Gen. Green Clay Smith, a Kentuckian, took over command of the First Brigade of the Army of the Ohio. The regiments in his unit had a reputation for harboring slaves. In less than a week after his appointment, Smith ordered Col. Moses Wisner of the Twenty-second Michigan Infantry to allow no slaves within his lines. "Citizens must not be interfered with in the rights of their property," and confiscation could only be initiated by headquarters. "I hope, Colonel, you will see that this order is fully executed," Smith concluded. The Eighteenth Michigan Infantry Regiment was moving into Central Kentucky during the same period, arriving in Lexington on October 22, 1862. As the regiment reached Fayette County, the troops were surprised, and a slave was removed from the ranks. The attempt to seize another failed. Within a few days, the new regiments from the Midwest had Central Kentucky in an uproar. In November, Col. Marc Mundy of the Twenty-third Kentucky Infantry Regiment wrote Lincoln that the Eighteenth Michigan was holding no fewer than twenty-five slaves belonging to himself and to loyal neighbors. The Michigan commander refused to turn the slaves out of his lines, justifying his action by the preliminary emancipation proclamation and the new articles of war. A colonel of another Kentucky regiment secured a writ of replevin from the Fayette County Court to reclaim the slaves, and the Michigan infantry used force of arms to prevent the sheriff from executing the writ. On November 15 the colonel of the Eighteenth Michigan Regiment was arrested, and his sword was taken from him by orders of the commanding general because he refused to give up slaves who came into his lines. The Nineteenth Michigan Infantry Regiment was also stationed near Lexington, and by November it had sheltered several slaves in its camp. A white man chased one of the slaves sent to pump water, and a sergeant with four men returned to the pump with the black, seeking to protect him. When they came back to the camp, they found three whites there to claim the slave. With the tacit consent of the colonel, the soldiers and the black defied the whites.[26]

The citizens of Lexington were furious. A protest meeting was held, and resolutions condemning the action of the regiment were passed with only one dissenting vote. A committee of three presented the grievances to General Granger, commander of the District of Central Kentucky, and requested that he furnish the committee with the number and names of the slaves detained in the various regiments. The committee also wished to know if the army in Kentucky intended to override the civil law of the state. Granger referred the communication to Gen. H. G. Wright, commander of the Army of the Ohio. Wright assured Granger and the committee that the army would not violate any Kentucky law that did not contravene the laws of Congress. He denied the request that he furnish a list of the names of the blacks who were with the regiments, since, he said, the meeting had set itself up as a court of inquiry. The slaveowners of Fayette County were less than satisfied. The editor of the *Lexington Observer and Reporter* complained that Wright had said "nothing to commit" himself on the vital question of army resistance to the recapture of slaves.[27]

The reason for Wright's failure to take a stand was the abdication of positive leadership on the slavery problem by Gen. H. W. Halleck, commander in chief in Washington. During October and November 1862, Granger forwarded to Halleck through Wright a number of complaints from the citizens of Central Kentucky charging that soliders and officers were kidnapping slaves out of the lines. Halleck's answer indicated that there was evidence of a policy change under way in Kentucky, but he respectfully referred Wright to the laws of Congress and the president's proclamation. Wright was left entirely on his own as to the interpretation of these measures and their application to the state.[28]

The most serious dilemma on the slavery question which faced the Army of the Ohio was the conflict concerning the army's policy in Kentucky between General Gillmore and Col. William L. Utley of the Twenty-second Wisconsin Infantry. In October, Gillmore issued General Orders No. 5 requiring that all contraband be left behind in Northern Kentucky when the division moved forward the next day. As the Twenty-second Wisconsin marched out of Camp Wells, Williamstown, the next day, the soldiers concealed two black youths whose owner was searching the ranks for his slaves. Three days later when the division established camp near George-town, Gillmore ordered Utley to send four slaves in his regiment, belonging to loyal citizens, to the general's quarters. Utley and the regimental officers later insisted that the owners of the slaves were notorious Confederate sympathizers who lived near Camp Wells. Utley's view of Union support in Kentucky, however, was extreme. He believed there was "no such thing as unionism in Kentucky." At the time Gillmore ordered the delivery of the slaves, there were at least eight or ten slaves in the regiment. The colonel refused to deliver them on the grounds that the request was contrary to the act of March 13, 1862, and the president's preliminary declaration of emancipation. On October 22, Gillmore issued General Orders No. 9, announcing that the practice of enticing slaves into the lines had become an evil of such magnitude as to demand an immediate remedy. He asked the guards and pickets to refuse admittance of contraband into the lines. All slaves within the lines were to be taken at once to the quartermaster. Gillmore defended his order as "fully justified by law" and "eminently politic," and he reported that although it was opposed by many at first, most eventually accepted it.[29]

Concerned about trouble between the troops and the citizens in Central Kentucky, Wright went to the region with the intention of issuing an order barring slaves from the camps, but he refrained, seeing that Gillmore had already initiated such a measure. Wright reported to Halleck that in his opinion, Gillmore had acted correctly.[30] According to the editor of the *Lexington Observer and Reporter,* the general orders printed in the issue and his interviews with Gillmore were convincing evidence that the slaves would be driven from the camps. The general next moved to post all of the fugitives in the regiments to a separate brigade for assignment to a work detail. Utley refused to send his unit's slaves, however, claiming that the regiment had only enough for its own needs, even though Gillmore threatened him with court-martial. The colonel was supported by Ohio and Michigan regiments in the division and successfully maintained his ground despite the general's repeated requests that he conform to orders.[31]

The community of Georgetown became so agitated that violence seemed imminent. The townspeople threatened to seize the blacks from the ranks of the Twenty-second Wisconsin Regiment, and the Tenth Kentucky Cavalry, also a part of the division, was reported willing to fight the Wisconsin "abolitionist" unit on account of its resistance to the recovery of fugitive slaves. Gov. James F. Robinson, who resided in the city, appealed to Granger to have the slaves driven from the camps, but the general saw the problem as originating with the slaves, over whom the army had no authority. Nevertheless, all the regiments were sent to Lexington except the Twenty-second Wisconsin, which was assigned to guard the supply cars until they were moved out a day or so later. Georgetown citizens then threatened to seize the slaves in Utley's command as the regiment marched out of the city. Governor Robinson again urged the colonel to give up the slaves and called to his attention the great danger of conflict with the citizens, but Utley refused to yield, stating that if resistance were offered, he would level the town. The next day the regiment marched out of Georgetown with loaded muskets but without incident. Failing to secure aid from

Granger, Robinson went to Washington to confer with Lincoln on the problem of fugitive slaves.[32]

Robinson was not the only high state official to seek the president's help in dealing with Utley. When the Twenty-second Wisconsin Infantry came into Central Kentucky, a slave boy owned by supreme court justice George Robertson came into the camp and begged for protection. He had been rented out and cruelly mistreated. Before the regiment left Georgetown for Lexington, Robertson came to claim the boy. Utley allowed the black to decide to stay in camp. The colonel was subsequently indicted by the Fayette County grand jury, but he repelled the sheriff, assuring a Wisconsin friend that the warrant would not be served as long as there was "a man left" in the Twenty-second Regiment. Robertson, who knew Lincoln professionally, wired the president and urged him to require the army in Kentucky to give up fugitive slaves, because the refusal of some officers to do so was calculated to "provoke a conflict between citizens and soldiers." The next day Lincoln drafted a reply, which he probably decided not to send: "I may as well surrender this contest directly as to make any order, the obvious purpose of which would be to return fugitive slaves." Eight days after writing Lincoln, Robertson still had not received an answer. He then wrote John Crittenden, asking that Crittenden call Lincoln's attention to the crisis that was brewing in Kentucky because of the action of "four abolition" regiments. "Our people are already ripe for popular uprising against military usurpation and defiance of our laws," he warned. In a letter of November 19, Lincoln was informed by Utley that he had been indicted because he had stood "by the Constitution," had obeyed "the laws of Congress," and "had honored the proclamation issued on the 23rd day of September." "To you I now appeal for protection," he wrote. To resolve the dilemma, Lincoln offered to pay Robertson "any sum not exceeding five hundred dollars" if he would convey the title of his slave to Utley so that the boy could be made free. Judge Robertson followed Utley on to Nicholasville and attempted to persuade Gen. Absalom Baird to intercede, but the general informed him that he must deal directly with Utley.[33]

An officer of the Eighteenth Michigan had a fifteen-year-old black girl also belonging to Robertson ("You may guess for what," Robertson hinted to a friend). Gillmore put the regimental colonel on trial by court-martial for not obeying his orders on the slavery question.[34]

When the Ninety-second Illinois Infantry arrived at Camp Dick Yates in Montgomery County early in November 1862, Col. Smith D. Atkins asked citizens to keep their slaves at home, as the regiment would not be used to return fugitives. Almost immediately the soldiers were accused of enticing blacks from the kitchens and fields in the community. Col. J. C. Cochran of the Fourteenth Kentucky Regiment and commander of the Demi-Brigade then began to grant a large number of orders to slaveholders commanding Atkins to deliver up fugitives to their owners. The slave named in Cochran's first directive was put out of the lines and was advised to flee across the Ohio River. Following this incident, Atkins consulted Lincoln's preliminary proclamation and found that the chief executive had included a provision ordering the military to obey and enforce the article of war of March 13, 1862, which prohibited the use of the army to return fugitive slaves. When new orders came from Cochran, they were refused on the grounds that the directives were contrary to War Department General Orders no. 1391, issued September 24, 1862, which made the provision in the proclamation mandatory for all army commanders. The complaints against the Illinois soldiers grew louder, and after local citizens urged that the regiment be removed from the country, it was sent to Central Kentucky.[35]

As the Ninety-second Illinois Infantry moved into Clark County with some twenty slaves it had refused to give up, the citizens of Winchester threatened to chastise Atkins's regiment with the aid of the Fourteenth Kentucky Infantry, stationed in that county seat. The Illinois soldiers entered the city with loaded pieces and fixed bayonets, and a clash of the regiments may have been avoided only because their paths did not cross. The Ninety-second Illinois Infantry camped in Winchester for one night. Although the officers of the Fourteenth Kentucky Infantry called at the camp of the Illinois unit, they were not permitted to enter. They presented a written complaint to Atkins against the regiment's practice of taking the blacks of loyal citizens. The next morning the sheriff of Clark County served several summonses on the colonel for stealing slaves, but the notices were ignored.

After the regiment had established camp in Lexington, citizens of Fayette County took up the protest. General Granger's Order No. 15 of November 4, which required commanders to expel slaves from camp, was effectively evaded by applying it only to blacks not employed by the officers. One slave was ejected as a token compliance. As tension grew, a mob broke into the ranks of the Ninety-second Infantry and attempted to carry away some blacks. Atkins succeeded in turning away the would-be abductors. The Fayette Circuit Court issued a writ for the return of a slave, but the colonel refused to honor the court document even though the owner also had an order from Gillmore. In the meantime, Robertson brought fifteen suits in the Fayette County Court for residents of the county against officers of regiments in the area. Finally the Ninety-second Regiment moved on to Jessamine County to join General Baird's Third Division at Nicholasville.[36]

General Wright had feared trouble between citizens and soldiers in Lexington and Georgetown, and tension had reached the point of explosion in other communities in the state. The problem became so critical at Munfordville that a citizen hurriedly dispatched a message to the headquarters of the Department of the Cumberland warning that "unless some change" was speedily made, a collision was very likely. Wherever Union troops moved across the state, the local population was greatly agitated by the army's disregard for property rights in slaves.[37]

During the summer and autumn of 1862, almost all the wells in Kentucky were dry. Often without water for hours and exhausted from long, hot marches—and sometimes short of food—the soldiers were in no mood to coddle Kentucky slaveholders. They continued to welcome the slaves who came into their ranks, and in Louisville they protected blacks as comrades in arms.[38] A soldier of the Twenty-fifth Michigan Infantry wrote the *Grand Rapids Eagle* on November 30, 1862: whether Democrat or Republican, nine-tenths of the soldiers intended to "use up slavery."[39] As the Seventy-seventh Illinois Infantry passed through Frankfort on the way to Louisville in mid-November, the rear guard was relieved of two slaves by the citizens. The blacks were retaken after a show of force by the soldiers, but a collision between the regiment and the provost's guard of Frankfort had been narrowly averted.[40]

On November 12, 1862, the portion of the command of the Army of the Ohio serving in Kentucky was divided into three districts. Gen. J. T. Boyle, a native of the state, was made commander of the Western District of Kentucky, On Novemer 27 he issued Order No. 2, requiring all commanding officers to prohibit slaves from entering their camps. All officers and soldiers were "forbidden to interfere or intermeddle with slaves in any way," and all slaves within the camps were to be "placed beyond the guard lines" and were not to be permitted to return. Boyle also required that all violations be reported directly to him. Later he sought to account for the presence of any slave in a camp within the district. His brigade commanders issued orders of their own barring slaves. Boyle's order went into effect at a time when the commanders in most other states were declaring that slaves coming from Confederate states were to be free when they entered Union lines.[41]

During November and December 1862, soldiers streamed into Louisville to await embarkation downriver. Many of the blacks who had been impressed to dig entrenchments had been released, and they wandered into the ranks of the newly arriving regiments. A Louisville slaveholder found his slaves serving in the Seventy-ninth Illinois Infantry Regiment. After seeing four generals and being stalled by delaying tactics, the slaveholder secured an order for his slaves from General Boyle only to find himself driven from the camp at bayonet point by a squad of soldiers under orders from the colonel. The regiment justified its refusal to deliver the slaves by referring to the articles of war adopted March 13, the Second Confiscation Act of July 17, and the preliminary emancipation of September 22.[42]

On November 19 the Seventy-seventh Illinois Infantry Regiment arrived in Louisville with a number of blacks still attached. Several owners followed the troops into Louisville and attempted to reclaim their slaves, but they were prevented from doing so by the soldiers. The chief of police and twenty-five deputies were also repelled when they tried to seize two blacks driving a team of horses pulling an army wagon. A short time later a black attached to the regiment was arrested and jailed. A squad of soldiers threateningly advanced upon the jail, but it did not attempt to recover the black. Finding it difficult to take blacks aboard the boat, an officer smuggled two of them across the Ohio River and set them on the road to northern Illinois. They were captured in Indiana, however, and were returned to their owners in Kentucky.[43]

As the number of troops in Louisville increased, the number of slave-owners who followed the regiments into the city grew. Slave hunters and kidnappers saw opportunities to profit, and the local agitators hoped to exploit the situation. In January 1863 hostility toward the Emancipation Proclamation increased the bitterness. Late in the month a slave was shot and killed when he resisted efforts to drag him from the ranks of a marching regiment. The next day the soldiers of the Twenty-second Michigan Infantry at bayonet point prevented the seizure of a black from their ranks. Some citizens threatened to board the boat and to take the slave by force, but more level heads arranged for the sheriff to present their complaints to General Wright, who had just arrived in the city.[44]

On January 1 the Ninety-second Illinois Infantry arrived in Louisville. The county sheriff greeted them from the sidewalk with a hundred deputies, but he did not interfere. A citizen stepped into the line of march and seized a slave; he was instantly clubbed to death by a soldier. Not a man broke rank, and the sheriff did nothing. The Twenty-second Wisconsin Infantry arrived in Louisville on February 1 still in possession of Judge Robertson's slave boy. Seeing the black as the regiment marched through the streets, Robertson rushed into the ranks and seized him, but he was prodded by bayonets until he released the slave and retreated from the street. Attempts to seize two other slaves were thwarted. The boat was waiting for the regiment, and every black with the troops promptly boarded it. As a last effort to thwart the Twenty-second Wisconsin infantry in its determination to retain the slaves, the captain of the boat refused to get up steam until all blacks were removed, but he yielded when the colonel threatened to put him in irons and take over the ship.[45]

General Wright finally found it necessary to issue an order requiring that all units of the Army of the Ohio that were leaving the state prohibit slaves from boarding the transports. Boyle reinforced the measure by threatening to discipline any commanders who failed to uphold it. The order was evaded by most of the regiments, but some officers and soldiers openly resisted. The colonel of the Seventy-eighth Illinois Regiment flatly refused to comply, calling the injunction an insult. He told Boyle's adjutant that civil officers might search his transports but that neither he nor his men would hunt slaves. The colonel was arrested and was scheduled for court-martial. By the end of 1862, units of the First, Second, and Third army corps were concentrated in Louisville under Gen. A. M. McCook, T. L. Crittenden, and C. C. Gilbert. Many of the officers under Gilbert expressed a determination to pursue a course similar to that of the colonel commanding the Seventy-eighth Illinois Regiment but without using his forceful language. "The larger portion" of General Granger's division did the same. The efforts of proslavery citizens to organize groups to seize slaves from the ranks of marching troops heightened the excitement among the troops and contributed to their resistance to the orders. The ebullition of the people, increased, in turn, and a serious clash was probably avoided only by the departure of many of the regiments to the Cumberland.[46]

The generals were slow to apply the principles of the articles of war and the Confiscation Act of 1862. No confiscation took place in Kentucky. Several commanders did, however, brigade the blacks in labor details when they were already in the camps. Colonel Utley charged that his regiment had been under five or six different brigade generals all of whom had been "chosen for their adherence to the Kentucky policy." The division and brigade commanders, however, soon saw that an adherence to the policy of keeping slaves out of the lines undermined morale. Gen. James S. Negley refused to help a slaveholder regain three slaves "in the absence" of a specific order from his commander. To do so, he wrote, would be "prejudicial to the harmony and discipline of the troops." Ornsby M. Mitchell admitted to Secretary of War E. M. Stanton that he permitted some slaves in the camps to render services for the men. Gen. Samuel P. Carter asked that a nominal number of slaves be permitted to serve officers in the camps of the regiments.[47]

The regiments from the Midwest not only came into conflict over slavery with the civilian population of Kentucky but also clashed with regiments from Kentucky. On November 4, 1862, the Twenty-third Michigan Infantry Regiment on its way to Munfordville passed the camp of the Ninth Kentucky Cavalry. The Kentucky troops rushed the rear of the Michigan forces and seized a slave who was acting as the servant of a Michigan officer, claiming that the black was a runaway belonging to their major. Open warfare was avoided because the Michigan troops did not learn of the affray in their rear until an hour later. When a grand review of the troops in Louisville was planned on December 5, 1862, the hostility between the Kentucky units and those from farther north was so great that the Kentucky troops refused to appear in the dress parade with the Twenty-fifth Michigan Infantry and the Pennsylvania Cavalry. In April 1863, before leaving Kentucky, the Eighteenth and Twenty-second Michigan infantries clashed with Kentucky regiments because of differences about blacks and barely avoided violence. The immediate removal of the Michigan troops to Nashville probably prevented bloodshed. Before the end of the year, the Eighteenth Michigan Infantry fought with the Seventh Kentucky Cavalry at a circus in Nashville. One Michigan boy was killed and several were wounded.[48]

The president was aware that his border-state slave policy had deteriorated. Slavery, which should have been used to great advantage by the North, had become a serious obstacle to the success of the Union cause. It was clear to Lincoln that it must go. The constant complaints, charges, countercharges, and denials he received from the border states had grown louder and louder. The controversy in Kentucky and to a lesser extent in the other border states had kept alive "a spirit of hostility" to the federal government which divided and weakened the Union and held out hopes to the Confederacy that "someday the border states would unite with them."[49] Lincoln hoped to encourage the border states to take the initiative in abolishing slavery themselves, so that slavery in the secession states could then be dealt with. He "earnestly" appealed to the Union slave states to accept the "definite and solemn proposal of Congress" to initiate compensated emancipation. By December 1861, public opinion in the North had significantly shifted toward the acceptance of emancipation. The "friction and abrasion" associated with war were eroding the institution of slavery in the border states.[50] Congress had moved to an advanced position which was not compatible with the border-state policy of the army.

Kentucky refused any consideration of Lincoln's proposal for compensated emancipation. By July 1862, Lincoln believed that the emancipation of the slaves of the Confederate states might be necessary as a military measure. He had hoped to secure voluntary action in the border states before he moved to emancipate the slaves of rebellious states, but the progress of events required that he act before that problem was resolved. The Emancipation Proclamation significantly affected the posture of Kentucky in the war.

CHAPTER THREE

Emancipation

RADICALISM WAS GROWING in the North and in Congress. As early as November 1861, George Bancroft, while chairing a meeting to aid loyalists from North Carolina, stated: "If slavery and the Union are incompatible, listen to the words that come to you from the tomb of Andrew Jackson: 'The Union must be preserved at all hazards.'" he sent Lincoln a copy of the resolutions of the meeting along with a letter in which he revealed his sentiments on slavery. "Civil War is the instrument of Divine Providence to root out social slavery," he wrote; "posterity will not be satisfied with the result unless the consequences of the war effect an increase of free states. This is the universal expectation and hope of men of all parties." Lincoln knew Bancroft did not express the sentiments of an abolitionist. "The main thought in . . . your letter is one which does not escape my attention," he replied, "and with which I must deal in all due caution, and with the best judgment I can bring to it."[1]

By July 1862 the advocates of emancipation had become more numerous and increasingly bold. John Jay organized an emancipation convention of prominent conservatives of New York at Cooper Union. "Our old conservative solid men are ready for the most radical measures," Jay assured Charles Sumner.[2] On August 20 the *Boston Advertiser* reported that "the great phenomenon of the year" was "the terrible intensity" which the resolution for emancipation had acquired. A year ago, the editor recalled, "men might have faltered at the thought of proceeding to this extreme in any event. The majority do not now seek it, but . . . they are in a great measure prepared for it." Four days later Sen. John Sherman wrote his brother from Mansfield, Ohio: "You can form no concept of the change of opinion here on the Negro question. Men of all parties . . . who are determined to preserve the unity of the government at all hazards, agree that we must . . . make it in the interest of the Negroes to help us."[3]

Lincoln felt the pressure of Northern sentiment. On July 12, when he called the border states' congressmen and senators to the White House, the president told them that by not moving to resolve the slavery problem, he "gave dissatisfaction, if not offense, to many whose support" the country could not afford to lose. "And this is not the end of it," Lincoln added. "The pressure, in this direction, is still upon me and is increasing." By accepting gradual compensated emancipation, as Lincoln had proposed in March 1862, the Union slave states could relieve him. Two days later the lawmakers rejected the president's proposal.[4]

On July 22, Lincoln read the draft of the preliminary emancipation proclamation to his cabinet. His Kentucky friends James and Joshua Speed were in Washington at the time, and the president asked for their opinions of the document. Joshua advised against issuing the proclamation, because it would alienate most of the people of the state. "The Negro," James warned Lincoln, "cannot be emancipated by proclamation. . . . Let the Negro be no party to the force which is applied for his liberation."[5] For Lincoln, however, the counterpoise had shifted. Now the opposition of the advocates of emancipation in the North "involved more serious consequences than offending the border states." Nevertheless, the president's concern about the reaction of Kentucky to the emancipation of the slaves in the Confederate states led him to send Cassius Clay to assess the attitude of the state legislature.[6]

Lincoln's proposal was a "new departure" that caught most of the cabinet members by surprise, for until July 22, "in all . . . previous interviews, whenever the question of emancipation . . . had been alluded to, he had been prompt and emphatic in denouncing any interference by the General Government with the subject."[7] But the blacks had reduced his border-state slave policy to a shambles. While they had wisely refrained from organized violence against the institution of slavery, they had, in large numbers, simply refused to play the part of slaves any longer. Firmly supporting the Union cause, they exerted great pressure on the federal government to enact emancipation. Although Lincoln's role was significant, the slaves were not his helpless beneficiaries. If the blacks themselves had not taken the initiative to abandon slavery, there would have been no emancipation in 1863. The husband of Hattie Cash of Canton, Kentucky, took a typical course of action. He "ran away early and helped Grant . . . take Fort Donaldson [sic]," telling his wife "he would free himself, which he did." The slaves' ally was less Lincoln than the soldier in the ranks of the Union army. The Northern soldiers stationed in the state questioned the loyalty of their Kentucky generals and seemed more interested in the destruction of slavery than in obeying orders. Many delighted in singing songs about the legendary Brown and other sensitive subjects in order to irritate the local population. The border states had rejected gradual compensated emancipation, and a new policy had become necessary. "We had about played out our last card, and must change our tactics, or lose the game,"

Lincoln related months later to an acquaintance. "I now determined upon the adoption of the emancipation policy."[8]

When the president issued his preliminary emancipation proclamation on September 22, 1862, it incorporated little of his own plan for resolving the slavery question.[9] Military demands forced him to act in a manner he had never designed. Lincoln, however, profited from the bitter experience gained during his protracted efforts to prevent slaves from using the Union army as a vehicle to freedom. His strategy for effecting his new policy was to capitalize upon the two forces that had defeated his former plan: the certainty that blacks would seek liberation and the assurance that the Northern soldiers would assist them in their quest.

The overwhelming mass of the people of Kentucky strongly opposed the proclamation, but a minority had actively worked for emancipation from the beginning of the war. A group of several hundred Eastern Kentucky citizens under the guidance of the American Missionary Association (AMA) had petitioned Congress to emancipate the slaves in 1862. In September, before the preliminary proclamation was issued, a Kentucky AMA missionary proposed to Lincoln that the slaves be freed.[10] Afterward, on October 3, John Fee wrote to him, in care of the AMA, that the time was ripe for a declaration of general emancipation. The Confederate invasion of 1862 had brought a change in many who had violently opposed emancipation. The acts of the Southern army had converted them into practical abolitionists, Fee reported.[11] The voices of the advocates of emancipation in Kentucky, however, were few and weak, and they had no instrument by which to influence public opinion.[12]

The president's action shook the faith of some of the most determined Union men in Kentucky. T. S. Bell reported to Holt in Washington that "many of . . . the most faithful men" were "expressing doubts as to Lincoln's ability," but a Kentuckian who wrote to the *New York Tribune* found that the proclamation had not affected the loyalty of staunch Union men. He toured more than fourteen counties and concluded that "halfway conditional [Union] men had become advocates of the South, and that secessionists had broken their silence with traitorous speeches."[13] A military agent from Tennessee, stationed in Louisville, held a similar opinion. The proclamation had an injurious effect in Kentucky and might yet "produce most serious difficulties and embarrass the suppression of the rebellion," he informed Andrew Johnson.[14] The extent of the alienation was revealed at an anti-emancipation convention on September 27, in Frankfort; several speakers severely denounced the president, and the meeting passed resolutions proposing resistance to the proclamation.[15]

On November 21, Lincoln had an interview with a group of unconditional Union Kentuckians. In the course of the conference, they reported, the president had said "he would rather die than take back a word of the proclamation." Lincoln dwelled on the advantages that gradual emancipation offered Kentucky, and he urged the delegation to persuade the state to follow the example of Missouri in moving to accept the scheme.[16]

The army in Kentucky was divided on the preliminary emancipation proclamation. The mass of soldiers, particularly those from the North, accepted it as a military necessity, a measure which would aid in overthrowing the rebellion. Many also saw in it the hand of an overruling Providence directing men to render a benevolent act. A soldier of the Forty-fourth Ohio Infantry Regiment stationed in the state reported that the proclamation was "received with general satisfaction" in his regiment. He could not see why the president did not apply the measure immediately.[17]

A soldier in the Twenty-sixth Kentucky Infantry who had only recently returned to camp from his home in Simpson County was not inclined to side with those who were cursing Lincoln. He was willing to see the Constitution set aside until the rebellion was crushed, if necessary.[18] He was not the typical Kentucky soldier, not even representative of his own regiment. Some native troops were inclined to doubt that the motive for the proclamation was really a military necessity. A soldier from Eastern Kentucky in the Seventh Kentucky Infantry Regiment was convinced that the president's objective was to free the slaves, that he would avoid concluding the war until he had achieved that end.[19]

The hostility between the Kentucky regiments and the Northern troops was already a serious problem before September. With the announcement of the proclamation, the bitterness increased. An officer of an Illinois battery stationed in Kentucky wrote Lyman Trumbull in November that the Kentuckians in the army were "more than half opposed to the North, and in sympathy with the South." The officers were "more than half Rebels," and they held all the highest ranks in the commands, he complained. One regiment from the North was recalled from the state after serious trouble with a Kentucky unit over slavery. Such conflict became so heated and violent by December 1862, that General C. C. Gilbert was sent to investigate the controversy. He suggested that Boyle ask Generals Wright and W. S. Rosecrans to order the regiments to the passes along the southern border of the state, where they would battle the Confederate armies and would forget their differences.[20]

The preliminary emancipation proclamation enjoined the military and naval forces "to observe, obey and enforce" the Confiscation Act of July 17, 1862, and the articles of war of March 13, 1862, which prohibited the delivery of an escaping slave unless the owner was loyal. The slaves of rebel owners were to be free when they came into Union lines.[21] The War Department's General Orders No. 139 of September 24, 1862, did not provide for any exceptions in the application of the proclamation. The commanders in Kentucky generally concluded that since the order was not absolutely explicit, it did not apply in all respects to the local conditions. The regimental officers were directed to permit claimants to recover slaves within the lines, provided the blacks' service was not required by the army. No inquiry was required to determine the loyalty of the slaveholders.[22]

On October 27, Col. John McHenry of the Seventeenth Kentucky Infantry in the field near New Market issued a special order announcing that slaves were prohibited in the camp of his regiment and that after a lapse of two weeks any blacks within its limits would be delivered to owners or agents upon application, regardless of whether the latter were loyal or disloyal. McHenry had apparently become exasperated at finding himself accompanied on at least one occasion "by a northern regiment with seventy or eighty stolen slaves each mounted on a stolen horse." The order was published in the Kentucky newspapers and was reprinted outside of the state. McHenry had apparently decided to cut the Gordian knot and to challenge the emancipation proclamation, as his order was a direct violation of regulations that Lincoln had ordered enforced. The colonel was dismissed by his commander, and although Lincoln preferred to treat him with leniency, Secretary of War Stanton had his way and the dismissal was sustained. Excitement ran high. McHenry's heroic war record was set before the public by a press that made him something of a martyr to the slaveholder, and the Kentucky legislature, after much heated argument, passed a resolution praising his action.[23]

Other officers of Kentucky regiments openly resisted the proclamation. Lt. U. S. Johnson, also of the Seventeenth Kentucky Infantry and a brother of Col. Adam Johnson of the Confederacy, sent his resignation to General McCook because of his opposition to emancipation. McCook placed him under arrest and sent him in irons to the military prison. Two weeks later General Boyle discharged Johnson because no charge had been preferred against him and sent him back to his regiment. Shortly after returning, Johnson again tendered his resignation on the same grounds, and General Rosecrans, commander of the Department of the Cumberland and Ohio, dismissed him from service for "mutinous language, and insubordinate action."[24] Soon after the Battle of Stone River, December 31, 1862, some fifteen or eighteen officers of the Fifteenth Kentucky Infantry tendered their resignation without giving any special reason. All were sent back by Gen. Richard W. Johnson, who commanded the division. Within a few days some half-dozen or more of the same officers again sent in their resignations without stating a reason, and again they were turned down. Maj. Henry F. Kalfus turned in his resignation for a third time with the statement that he had entered the army to assist in suppression of the rebellion and now declined further participation because of the emancipation proclamation.

The commander had Kalfus placed under arrest by orders of General Rosecrans. He was stripped of his shoulder straps and was marched out of the lines at bayonet point after having been dishonorably discharged.[25]

Before the Kalfus matter was settled, Colonel Cochran and other officers of the Fourteenth Infantry resigned because of the president's proclamation. More than a hundred men deserted the Twenty-fourth Kentucky Infantry, and when that Regiment was ordered away from Frankfort, there was such mutiny in the ranks that the unit had to be escorted aboard the cars under the guard of the bayonets of the Forty-fourth Ohio Infantry. A false rumor that spread through Kentucky attributed to Unionist Robert J. Breckinridge the statement that "there was but one thing for Kentucky to do," namely, "to call back all the troops that she had sent into both armies . . . and drive the Yankees from her soil." There was a movement under way among the officers of the Kentucky regiments in Tennessee to have their troops sent back home. Many of the Kentucky regiments under Rosecrans were so depleted of forces that there was talk of combining some of them. All of the officers in the Twentieth Kentucky Infantry except the colonel, who was sympathetic, planned to resign when Lincoln made the proclamation final on January 1; many carried out their intent by giving such excuses as business or health. More than sixteen officers in S. D. Bruce's Twenty-second Brigade resigned because they were required to remain in the South while Northern regiments stole their slaves. As the epidemic of resignations spread through the Kentucky troops, Col. J. H. Ward, commander of the Twenty-seventh Regiment, issued an order reminding his men that it was their duty "as soldiers to suffer anything, even unto death," as long as there was the least hope of establishing the Constitution and perpetuating the Union. He informed them that the president who had issued the "odius [*sic*]" proclamation had only two more years to serve before his term expired. That the resignations and departures did not reach massive proportions and cause a military crisis in the regiments of Kentucky was due only to the strong measures taken by Rosecrans and Stanton and to the fact that the sentiment against the proclamation did not run as deep in the ranks as it did among the officers.[26]

When Lincoln issued his preliminary proclamation, it was taken as a signal by the Kentucky slaves to rush into the lines of the Union army. Mary Crane, a former slave, years later vividly recalled the event in Larue County. "When President Lincoln issued his proclamation, freeing the Negroes," she recollected, "I remember that my father and most all of the other younger slave men left the farms." The announcement of the preliminary emancipation proclamation also caused fear that the slaves in Kentucky would rise up. A correspondent for the *New York Tribune* in October found much evidence of dread of an insurrection. One planter was willing to wager a thousand dollars that there was not a slave in Kentucky who had not heard of the president's action and did not understand exactly what it meant. The slaveholders agreed that every time the blacks "heard a drum beat, their whole nature was aroused." Cases of violence between owners and slaves appeared to be growing, and many observers were convinced that this increase could be traced directly to the proclamation. In November the *Lexington Observer and Reporter* asserted that there was a widespread, if not universal, belief among the slaves that they were to be free on January 1, 1863. The journalist suggested that the community prepare for the eventuality by setting up an elaborate patrol system. The *Louisville Journal* reprinted the *Observer*'s article and stated that the facts were strongly corroborated by another source in Lexington. A similar situation prevailed in Louisville, the editor wrote, but he hoped that nothing more serious than a general rush to excape would take place. In the countryside, however, "the evil may be greater," he warned.[27]

A Louisville citizen was convinced that the proclamation had come because the "northern fanatics" had become enraged by their failures and had decided to turn the war on women and children. He predicted that whites would have to slaughter the blacks in self-defense. A citizen writing to the *New York Tribune* from near Corinth, Mississippi, reported that blacks from Kentucky who were with the Union regiments had assured him that the Kentucky slaves were "ripe for revolution," and a Union man of Southern Kentucky asked the local commander to use his influence with the adjutant general of the state to keep a company of cavalry in the country until "the infernal proclamation" had died away, because the community "anticipated trouble" with blacks after January 1. The *Louisville Journal* appealed to the black preachers to spread among their flocks word that the proclamation did not apply to them. "It is a well-known fact that an impression prevails to a considerable extent among the slave population of Kentucky that they will be free on the first of January under the proclamation," the editor reported.[28] The danger of an insurrection in Kentucky, however, was largely imaginary. The blacks had too much common sense to endanger their new-found freedom by a reckless action that would unite the whites in opposing their increased liberty.

The president's annual message of December 1, 1862, removed what faint hope of preserving slavery still lingered among the opponents of emancipation in Kentucky. Lincoln made it clear that the emancipation commitment would stand, but he still offered compensated emancipation for the states that accepted his proclamation before January 1, 1863.[29] The response to his message indicated that public opinion had not become more favorable in Kentucky since September. Dr. Breckinridge, who had played such a significant part in the work of keeping Kentucky in the Union, protested against the president's proclamation policy. He termed it "unconstitutional, uncalled for, inexpedient and dangerous." But "we share, with all the power of our being," he declared, "the conviction that the rebellion should be crushed, and that the national existence should be preserved." The reason Breckinridge objected to the emancipation policy was because he "believed in the Providence of God," and it seemed to him "a folly, if not a sin, to attempt to frustrate the course of Providence—whether by hastening or by retarding it."[30] The response of the editor of the *Observer and Reporter* on December 6 was typical of the reaction of the press in Kentucky to the president's message. He asserted that the document would be read "with the deepest mortification by every true lover of his country," because Lincoln had evinced "an utter disregard, not only of his constitutional obligations, but of his own pledge."[31]

The Emancipation Proclamation, issued on January 1, was greeted with a storm of disapproval. Practically no one could be found in Kentucky who publicly supported Lincoln. The press condemned Lincoln for having broken a sacred promise not to make war on slavery. After January 1, attention focused on the meeting of the Kentucky legislature and the governor's message of January 8. General Wright had heard rumors, which he was inclined to believe, that the governor would support the General Assembly in measures to legislate the state out of the Union. Wright proposed to arrest all legislators who spoke in favor of such action or voted for the withdrawal of the state. General Halleck advised him to act with discretion and to make no arrests that would appear to jeopardize freedom of speech.[32]

Governor Robinson's message was considered the critical factor in determining the measures that the legislature would take in reference to the Emancipation Proclamation. Members of the inner circle of the unconditional Unionists met in Louisville and spent the day before the General Assembly convened trying to line up legislative support for the president's proclamation. One of the members contacted the governor and found him "very excitable on the subject." Although the Unionist was convinced that the governor's message was already firmly fixed, he offered a few suggestions. The friends of the proclamation secured the service of Parson W. G. Brownlow to speak in favor of the proclamation in Louisville on the day after the governor's message. It was believed that Brownlow's speech produced the hoped-for effect, at least to some degree, and the next night Brownlow was persuaded to speak in Frankfort. Brownlow contacted many of the legislators and privately warned them that any action against the proclamation would give aid and comfort to the rebellion. He spoke to the same effect in the Masonic Temple at Frankfort. Despite all the lobbying in favor of the administration by Union men in Frankfort, Brownlow was convinced that the Kentucky legislature would take "strong action" against the proclamation.[33]

In his message to the legislature, the governor charged that the president had "lent too facile an ear to the schemes of abolition partisan leaders," who had blinded his better judgment, had alarmed his fears, and had "induced him to publish a manifesto from which nothing but evil" could flow. Robinson urged the General Assembly to reject the president's scheme of compensated emancipation, which he saw as especially aimed at Kentucky. He condemned the proclamation as "an inducement to servile insurrection" despite the attempt to disguise its purpose. The governor was certain that emancipation was an act of usurpation that would inflame the South with "inextinguishable hatred."[34] William C. Goodloe, provost marshal of the seventh district of Kentucky, was bitterly opposed to the position of the governor, which he believed was calculated to place Kentucky in rebellion.[35]

The Unionists dominated the legislature, but in caucus they represented a wide diversity of opinion. After a few meetings of the caucus, it became clear that most of the members wanted resolutions that calmly and with dignity expressed disapproval of the policy of the government. In a letter to Governor Robinson that was read in the legislature on January 26, John Crittenden warned that extreme action would only aid the Confederacy. He believed, however, that Kentucky should not submit "in silence to the unconstitutional and odious acts" of the president. Crittenden maintained that the best course was for the state legislature to pass resolutions declaring the proclamation "unconstitutional and void." The president's proclamation was "but words. We can fight them with our resolutions," Crittenden urged.[36]

The Kentucky House of Representatives divided into three factions on the issue of the proclamation. The Union Democratic party was led by Joshua F. Bell. It was called "the straight out Union" party by its supporters in the legislature. The Union party was content to limit legislative action to a dignified protest against the proclamation. The party of political opposition to the administration was the Peace Democrats, or the "straight-out secession party," as it was called by its opponents. It was in favor of withholding men and money from the federal government or of giving the governor power to recall the Kentucky troops when he thought there was a need for such action. The members of the legislature who considered themselves Democratic opponents to the administration met in caucus and drew up measures condemning the president for permitting the army to entice slaves from masters at bayonet point and for flouting the laws and courts in Kentucky. The third party was a middle-of-the road party led by Nathaniel Wolfe. It disagreed with the Bell faction only as to the form the measure should take. The Wolfe party wanted an address drawn up in the form of the Bill of Rights and the Declaration of Independence, to which would be appended a set of resolutions. This idea had some backing among the constituents. The first of a series of Democratic Union party county meetings, held in Montgomery County early in 1863, urged the state legislature to issue an address and to call a national convention in April to adopt measures to preserve the Constitution. The Legislature was asked to "indignantly reject" compensated emancipation and to repudiate the right of the federal government to use the public treasure for such a purpose. Despite the varying shades of sentiment, the secession-minded members were isolated, and the other two parties drew up the report.[37] The house rejected a minority report which instructed the Kentucky delegation in the U.S. Congress to refuse to vote men and money to continue war in its "perverted" form and proposed to send a delegation to Washington and Richmond to try to secure peace. Instead, the house voted by a large majority to remove the address from the majority report and sent the measure to the senate. The senate accepted the house measure with a slight modification, and on March 2 the legislature passed the resolutions which pronounced the proclamation "unwise, unconstitutional and void" with only three negative votes in the house and none in the senate. The resolution rejecting compensated emancipation passed unanimously in the house and with only James Speed voting in the negative in the senate. The Kentucky delegation in Washington joined the state legislators in denouncing the proclamation.[38]

The activities of the military concerning emancipation reached a high point during the period from October 1862 to January 1863. Early in 1863 a considerable number of the Union troops moved from Kentucky to the lower Ohio Valley, and the occasion for friction between the soldiers and citizens was reduced. The debates that had been conducted between the regiments had largely run their course, and interest was shifting to new questions. Joseph C. Breckinridge, son of R. J. Breckinridge of Danville, reported that not many of the men in his Kentucky regiment became "excited upon the Negro question. They seem to think 'damn it,' " he wrote from a station outside Kentucky. The proclamation continued to occupy the attention of some of the Northern regiments and men. Gen. James M. Shackelford, a native of Kentucky, prohibited speeches and debates by soldiers on the proclamation. When he heard a sergeant "haranging the men on Lincoln and the Proclamation," the general called him in and told him that he was in a military camp for military service and must leave politics alone.[39]

In March 1863 the chaplain of the Twenty-fifth Wisconsin Infantry in one of the churches of Columbus, Kentucky, prayed for the freedom of the slaves. The soldiers of the Twenty-fifth Wisconsin Infantry Regiment lost no opportunity to inform the blacks that they were free. The Northern regiments were upset by an order in February 1863 from Gen. M. D. Manson, commander of the District of Western Kentucky, to Col. Marshal W. Chapin, stationed at Bowling Green, instructing him to comply with

Boyle's order to expel all Negroes from the camps. Some of the regiments obeyed the order, but the slave hunters failed to capture their quarry, and the next day the blacks were back in camp. Chapin's own regiment, the Twenty-third Michigan, refused to obey the order and sent a vigorous protest signed by twenty-five officers to Gen. William Rosecrans. A colonel in another regiment also sent a protest, and the line officers in the brigade held a meeting and drew up a protest which was sent through the channels of the command. The 102nd Ohio, 111th Ohio, and the 129th Illinois infantries joined the Twenty-third Michigan in refusing to expel blacks from the camps. By March 5, the order to expel the blacks had been renewed by a directive from Gen. H. M. Judah, who required that the slaves not be permitted to return. In order to evade the directive, some of the slaves were sent to Tennessee with officers who were being transferred to Nashville. Early in April 1863, even after being ordered by General Manson to turn slaves belonging to loyal Kentuckians out of their lines, the Eighteenth and Twenty-second Michigan infantries refused. The Michigan regiments were leaving and insisted that they were acting in accord with federal laws and War Department regulations. Manson ordered them not to leave the camp until the matter was settled. He called out the Sixteenth Kentucky Infantry to detain the trains until he ordered departure, and he prohibited unauthorized persons from entering the cars. Manson telegrammed Boyle and received his backing on the action taken against the Michigan regiments. The Michigan regiments were forced to yield and departed, leaving five slaves behind. But Boyle had serious trouble closer to his headquarters. Col. Orlando H. Moore, provost marshal at Louisville and a soldier of the Twenty-fifth Michigan Infantry, refused to enforce the general's order, which he viewed as trampling on the Emancipation Proclamation. He criticized the seizure of slaves who were subsequently jailed and then sold back into slavery. Boyle reinstated the provost marshal after Stanton ordered that the blacks be released from the jails if evidence revealed that they came from the Confederate states.[40]

In May 1863, a post commander in Louisville told a journalist that a large majority of General Rosecrans's men had come into the war friendly to slavery, but "not one of them would now consent to any peace that did not destroy it root and branch." He himself had left home a Breckinridge Democrat; "and now, sir," he added, "I'm as black an abolitionist as Wendell Phillips." The colonel could better have described himself as a nationalist; the nationalists cared little for the welfare of the slave but hated the slaveholder. Many of the abolitionists, such as Col. Stanley Matthews, who edited the abolitionist *Cincinnati Herald* in the 1840s, showed a great deal of empathy for the slave. Matthews wrote his wife on January 23, 1863: "I wish I were out of this arena of bloodshed." The nationalism of the

Northern troops was appropriately expressed by a resolution adopted by an Indiana regiment: "We are in favor of every measure that is calculated to weaken our enemy and destroy his resources."[41]

Bell I. Wiley, the leading authority on the Union soldier, in his informative study *The Life of Billy Yank* says of the Union soldiers, "Some fought to free the slaves, but a polling of the rank and file through their letters and diaries indicates that those whose primary object was the liberation of the Negroes comprised only a small part of the fighting force." Wiley states, "It seems doubtful that one soldier in ten at anytime during the conflict had any real interest in emancipation per se."[42] Still, a poll taken in Kentucky revealed that the Northern soldiers were overwhelmingly in favor of emancipation, and the records show that they were almost equally supportive of the Emancipation Proclamation after it was issued. In their efforts to destroy slavery the Northern soldiers were enthusiastic and determined. Some hated the institution and wanted it abolished; others wanted the slave to work for them. I examined regimental histories, diaries, and manuscript letters of the soldiers of the North in Kentucky, as well as letters published from September, 1861 to March, 1863 in newspapers in the Midwest. Before the Emancipation Proclamation was issued, letters and diaries of the soldiers indicate that more than 86 percent from the North who expressed an opinion favored emancipation. At this time soldiers seldom indicated the sentiment of their regiments. After the proclamation was issued, more than 76 percent of the soldiers who registered their opinions were in favor of emancipation, and the soldiers usually indicated that their regiments agreed with them. That a higher percentage voiced sentiments in favor of emancipation before September 22 is explained by the fact that an expression of opinion did not go beyond an intellectual commitment and was often an emotional response that reflected anti-Southern sentiment. The Conscription Act March 3, 1863, provided for military draft of the slaves, and the army discouraged the use of blacks as personal servants. To some extent, this law accounts for the decline in the percentage of soldiers favoring emancipation after the Emancipation Proclamation was issued. Since the issue was real after September 22, it called up some latent opposition that was not articulated as long as the question remained theoretical.[43]

The Emancipation Proclamation also led to a realignment of parties in Kentucky. The States' Rights party, which had been made powerless after the resignation of Governor Beriah Magoffin, revived after January 1, 1863, and became the refuge of many Unionists who ceased to support the administration because of Lincoln's new policy. The States' Rights party believed that the time was ripe to recover its lost prestige in Kentucky. A call was sent out for a state convention, in Frankfort, on February 18, six months before the election, to nominate a governor and other officers. The Unionist *Frankfort Commonwealth* claimed that the States' Righters chose this time because they believed the "odiousness of the radical acts of the administration had prepared, or was rapidly preparing, the Kentucky mind for revolt against the Union." The editor declared that the States' Righters "openly proclaim sympathy with the rebel cause, secretly sending clothing and provisions to rebel prisoners, and flaunt 'sesesh' flags and badges in the face of Union people."[44] On February 17, the house of representatives voted 40 to 36 to refuse the use of its hall to the States' Rights convention.[45] After the States' Rights party had been called to order in Metropolitan Hall, Col. S. A. Gilbert, in command at Frankfort, entered the hall accompanied by troops with fixed bayonets and required the body to disperse.[46]

On the same day that the States' Rights party met in Frankfort, Jesse W. Fell, an Illinois friend of Lincoln, who was in Louisville at the time, wrote an Illinois Unionist: "the denunciation of Mr. Lincoln, and his emancipation policy" was "bitter and universal" in Kentucky. He feared that troops being raised in Kentucky for the Union would ultimately be turned against the government. "Kentucky loyalty means loyalty to slavery," Fell wrote to Lincoln. Cassius M. Clay also saw the situation as critical. He had pressed Lincoln to issue the proclamation, and now he urged the president to put an end to proslavery leadership by replacing McClellan with Benjamin F. Butler,[47] but the situation was not as critical as it seemed. In the countryside, where the property of the people had been despoiled by Confederates and guerrillas, the people were in no mood to cast their lot with the Confederacy.

Most of the Democratic Union party county organizations held conventions from February to March in preparation for the August election. The question of emancipation occupied much attention. All of the county Union Democratic conventions passed resolutions opposing the president's proclamation but insisted that they were unalterably attached to the Union.[48] Although there is no record of a political convention in Eastern Kentucky, John Fee addressed a meeting in Lewis County on the importance of sustaining the government, the proclamation, and immediate emancipation. A clergyman in Laurel County, also in Eastern Kentucky, reported that some people were pleased with the proclamation and others were unhappy because the president had not issued a general emancipation proclamation abolishing all slavery.[49]

The Union Democratic party at its convention in Louisville on March 18–19 sustained the position of the legislature with respect to relations with the federal government. The convention was composed of decidedly unconditional Union men who showed their displeasure when a politician from Indiana "assailed Lincoln and his war policy." The delegates nominated Joshua Bell for governor.[50] When Bell withdrew, the Union Democratic central committee selected Thomas E. Bramlette to replace him. Many Unionists would not accept Bramlette because of his radicalism (agrarianism) and split off to form an opposition. The growing desire for peace was probably more important in creating the opposition, but the most powerful force in convincing many that they wanted peace was the disillusionment resulting from Lincoln's new policy. In June, a group of dissenters called on Charles Wickliffe to run for governor. Wickliffe announced that he would stand for election without calling for a convention. The party was called the Peace Democrats, and the president's proclamation was the principal issue in the election of August 1863. The Confiscation Act, martial law, and the possible arming of slaves trailed far behind the Emancipation Proclamation as significant issues in the election. No Union Democratic candidate supported Lincoln's policy. Bramlette was critical of Lincoln's proclamation, but he insisted that correction could be secured through the ballot box. He made a distinction between the government and the administration and supported the former but opposed the latter.[51] Wickliffe assured the voters that if he were elected, he would urge Congress to pass a bill to require the president to retract his Emancipation Proclamation. Wickliffe maintained that the state should withhold men and money if necessary to secure a change in the administration's policy.[52]

The presence of the army affected the election, but it was not a decisive factor. The legislature had passed a law disfranchising all persons who had been expatriated. Governor Robinson issued a proclamation in July announcing that the expatriation law would be enforced. Fear of the consequences caused many to refrain from voting, because the state was under martial law and the army could act in the election. The program of the Peace Democrats appealed primarily to those who could not safely vote without fear of incriminating themselves. The Union Democrats won the election. Bramlette took office, and most of the Union congressional candidates did so as well. The Union Democrats made almost a unanimous sweep of both houses of the state legislature.[53]

The election had been contested on the issue of slavery, and most of the voters in the state had no interest in the institution. The theft and destruction of property in the state by the Confederate armies during the summer and autumn of 1862 had deepened the resentment against the Southern government, so that few thought of casting their fortunes with the Confederacy. T. S. Bell, the strong Unionist and physician of Louisville who kept well informed concerning public opinion throughout the state, judged public sentiment correctly in an article under the penname "Kentuckian" in the *New York Times*. "There has been no time since this rebellion commenced," he wrote, "when the mass of loyal men of Kentucky were more firmly resolved to tear up root and branch of this rebellion." The sentiment against slavery in Kentucky was stronger than public pronouncements indicated.[54]

Gen. A. E. Burnside took command of the Department of Ohio just as the political campaign was moving into full swing. At the same time, the steady stream of contraband slaves that had been drifting into Kentucky turned into a torrent from Alabama, Georgia, and Mississippi under the impact of the proclamation. The state government of Kentucky claimed authority over all slaves who were found within its borders. The county sheriffs seized them and put them in jail. After advertising for the owner to claim his slave, the jailer sold the fugitive at public auction after thirty days. The law had required sale after a confinement of eight months, but the number of contraband arriving in Kentucky became so great that the period was reduced to make space available in the jails. In the larger cities the prisons were filled, and slaves were sent to rural counties for confinement. The newspapers in Louisville, Frankfort, and Lexington contained hundreds of advertisements for runaways. Some private slave traders kept pens and regularly seized the transient blacks from the Confederate states and sold them. The law of Kentucky which provided for the sale of unclaimed slaves was in direct conflict with the president's Emancipation Proclamation. The radical Republican and abolitionist newspapers reprinted the advertisements of the Kentucky press and called on the federal administration and the army to enforce the proclamation in Kentucky.[55]

On April 23, Judge Advocate Gen. Joseph Holt voiced the opinion that slaves from the Confederate states coming into Kentucky were free under the articles of war and the Second Confiscation Act of July 1862 as well as by the president's proclamation. Sales of these slaves were void, and no claim of the county for a black's expenses while in custody of the state should be recognized. The opinion was sent to Stanton and Burnside. A dispatch from Louisville which appeared in the *National Intelligencer* of Washington on April 29 indicated that slaves were being sold in Louisville in violation of the president's proclamation. Stanton wired Burnside instructions to see that no captives of war were returned to slavery in violation of the proclamation and the acts of Congress. On the same day Stanton sent Holt's opinion to General Halleck, and Burnside received an order from Halleck to comply with the interpretation of the proclamation rendered by the judge advocate.[56]

General Burnside issued General Orders No. 53, dated April 28, which stated that "in accordance with the spirit of the Proclamation" army personnel were prohibited from impeding the civil processes in the recovery of slaves and were forbidden to aid in their escape. On paper this order gave the Kentucky slaveholders protection against regiments that were determined to destroy slavery by military force. The orders also prohibited any interference with the freedom of slaves who had been made free by the president's Proclamation.[57] General Boyle relayed the policy to post commanders with his own orders, and a serious attempt was made to enforce it.[58]

Burnside then appointed a commission to oversee the enforcement of freedom for contrabands. When Buell's army returned to Louisville to defend Kentucky in the autumn of 1862, approximately a thousand slaves came with him from Tennessee. They were picked up by the sheriffs in the counties around Louisville and were sold for prices ranging from $450 to $200. The commission tracked down and confiscated many of these blacks and put them to work at $10.20 per month on public works. Many of the slaves were located in an eleven-county area around Louisville, but the county sheriffs would not cooperate. The commisssion could recover the slaves only by sending a detachment of soldiers to remove them from the jails before they were sold, but it was impossible to detach enough soldiers from military commands to handle such a comprehensive task. The regions around Henderson and Owensboro were the worst offenders. As late as September 1863 the *New York Tribune* reported that blacks coming from the South were regularly arrested and put in jail to be sold in Southern Kentucky, but by the end of 1863 the enforcement of freedom for contraband was generally successful in the area of Louisville, Frankfort, and Lexington. Success was primarily due to the fact that the army worked out a successful policy of retaining slaves in the Confederate states as agricultural laborers or soldiers.[59]

CHAPTER FOUR

Military Enrollment

THE GENERAL MILITIA ACT and the Second Confiscation Act passed by Congress in July 1862 had authorized the president to recruit black soldiers, but Lincoln did not immediately use the provisions of these acts, and blacks were seized to assist on public works before a procedure evolved for receiving them into the service. The Militia Act provided for the enrollment of all able-bodied male citizens between the ages of twenty and forty-five "for the purpose of constructing entrenchments, or performing camp service, or any other labor, or any military or naval service for which they may be found competent." The president was also given power to emancipate any black soldiers who enlisted and their families as well if the former masters were rebels. Under the Second Confiscation Act the president could employ persons of African descent as needed to suppress the rebellion.[1]

The army's need for laborers first led to formal impressment of many slaves and contrabands, sometimes for long periods. The slaves of the disloyal were the first to be recruited, but military needs and the blacks' eagerness to serve slowly undermined the exclusion policy. As early as March 1862 the provost marshal in Louisville was combing the workhouse in search of able-bodied men. By the middle of August the army engineers in Kentucky had requested between 200 and 300 blacks to work in timber operations to furnish wood for military bridges. On August 25, an impressment of slaves was imposed on slaveholders of Fayette and Madison Counties who had been declared Confederate supporters or sympathizers. The newly formed labor brigades were to repair military roads from Rockcastle County to Cumberland Gap. The number desired in the impressment was 1,200, and John Hunt Morgan's hemp factory served as a barracks staging area for the blacks.[2]

When Confederate forces threatened to seize Louisville and Cincinnati during the invasion of Kentucky in the autumn of 1862, labor brigades of blacks and newly impressed slaves were set to building fortifications and to digging rifle pits and embankments in the Cincinnati-Covington area.

Owners were promised compensation for the use of their slaves on proof of loyalty. In the crisis, both blacks and whites answered the call for laborers and worked together without regard for class or race. Eight thousand civilians and soldiers labored on the fortifications, and 600 blacks worked under the immediate command of other blacks. After long hours of labor the blacks went through military drill as the soldiers watched and cheered.[3]

When it was reported that Morgan had taken Glasgow, General Wright issued an order commanding that all available males, both black and white, be assigned to build fortifications for the defense of Louisville. General Boyle had already begun to impress the slaves of rebels, and of other individuals who had assisted the Confederacy, for the purpose, and during the crisis he extended impressment to the slaves of loyal citizens.[4]

Even before the autumn of 1862, one of the most common complaints of the new white recruits was the hardship of manual work in labor brigades. When they wrote to local leaders back home, the politicians passed the grievance on to Washington and urged that blacks be drafted to perform this service. After the emergency was over, General Boyle continued to make use of contraband labor on a large scale, and in December, he ordered the provost marshal to release the Negroes from jails and from the pens for runaway slaves so that they could work on military projects.[5] Becoming aware of the new policy, blacks flocked to the military prisons so that they would be sent to labor on the fortifications.[6] The slaves were anxious to contribute to the support of the government. Since Negroes had always been barred from the militia by law, they correctly concluded that their new status was a step in the direction of securing recognition as free men. The slaves of disloyal owners received wages as well as subsistence, and at least some of the workers in the private sector, regardless of the status of their owners, received a bonus or incentive payments.[7]

Early in 1863 the number of impressments increased, and less distinction was made between the slaves of loyal and disloyal slaveholders. A controversy began to brew. Union slaveholders were always assured pay for the services of their slaves, but they objected to the new demands. One of the chief reasons for the greater use of slaves was the shortage of labor to maintain the railroad. On March 2, James Guthrie, president of the Louisville and Nashville line, asked General Boyle to impress three or four gangs of blacks, or approximately eighty slaves, to work on the tracks. Boyle hoped to secure half of the necessary labor by emptying the military prisons and the Negro pens in Louisville. Thereafter the railroads increasingly used slaves, and the owners of mail packets and steamboats that operated along the Ohio River and in Western Kentucky turned to the army for similar assistance.[8] In March 1863 the impressment was extended to Bourbon County in Central Kentucky and was renewed in Fayette County for the purpose of building fortifications and digging trenches in Lexington. The post commander in

Lexington who was in charge of the labor scolded the Union slaveholders for trying to shirk their patriotic duty by evading the impressment and for failing to contribute their slaves freely, as had the rebels, who felt fortunate that they did not have to work in the trenches themselves.[9]

On January 12, 1863, the radical Republican Thaddeus Stevens of Pennsylvania introduced in the House of Representatives a bill calling for the enlistment of 150,000 blacks. The bill was bitterly debated for the rest of the month. The Kentucky congressmen bore the brunt of the opposition to the measures[10] and a member of the lower house of the Kentucky legislature wrote John Crittenden that a storm of popular protest was raging. He doubted that the moderates could prevent the adoption of the threatening resolutions. After receiving the correspondence, Crittenden took the floor of Congress. He predicted that the citizens of Kentucky would not allow recruiting officers to set foot on their farms and that the new policy would arouse extreme hostility to the federal government.[11] Before the measure passed the House of Representatives, the bill was amended to exempt the slaves of loyal citizens in the slave states that had been excluded from the president's proclamation; recruiting offices would not be set up there.[12]

When the bill was sent to the Senate, the measure was struck down in the committee which was working on the Conscription Act of 1863. The chairman reported that the power requested by the new bill had already been granted by the act of July 17, 1862.[13] The Conscription Act of 1863 provided for enrollment of all men subject to the draft as a preliminary to conscription or enlistment. The act listed the classes of individuals who were exempt from conscription, and since blacks were not mentioned, the president ordered the War Department to develop a policy for their enrollment. The War Department set up a Bureau for Colored Troops in the office of the adjutant general. No person would be permitted to recruit black troops unless authorized by the War Department. Alarmed at this new development, John Boyle, adjutant general of Kentucky, who was in a position to test public sentiment, urged John Usher, secretary of the interior, to intercede in the case of Kentucky. The enrollment of slaves in the state could only be enforced at the point of the bayonet, Boyle declared. He predicted that 75,000 men would take to the field "to keep a miserable few hundreds of slaves from being taken away." Weeks passed, and the new system proceeded as planned by the administration. By June the national enrollment of blacks and whites was under way. In Kentucky, free blacks, but not slaves, were to be included. The army did not publicize its plans for the freedmen in the state, but the provost marshals and registration officer were sent into the field with forms and instructions.[14]

By the last week in June, the commanders in Kentucky had become aware that the enrollment of free blacks was pending. General Boyle immediately communicated to James B. Fry, the provost marshal general in

Washington, his fear that the measure would "revolutionize the State and do infinite and inconceivable harm." "Not an honest loyal man in the state" would support the plan, and it would "meet decided opposition." Boyle explained that there were only 4,130 free black males in Kentucky and that possibly only one-eighth were in the age group subject to the draft. By drafting these, he predicted, the army would lose 10,000 other recruits. Boyle urged Fry to confer with the president on the subject. W. H. Sidell, the provost marshal for Kentucky, sent a similar dispatch to Fry, and the next day Boyle telegraphed Lincoln. In response, Fry informed Boyle and Sidell that there was no "infinite and inconceivable harm" in determining how many free Negroes resided in Kentucky. Why should Kentuckians revolutionize the state? The army sought to do only what the Census Bureau had done.[15] In the meantime General Burnside, too, had telegraphed Lincoln to express his alarm. The president sent Boyle and Burnside identical telegrams assuring them that the plan in Kentucky was limited to enrollment of the free blacks. He promised not to go beyond that point until he understood the question better.[16]

Burnside nevertheless persisted in his effort to secure a change in the provost marshal general's orders. He informed Lincoln that if free blacks were drafted in Kentucky, the army would secure no more than 300 from that class and would lose many other men. Burnside thought the enrollment of the free blacks properly belonged to the state, which needed them as laborers, and added that an order was about to be issued to impress them for work on the military roads. "I sincerely hope the enrollment may be stopped," he concluded. Lincoln forwarded Burnside's second dispatch to Secretary of War Stanton and noted on it, "I really think the within is worth considering."[17]

On July 4 Boyle wrote Fry a second time. The enrollment of free blacks, he said, had already resulted in a decrease in the enlistment of volunteers. Bands of guerrillas were forming throughout the state and were "encouraging opposition to enlistments in every way." Boyle warned that the state was on the verge of revolution. Boyle then contacted Bland Ballard, the federal district judge of Louisville, who expressed the unofficial opinion that the act had not "contemplated the enrollment of persons of African descent." Boyle asked the judge to communicate his opinion to Lincoln and to use his influence to secure a change in the War Department directive. Ballard advised the federal administration that the opposition to the enrollment of blacks was "well nigh the universal opinion" in Kentucky and would "do much harm." Ballard's view was echoed by N. C. Grier, the provost marshal of the nonslaveholding northeastern section of the state. An antislavery man, Grier reported that the enrollment of blacks could not be undertaken without the aid of the army.[18]

Early in July the press and state officials in Kentucky learned of the federal government's plan. The state authorities remonstrated against it. Aware of public feeling on the issue, Thomas Bramlette, who was campaigning for governor in Covington, made public pledges to "sweep away emancipation, confiscation [and] negro regiments"[19] by providing the necessary leadership to help defeat the Confederates. The Kentucky press informed the people that the president had not intended to enroll the free blacks as a preliminary to arming them but instead might employ them as laborers; Lincoln had as yet settled on nothing but a census. This reassurance was not enough to quell the public outcry. The principal complaint was that the enlistment of free blacks would imperil slavery. The *Louisville Journal* expressed confidence that the president would respect the wishes of the people of Kentucky. In view of the uproar, on July 22, 1863, the provost marshal general instructed the provost marshal for the District of Kentucky that an enrollment of the blacks need not be made if it had not already been completed. The information was promptly forwarded to the marshals in the subdistricts.

The enrollment of free blacks was still the most exciting topic of discussion on election day in August. Bramlette was elected to the office of the governor, and in his inaugural address he discussed the question of slavery. The employment of Negro troops, he said, would severely weaken the value of slaves belonging to loyal Kentuckians. He denounced the arming of blacks as an "uncalled for and needless experiment" which catered to the worst "passions of the extreme abolitionists."[20] The governor remained hostile to any signs that the army planned to enlist blacks in Kentucky.

On August 5, Adj. Gen. Lorenzo Thomas informed General Burnside of the Department of the Ohio that the secretary of war had authorized him to raise and organize into regiments of ten companies each as many troops of African descent as he was able to secure. Since Burnside commanded Kentucky, with headquarters at Cincinnati, his operations on Kentucky's border would undermine the security of slavery in Kentucky. The recruitment in southern Ohio and Indiana had already drawn extensively on fugitives from Kentucky. As the recruiting progressed, their numbers would increase.[21] Bramlette immediately asked the president to notify him if blacks in Kentucky were to be enlisted, as he hoped to avoid "the dire effects of such a movement upon the interests" of the people. "I can offer controlling reasons of law and policy against such action in Kentucky," Bramlette wired the president.[22]

Finally, on October 1, 1863, Stanton sent Lincoln a memorandum which, according to the secretary, conformed to the views expressed earlier by the president. The memorandum stated that blacks, both free and slave, would be enlisted in Tennessee, Maryland, and Missouri but not in Kentucky because military authorities in the state had impressed 6,000 blacks to build military roads. Two weeks later, on October 17, 1863, Lincoln called

for 300,000 men to meet the military needs of the nation. Kentucky's quota
was 12,701. The states were to call for volunteers, and any deficiency was to
be filled by a draft on January 5. Rumors again spread through Kentucky
that the state's slaves were to be armed. Bramlette saw a dispatch from
Washington in a newspaper announcing that the War Department would
issue an order to enlist slaves in Kentucky.[23] Within the week, however, the
state authorities of Kentucky had received fresh assurance that the blacks of
Kentucky would not be enlisted.[24]

Immediately after passage of the Conscription Act of March 3, 1863,
Lincoln had made a determined effort outside Kentucky to recruit as many
blacks as possible for military service. By July thirty black regiments were
being organized, and some were already in the field. Although freedmen
and slaves were not drafted in Kentucky, by the end of July 1863, the army
in the state was more heavily relying on them for military labor. On July 25,
General Boyle formalized the policy on impressment by issuing General
Orders No. 37. The slaves of the citizens who had "no more men and no
more money to suppress the rebellion" would be the first to be impressed,
and loyal citizens would not be asked to turn over their workers "unless
absolutely necessary." Early in August, Boyle issued General Orders No. 41
for the impressment of 6,000 black laborers from fourteen Central Kentucky counties to extend the railroad from Lebanon toward Danville. The
slaves were to be impressed from the counties through which the railroad
passed, and owners were warned that if they failed to deliver their quota, all
the slaves they owned would be seized.[25] On September 2 there followed a
special order to impress 500 blacks to supply firewood for the Louisville and
Nashville Railroad, and three weeks later another order provided 100 for
the Louisville and Frankfort Railroad for the same purpose.[26]

Near the end of 1863, it was becoming more necessary to draw on loyal
citizens for impressed labor, but an effort was first made to tap more fully
the stream of contrabands that was flowing into Kentucky from the South.
In October the public was notified that all blacks abroad without passes
would be picked up and sent to work on fortifications or other military
projects.[27] The new policy took effect and served to regulate the movements
of Negroes to the satisfaction of civil authorities. As the colder weather of
the winter of 1863–1864 approached, however, the laborers began to try to
evade impressment because of the hardships of working outdoors. The
complaints became louder and more general, and the army tried to make the
program more flexible to answer grievances. Exemptions were extended to
slaveholders who were grazing army livestock as well as to citizens with a
contract to furnish firewood to the railroads. Owners whose slaves were
subject to impressment were given the option of hiring their blacks to the
railroads.[28]

Slaveholders continued to protest bitterly, particularly in Madison and

Bourbon counties, and the colonel in command in Bourbon County threatened to arrest and imprison anyone who disobeyed the order or obstructed "its execution." By January 1864, Camp Nelson, in Jessamine County, had become recruiting center for blacks in Central Kentucky. Slaves impressed for limited duty were sent there along with those who had been newly impressed to work on military roads. The number of Negroes in the service in Kentucky was by now so great that disinterested and informed observers feared that the harvest of corn and other crops would be seriously restricted.[29]

With the recruitment of blacks going forward along Kentucky's borders starting in mid-1863, it was not long before recruiting agents were soliciting black volunteers within the state. Slaveholders reported that recruiting agents were enticing their slaves to go elsewhere to enter military service. On December 10, Governor Bramlette received a communication from Edward Cahill, an army captain, who said he had been ordered to Kentucky to recruit free blacks for the army. He asked the governor's consent and cooperation. Bramlette rejected the captain's proposal in a published letter reiterating that in deference to Kentucky's "peculiar position, and to avoid unnecessary aggravating the troubles of loyal men of Kentucky," the authorities in Washington had agreed not to recruit blacks in the state.[30] Two officers of the First Michigan Colored Regiment then solicited Boyle's aid in a similar recruiting mission in Kentucky. Boyle referred the letter to Bramlette, who sent the Michigan officers a copy of his letter to Captain Cahill. The governor warned the Michigan officers that "summary justice" would "be inflicted upon anyone attempting such an unlawful purpose." Negro recruiters would "endanger their own liberties if . . caught within this state," he warned. The editor of the *Louisville Journal* declared that "the action of the Governor" would "receive the hearty approval of every true union man in the Commonwealth." A Kentucky soldier stationed at Cumberland Gap also applauded and added: "He [the governor] will be sustained by every true Kentuckian, and many of them are willing to sholder [sic] their muskets and meet any opposition force that would attempt to carry out" such recruitment. Kentucky was nevertheless overrun by brokers who enticed one or two slaves or free blacks to leave the state and enlist. In addition, many communities in the Northwest offered large bounties for substitutes, and the brokers could profit by selling blacks as substitutes to fill local quotas.[31]

Late in January 1864 Richard Cunningham arrived in Paducah with a commission from the War Department to recruit 1,200 blacks for an artillery regiment. The counties west of the Tennessee River in Kentucky were attached to the District of West Tennessee. The adjutant general of Kentucky telegraphed the War Department for an explanation and discovered that Lucien Anderson, the congressman for the First Congressional

District (Paducah), had approved of the recruitment. Anderson had formerly been kidnapped by Confederate raiders and had become Kentucky's most
radical congressman. Cunningham, who was assisted in his recruitment by
black troops, caused much excitement by his vigorous methods of operation. He undertook to "conscript" black merchant marines from a steamboat, and a pitched battle broke out when the sailors were aided by white
soldiers. On a recruiting trip into Union County in Western Kentucky,
Cunningham impressed a steamboat to aid in his activities. Cunningham
continued to arouse bitter opposition in Western Kentucky until a late as
July 1864.[32]

Recruiting camps were located at Nashville, Clarksville, and Fort
Donelson in Tennessee and in the northwestern states along the north bank
of the Ohio River. It was not necessary to entice the Kentucky slaves into
these camps. The servants of both the loyal and Southern sympathizers left
Southern Kentucky for these camps by the "hundreds and thousands, and
received protection against being reclaimed by their masters." In December
1863, a group of leading citizens of Southern Kentucky petitioned the
secretary of war for removal of the recruiting stations on Kentucky's borders
to a point farther from Kentucky.[33]

The citizens of Christian County in Southern Kentucky sent a committee of two to confer with the governor concerning the problem of slaves
fleeing to Fort Donelson and Clarksville. As the problem was rapidly
increasing, several weeks later, twenty-four loyal citizens petitioned the
governor for "relief" from an evil that was driving them to ruin. Benjamin
H. Bristow, who represented Christian County in the legislature, informed
the governor that he had received several complaints from constituents.
"They say that the Negroes are going off from Christian County by droves
and are met at the state line by armed soldiers and escorted to the recruiting
camp at Clarksville," he wrote Bramlette. Bristow suggested an appeal to
Governor Johnson of Tennessee and to Gen. L. H. Rousseau in command
in the region.[34]

A Hopkinsville correspondent for the *Louisville Journal* reported that
hundreds of slaves were leaving Christian and Todd counties every night for
Clarksville, and many blacks were sent back to recruit others who were less
inclined to leave. The situation was so critical that Bramlette and the citizens
of Christian County persuaded Bristow to go to Washington and confer
with Lincoln and Stanton on the problem. Bristow hoped to convince them
that the camp should be moved farther south, but the administration would
offer Kentucky only credit in the draft for all blacks who had fled to the
army.[35]

In his annual message in December 1863, Governor Bramlette brought
up the subject of arming blacks. "We think, and most earnestly, that it is
better to use none but the white man to fight our battles," he asserted. He

believed it was just "as revolutionary and disloyal to subordinate the government" to the question of the Negro's freedom as it was to the question of maintaining his enslavement.[36] Despite his strong position in the message, the governor was willing to compromise. He realized that Kentucky needed the cooperation of the army to prevent slavery from collapsing immediately. The enslavement by Kentucky of blacks freed by the Emancipation Proclamation who had fled from the South continued to be a point of irritation between the state and the army. In February 1864 Bramlette sent a special message to the legislature of Kentucky on the subject of fugitive slaves from other states who had been freed by the president's proclamation. Although the governor still considered these blacks to be slaves, he agreed that the rebellion of the former masters nullified their claims to ownership. He probably considered the freedom of movement of the contraband in Kentucky to be intolerable because, again, it threatened the institution of slavery in the state. Bramlette asked the state legislature to provide special legislation for this class of blacks to resolve the conflict between the county government in Kentucky and the army. The governor probably had in mind laws which would permit cooperation of the state with the army in removing contrabands from the soil of Kentucky by enlisting them in the army and possibly crediting the state with the enlistment to meet its quota. Such a system would decrease the operations of the draft brokers and kidnappers and would also end the seizure and sale of contraband by the county sheriffs, which seemed likely to cause future collisions between the state and the army.

Despite Bramlette's appeal, however, the legislature failed to act in the matter. The General Assembly remained opposed to arming slaves in any part of the Union. The emotions of the legislators were inflamed by the newspaper reports that the secretary of war had flagrantly violated the pledge made to the governor that the slaves of Kentucky would not be armed. Although the press was not specific, the matter in question was doubtless the recruiting of slaves in the District of West Tennessee in Western Kentucky. The legislature had already committed itself to an uncompromising position. As it declared on February 18, it considered "the enlistment of Negroes as soldiers into the armies of the United States . . . impolitic."[37]

On February 1, 1864, Bramlette wrote Lincoln that he was dismayed to learn that recruiting posts had been set up in Paducah under the authority of the War Department. The governor noted that as chief executive of Kentucky he had personally sworn to see that the laws were faithfully executed. "I never shrink from responsibility, when duty demands action," he declared. "But as it is my earnest desire to avoid even the semblance of disturbance between the civil authorities of my state and any of the departments or agents of the Federal Government, I beg leave to invite your attention to the grave question which this action involves." Bramlette argued that slaves could not constitutionally be called out by the president. Individuals sent to recruit slaves in Kentucky had "no competent authority to shield them from the penalties" of violating the state's laws. They were "guilty of a felony punishable by confinement from two to twenty years," he warned. "I must interpose such power as I possess to stay the evil and you will stop those who have been sent to violate our laws, and assist me in staying the tide of passion which such acts provoke." The governor called on Lincoln to act promptly to remove the "evil" and thus to save the government the necessity "of arraying the civil powers of the state against these persons."[38]

Still another conflict between federal and state authorities occurred early in 1864, when Stanton sent Thomas to the Mississippi Valley to prepare the region for a fuller use of blacks in the military service and in agricultural pursuits in the South. Thomas had once owned slaves but had become a practical abolitionist as the war progressed. Because other states were so successfully recruiting Kentucky's black population, and many blacks were fleeing to join the army, Thomas was sure he could persuade Bramlette to draft blacks to fill the state's quota. When the two men met, however, the governor convinced Thomas that he should drop any immediate plan to enlist blacks in Kentucky.[39] By the end of March 1864 John Boyle had "authentic information" that a regiment of twelve hundred Negroes from Kentucky had been taken into service at Clarksville, Tennessee, a regiment of eleven hundred strong had been recruited at Columbus, Kentucky, and one of three hundred was mustered into service at Paducah. The adjutant general of Kentucky estimated that various other commands in Illinois, Ohio, Indiana, and Tennessee had enlisted 2,000 or more negroes from the state. The authorities of Todd County, Kentucky, filed certificates with Boyle's office showing that 285 slaves from that county had enlisted outside Kentucky. State authorities wanted to claim these blacks to fill the Kentucky's quota, but there was still no indication that the public was willing to consent to the enlistment and drafting of blacks within the state.[40]

In early 1864 the impressment of slaves in Kentucky began to end. In February, Gen. U.S. Grant revoked all orders in effect in the state, and General Burbridge, commander in Kentucky, terminated the practice on March 4. It continued locally, affecting a limited number of slaves, but post commanders were careful not to requisition the property of loyal citizens. By 1864 impressment clearly offered a less effective means of meeting manpower needs than the draft, even in Kentucky.[41] The impressment system had opened the way and had softened local resistance, as had the erosion of slavery and civil problems relating to the movement of free blacks in the state and recruiting activities nearby. As several observers had noted, if enlistment of blacks had been undertaken in Kentucky in May 1863, as it was elsewhere, an army of occupation would have been needed. As the spring of 1864 approached, however, the time seemed ripe, and radicals in Congress were determined that Kentucky should follow the lead taken by the other states.

CHAPTER FIVE

Slaves Go to War

FROM THE BEGINNING of the war, Lincoln had felt that Kentucky would be a "turning weight in the scale,"[1] and particularly since the federal government did not have great military strength in the state, he was inclined to respect the wishes of Kentuckians regarding the enlistment of blacks. Slaves were subject to the draft in all other states, however, and there was much opposition in antislavery circles to the special treatment given Kentucky. The antislavery newspapers bitterly denounced Lincoln for his forbearance. When Congress met in December 1863, several radical senators led by Henry Wilson of Massachusetts refused to accept Lincoln's pledge to Bramlette and demanded to know why the War Department had not enrolled Kentucky slaves. Secretary of War Stanton recommended that the Conscription Act be amended to eliminate various ambiguities, especially with respect to the procedure for inducting blacks, and Wilson introduced a bill for the purpose.[2] The new legislation explicitly stated that all able-bodied blacks between the ages of twenty and forty-five were part of the national force and were liable to the draft, although their owners, if loyal, would be compensated.[3]

Despite opposition to the enlistment of blacks in Kentucky, Wilson's bill received support from three of the states' congressmen. Lucien Anderson of the First Congressional District urged that loyal slaveholders be compensated for their slaves by the Federal government provided the state legislatures abolished slavery, but his resolution was defeated. During the debate Anderson expressed opposition to the conscription of the slaves of Union men in Kentucky, but when the bill came to a vote, Anderson supported the enlistment of slaves of Unionists with a bounty as compensation. Green Clay Smith of Covington and the Sixth Congressional District advocated confiscation of the slaves of Confederate sympathizers but refrained from suggesting that the slaves of Unionists be enlisted. Smith was absent when the bill passed, but he claimed he was for it and missed the vote because of illness. William H. Randall of the Eighth District, which contributed more volunteers to the Union army than any other district, also voted for the bill. The other five congressmen from Kentucky opposed the bill, with Robert Mallory spokesman. He declared that the attempt to enlist blacks from Union slave states was motivated by the "wish to demoralize and destroy the institution of slavery" and was 'a reckless crusade" which would work the destruction of the country if it continued.[4]

The Conscription Act passed on February 24, 1864, and J.B. Fry ordered Provost Marshall Sidell to begin enrolling free blacks and slaves in Kentucky on March 7. Fry asked that progress reports be sent to Washington on March 14, 20, and 25 (a final report). This timetable seemed unrealistically short, encouraging opponents to hope that the program would be destroyed if resistance prevented the schedule from being met. Sidell received a large number of protests in the Department of Kentucky, the most significant of which he sent to Fry along with his own endorsed opinion, warning officials in Washington of the seriousness of the continued opposition to the enlistment of blacks. Fry referred the communications to General Burbridge, the new commander of the Department of Kentucky, asking for a full report. When it came, the War Department issued Special Orders No. 140, which gave Burbridge "general supervision of the U.S. laws for raising men in Kentucky" and directed the provost marshal of Kentucky to regard any order from Burbridge as sufficient on the subject of enlistments.[6] Sidell ordered the provost marshals in all subdistricts to begin enrollment immediately. Some subdistrict marshals resigned rather than obey the order, and many others pleaded that they could find no enrollment officers. The enrollment was delayed for weeks. The most violent form of resistance involved the organization of guerrilla bands. All subdistrict marshals called for protection before they undertook enrollment, and Burbridge, a native of Kentucky, stationed one company near the headquarters of each provost marshal except in the First District at Paducah, which was under the command of the officer in charge of the District of West Tennessee. The provost marshal west of the Cumberland River was not able to enroll the blacks in Western Kentucky for several months, however, because of the failure to secure mounted troops in that area and because of the guerrilla operations in the region west of the Tennessee River. The military protection in Kentucky was never adequate except in the extreme eastern part of the state, where none was needed. Although units were initially supplied, the commanders of the army in Kentucky were unwilling to place a company in each district on a permanent basis, and troops were not freely furnished except in the case of single expeditions to effect a single object. The commanders pleaded "superior necessities" of troops in the field against Confederate forces.[7]

The regulations were later modified, but until then the consent of the master was required before a slave could volunteer, and many of the early enlistments came from slaves who had fled the Confederate states. As noted earlier, Negroes in Kentucky were enthusiastic about volunteering. Since blacks were not enlisted in Kentucky until two months after passage of the law of February 24, many continued to go to the Northwest to enlist. Even after enlistments had begun in Kentucky, the number of slaves who could secure the consent of their masters was limited, and the exodus to the North became greater because it was impossible for the masters to prevent it. In a few cases slaveholders brought in their blacks for enlistment and eagerly collected the bounty that was offered to volunteers. There was a growing feeling that it was better to use blacks to fill Kentucky's quota than to allow them to continue to cross the Ohio River and the Tennessee border to fill the quotas of other states. In every subdistrict partly because of the short time allotted but mostly because of the local opposition and resistance, the enrollment could not be completed according to schedule, and additional days had to be allowed. The delay restricted the enlistments that could be secured before the draft.[8]

Black enrollment was made more difficult because of the excitement created by the speeches of Frank Wolford, colonel of the First Kentucky Cavalry. Speaking to his regiment, which was stationed at Lebanon, Kentucky, Wolford condemned the enlistment of black troops, and he repeated his criticism of army policy in Danville. On March 10, 1864, after being presented with a sword by the citizens of Fayette County, the colonel denounced the order to enroll Negroes as "unconstitutional and unjust." He told the audience gathered in the Melodeon that it was "the duty of the people of Kentucky to resist . . . a violation of their guaranteed rights." The governor would protect the constitutional rights of the people, and the people should rally to his support as he worked to do so. Bramlette, an intimate friend of Wolford's, occupied a place on the platform when the colonel spoke. Wolford's position met with the approval of most of the Kentucky press.[9]

The speech caused great excitement in Lexington, Paris, and other communities in Central Kentucky, and there was fear that it had strengthened the opposition to the enrollment of blacks. The Union men in Kentucky were indignant, and William C. Goodloe, a Union judge of Fayette County who considered the addresses by the outspoken colonel to be "outrageous," called on Robert Breckinridge to counteract Wolford's influence by delivering a series of pro-Union speeches in Central Kentucky. In Lexington Breckinridge publicly defended the action of the federal government as justified by the law and the Constitution. Green Clay Smith also came to Lexington and supported the enrollment act, calling it the law of the land. To check the outbreak of widespread open resistance to the enrollment of blacks in Kentucky, the provost marshal general ordered Wolford's arrest, but the colonel was released on his promise that he would "report for trial at a designated time and place."[10]

Wolford's position echoed that of Governor Bramlette, who had declared in a public letter on January 2 that he would not tolerate the enlistment of the state's Negroes. When a legislative representative informed Bramlette in late January that black troops were being recruited in Henderson County, Bramlette announced that he would pardon anyone who shot the scoundrel responsible. He would, he said, use the entire force of the state to prevent the recruitment of blacks. Before Wolford delivered his address in Lexington on March 10, Bramlette wrote Lincoln a dispatch dated March 8 that was apparently not sent until March 13; the document asserted that the Governor would execute the laws of Kentucky against all who attempted to take slaves from their owners without consent. Before the president could respond, the provost marshal of Boyle County wired Bramlette on March 10: "I have commenced the enrollment of Negroes here. Some persons refuse to give in their lists until they know what the State Authorities intend to do. Please advise me." On March 12, Bramlette telegraphed his reply: "If the President does not upon my demand stop the Negro enrollment I will. I am waiting his answer." The next day Bramlette wired Robert Breckinridge that he desired to consult with him immediately.[11]

Breckinridge arrived in Frankfort on March 15 and joined Theodore S. Bell, General Burbridge, and A. G. Hodges in a conference with Bramlette in the Capitol Hotel. The governor produced a proclamation that he had drafted for release the next day to the people of Kentucky. It advised forcible resistance to the enrollment of slaves in the state. J. M. Kelley, the military telegraph operator at Danville, who was present and had an opportunity to see the document, thought it would be "a firebrand if published." Breckinridge and Burbridge believed that it would produce open conflict between the federal government and the state. The group conferred from eight o'clock until after three o'clock the next morning. Major revisions proposed by Bell, Breckinridge, and Burbridge produced a totally different document one-third of its original length. The governor argued against every change that was made,[12] but he published the revised version the next day in the *Frankfort Commonwealth*.

The proclamation of Governor Bramlette as published on March 16 recommended that Kentuckians quietly submit to black enrollment and trust to the American people for justice which could not be secured from the present Congress. The state's citizens should "submit to the laws and trust to legal remedies" and the ballot box.[13] The unconditional Unionists were relieved that internecine strife had been avoided; the conservatives were disappointed that Bramlette had retreated. Conservative John Jones of Paris complained: "We had just as well have no constitution and laws as not to have them enforced." Elder Aylette Raines criticized the governor for "backing down" in "a very awkward manner."[14] But William M. Pratt, a

Baptist minister of Lexington, praised Breckinridge for his role in persuading Bramlette to alter his "nullification proclamation," which had placed
Kentucky on the brink of open violence and bloodshed.[15]

The new and moderate position taken by Bramlette prevented open
conflict from occurring between the federal government and the state. In
part, the strong action that the army took in dealing with Wolford had
probably caused the governor to reconsider. Then, too, the position taken
by Bell and Breckinridge on the night of March 15 had made it clear to
Bramlette that the unconditional Unionists would support the federal
government against the state administration. For these and perhaps other
reasons, he abandoned his plan of sending Breckinridge to Washington to
negotiate with the administration. As events unfolded, it became clear that
conflict between Kentucky and the federal government would have brought
an immediate invasion of the state from north of the Ohio. The *Cincinnati
Gazette* predicted that Kentucky would be "over-run by the fresh swarm
that the northern hive would pour out upon such an occasion." A citizen of
Indiana informed Breckinridge that his state had "been looking on with the
deepest anxiety lest . . . some intrigue" carry Kentucky into the "vortex of
secession and destruction." Gov. John Brough of Ohio stood ready to take
firm action against the neighbor state. (Later in the year he advised the
federal administration that "nothing but a vigorous application of the
Maryland policy"—i.e., military occupation—would save Kentucky and
that the longer Washington delayed, "the more dangerous" Kentucky
became.)[16]

On March 22, 1864, Bramlette, Archibald Dixon, and Albert G.
Hodges, editor of the *Commonwealth,* left Frankfort for Washington to
confer with Lincoln on the coming enrollment of blacks. When knowledge
of the conference became public, M. M. Benton, an antislavery Unionist of
Covington, wrote Secretary of the Treasury Chase that the truly loyal men
of Kentucky hoped the president would stand firm on the issue. As matters
developed, however, the meeting resulted in an understanding that was
satisfactory to all concerned. The chief executive promised that blacks
would not be enlisted in any county in Kentucky that met its quota by the
enlistment of whites, and he added that any Negroes who joined the army
would be removed from the state for training. The second provision was
calculated to bring relief from the "unauthorized and offensive" (Bramlette's words) interference of officers, soldiers, and recruiting brokers with the
resident slaves. The president further assured the governor that any recruitment of blacks would be conducted without "collateral embarrassment,
disorder, and provocation." In a memorandum to Stanton, Lincoln set
down the points that Bramlette wanted the army to concede, noting that he,
the president, thought the requests "just and reasonable." On March 31,
Hodges wired Breckinridge from Baltimore: "Everything right. We are

coming home."[17] No official report of the Washington conference was made when the governor returned to Frankfort, but on April 2 Editor Hodges reported that Governor Bramlette had expressed his satisfaction with the visit to Washington.[18] Hodges was constantly asked to explain the agreement reached, and he turned to the governor. According to Bramlette, the president had agreed that officers and recruiting brokers would cease meddling with slaves in Kentucky. General Burbridge, who had been made responsible for seeing that the draft was conducted according to law, had already issued orders to correct existing abuses.[19]

The controversy concerning the enrollment and enlistment of blacks split the Union party in Kentucky. A call was issued by the Union Democratic central committee, controlled by George D. Prentice and James Guthrie, for a state convention to meet in Louisville on May 25, from which delegates were sent to the Democratic National Convention in Chicago. Former governor James F. Robinson, Governor Bramlette, Lt. Gov. R. T. Jacob, and Frank Wolford were active members of the party. The unconditional Unionists, dominated by Robert Breckinridge and Lucien Anderson, refused to recognize the convention as legitimate and held their own Union Democratic convention, sending delegates to Baltimore in support of Lincoln.[20]

The opposition to the enrollment of blacks did not cease with the agreement between Bramlette and Lincoln. Wolford remained as determined as ever in denouncing the arming of blacks. He had been joined by Lieutenant Governor Jacob. In January Jacob had addressed the senate on the subject of slavery and the war. Kentucky was "not fighting for the preservation of slavery," he had declared, nor was the state "fighting for its destruction." If the institution went down in the effort to maintain the Union, well and good; if it was saved in preserving the Union, well and good. All that Kentucky asked, he claimed, was that the enormous sacrifices not defy the Constitution but be incidental to the prosecution of a war for the maintenance of the Union and Constitution. Two months later, in March, Jacob had urged Lincoln to delay the enrollment of blacks because there was great danger of "producing an outbreak of a portion of our loyal people." "I dreadfully fear a conflict between the Federal and State authorities," he explained.[21] Jacob spoke in the Melodeon Hall in Lexington on April 2 and insisted that Lincoln had no more right "to destroy the Constitution than Jefferson Davis." The next speaker, Wolford, charged that the war "had been perverted from its original purpose to one of fanaticism. McClellan . . . prosecuted the war upon Christian and enlightened principles . . . ; he was opposed to stealing Negroes."[22]

Jacob and Wolford spoke at Lebanon and Paris later in April. At Paris Jacob declared that Charles I had been beheaded for lesser crimes than those of Lincoln. A correspondent for the *Cincinnati Gazette* accused Jacob of being opposed to the administration because the army would draft his own slaves. At the Union Democratic convention in Louisville, Wolford severely criticized Lincoln's letter to Hodges. "The doctrine of the letter was that of the despot," he charged.[23] Lincoln checked Wolford's political activities by ordering his arrest.

The War Department ordered Kentucky to raise 10,000 state troops for a term of six months. Bramlette appointed Wolford to raise and command them. The unconditional Unionists feared that the men would be used for the purpose of hindering the enlistment of blacks. William C. Goodloe believed that only individuals who, like Wolford, were hostile to the administration would be appointed to any command. "If the President does not stop the recruiting of these six months men, we shall have Civil War in Kentucky in ninety days," he warned. A Kentucky Unionist wrote Lincoln and predicted that the new troops would be "engaged indirectly," at least, in thwarting "the administration's method of putting down the rebellion." A committee of the Union League of Newport advised Lincoln that Wolford had openly avowed, evidently with the knowledge and approval of the governor, that under certain contingencies, he would lead the regiment against national forces.[24] The Unionists urged Robert Breckinridge to go to Washington to secure, among other things, the cancellation of the order. In the end, however, the recruitment effort was discontinued as the result of a misunderstanding.[25] Bramlette tendered 10,000 troops to the War Department who were rejected because their term was three months rather than the six months that Stanton had specified. Thinking the troops no longer needed, the governor ordered Wolford to dismiss them. When the error was discovered, the adjutant general of Kentucky claimed that it had not been possible to raise the requisite number of six months men because the army had begun its "unfortunate attempt" to recruit blacks in the state. With blacks called into military service, Boyle explained, potential white recruits had to remain at home to cultivate the land.[26]

If the original reason for arresting Wolford was to check his influence in promoting resistance to the enlistment of blacks, by July the administration simply wanted to prevent Wolford from drawing attention to the issue. Early in July, the military authorities in Kentucky rearrested him and charged him with discouraging enlistments. Wolford was to be released on the condition that he pledge to "neither do or say anything" that would "directly or indirectly tend to hinder, delay or embarrass the employment and use of colored persons, as soldiers, seamen . . . , so long as the U.S. Government chose to so employ and use them." Wolford replied that he could not "bargain for his liberty as a free man on any such terms."[27]

The governor published correspondence between Wolford, Jacob, and himself in which he blamed the federal administration for the failure to secure white volunteers in Kentucky. Bramlette charged that large farms had been wholly robbed of labor and that a considerable number of the blacks had been recruited to the credit of other states. The *Louisville Daily Journal* took up the complaint, blaming the Kentucky abolitionists, who had "prevailed upon Mr. Lincoln to violate his direct and solemn promise to Governor Bramlette that slaves in Kentucky should not be enlisted without the consent of the owner.[28] Hodges, who had become a strong administration supporter, did not follow the lead of the *Journal*. He informed Bramlette that the governor's part in the Wolford-Jacob correspondence was "the most imprudent act" of his life. Hodges assured Lincoln of Bramlette's loyalty to the Union but meanwhile wondered whether the governor was not being manipulated by men with very different aims.[29]

The Bramlette-Lincoln agreement finally broke down because most of the districts did not meet their quotas by sufficient white volunteers to make a draft unnecessary. On March 25, all nine districts in Kentucky were deficient, with a total deficit of 15,472 even after the number of Kentuckians who had entered the Confederate service had been subtracted from the quota for the state. An effective enrollment organization had plainly been lacking. Still, the unconditional Unionists argued that the effort to meet the Kentucky quota by recruiting only whites had failed for reasons unrelated to the arming of the slave and insisted that black enlistments were necessary. The draft came late in March, and a call was made for 9,186 men. Those who responded numbered 4,193; 4,993 failed to report. Some fled to Canada, others joined guerrilla bands, and still others, being forced to fight, sided with the Confederacy.[30]

When the March draft failed, the army began recruiting blacks in Kentucky. General Burbridge issued General Orders No. 34 in conformity with War Department orders on April 18. The provost marshal of Kentucky and his subordinates were directed to receive and enlist as soldiers all able-bodied slaves and free blacks of lawful age who applied. Any unauthorized person found recruiting blacks within the borders of Kentucky was to be arrested. Loyal slaveholders were to receive certificates of ownership and were to be compensated.[31] Now at last Kentucky's slaves had their chance. Large numbers from the counties in Central Kentucky came into the provost marshal's office and volunteered for service. In Boyle County the marshal opened his office for enlistment on a Saturday, and nearly a hundred joined. On Sunday almost twice as many were received. "Nearly everybody's black able-bodied men were gone or going," wrote a resident of the county. The *Covington American* reported that Negroes were arriving from the interior counties in swarms. About 200 were said to have come in three days. The draft quotas of many counties were reduced by these volunteers. The entire quota of Jessamine county was filled by black enlistments.[32] In Madison County, one hundred signed up on a single June afternoon.[33]

On June 1, Governor Bramlette sent a strong protest to Burbridge against the recruitment of Negroes. He claimed there was no authority for the action, that it violated the promises made to him by the president and the secretary of war. The protest received little consideration. Outraged Kentuckians threatened the slaves and often apprehended them on their way to enlist, sometimes beating, maiming, and even murdering them, according to judge advocate General Holt. Slaves who were rejected as physically unfit for service were in similar danger when they attempted to return to their homes. Between May 13 and July 1864, eight slaves were killed in Nelson County for attempting to volunteer. In Marion County, slaveholders caught two blacks attempting to enlist and cut off their left ears. Four owners whipped fifteen Negroes in Lebanon because they wanted to enlist. Nor were the provost marshals exempt from the violence. In Spencer County an agent was severely beaten and chased home. A Green County Marshal reported that the provost marshals were flogged when they merely spoke of enlisting slaves. When seventeen blacks left Green County to enlist, a mob of young men followed and whipped them. In Larue County a special agent was stripped, tied to a tree, and cowhided. In the course of the war seven provost marshals were slain in Kentucky either directly or indirectly as a result of the agitation. In May, Burbridge authorized the arrest of any person interfering with or discouraging voluntary enlistments, and early in June he ordered that blacks rejected for military service be given passes placing them under the protection of the army until they reached home.[34]

The regulations relating to the enlistment of blacks were made more flexible to meet the needs of slaveholders willing to cooperate with the army. The slave could be enlisted by the owner without the slave's consent, and the owner, if loyal, could pocket the bounty of $100 and could receive as much as $300 in the future if loyalty could be verified. The assistant provost marshall general of Kentucky announced that slaves would be accepted as substitutes for whites, and the provost marshal general later went so far as to permit whites and blacks to substitute for each other. The secretary of war authorized owners to induct into military service any slave found leaving a master and taking refuge in towns or camps.[35]

Force was not to be used to compel blacks to enlist, but many slaves were carried off without their consent. An Evansville correspondent for the *Louisville Democrat* reported that squads of soldiers were taking blacks from their beds in the dead of the night in Henderson and adjoining counties. On one occasion the provost marshal of the district raised a posse, recaptured the slaves, and turned the soldiers over to the commander of the post at Evansville. Lincoln received complaints from the vicinity of Henderson that blacks had been seized, carried off, and forced to enlist without their consent. The president ordered Lorenzo Thomas to investigate and correct the situation. Governor Bramlette also wrote two letters to Secretary of War Stanton and complained about the coercion of blacks. He particularly condemned the activities of Colonel Cunningham in Western Kentucky. Another correspondent wrote Lincoln that Kentuckians from Henderson to the mouth of the Cumberland River and up the Cumberland to Nashville had been turned into "rebel sympathizers" by the Negro problem. Governor Bramlette also received complaints from the citizens of Union County to the effect that 180 blacks had been forcibly taken by recruiting agents when the county was 452 short in its efforts to fill a quota that the citizens regarded as unjust.[36]

The confusion of authority in Kentucky contributed to the difficulty of enforcing the measures for enlisting blacks. In 1863 General Thomas was placed in charge of Negro recruitment. When the enrollment got under way, he moved his office to Louisville and issued General Orders No. 20 on June 13, 1864. A camp of reception was established in each congressional district, and Gen. A. L. Chetlain was to supervise the organization of black troops in Kentucky from headquarters in Louisville. Chetlain's approach was to send a Negro company into a section with orders to bring in all able-bodied blacks, using force if necessary. By July 4, 1964, he had assembled a full regiment in Louisville, and two other regiments were more than half filled. His method raised a storm of protest from the citizens and congressmen of Kentucky. On one occasion a black regiment intending to march through the city of Louisville on the way to a picnic ground found its permit revoked. As recruitment proceeded, crops suffered, and a committee of citizens went to Washington in late July to protest a labor shortage that was, they claimed, destroying the tobacco industry.[37]

Sidell complained to Fry that Negro regiments engaged in recruiting were "introducing much trouble and confusion." The provost marshal system had been set up by the Conscription Act of March 1863 to administer the enlistment and draft under the law, but Sidell said that his work was complicated, and the resistance to black enlistments increased, by confusion resulting from the existence of three authorities supervising the draft of blacks in Kentucky.[38]

When General Burbridge had first been charged with responsibility for raising black troops in Kentucky, he had sent them to Louisville without delay, placing most of them in the early period of enlistment on garrison duty so as to free white troops for active service. The general now complained to Thomas about the marauding by recruits under the command of Chetlain's officer. Burbridge argued that black enlistments conducted by him would create less hostility because he was a native Kentuckian and a large slaveholder and because the men he put in charge of black regiments were natives of Kentucky. The provost marshal general apparently agreed and reaffirmed Burbridge's authority in a communication to Thomas dated July 3. Thomas was asked to aid Burbridge in carrying out his plans, Chetlain was withdrawn from Kentucky, and Col. James S. Brisbin became superintendent of colored troops in Kentucky. Although three authorities in Kentucky had now been reduced to two, confusion continued to contribute to the difficulties involved in enlisting blacks in the state.[39]

Regardless of the agency responsible for black recruitment, the regulations governing the age and fitness of conscripts were applied very loosely. It was assumed that the young slaves did not know exactly how old they were, and it was generally suggested in Kentucky that no one be taken who looked younger than sixteen (as noted above, the regulations provided for recruits between the ages of twenty and forty-five). If an older man seemed to be in good health, the upper age limit was not strictly observed. Thomas had suggested that men who were not considered sufficiently fit could be used by the engineers, quartermasters, and commissary departments and this practice was followed. Although blacks were not to be compelled to enlist, only force of the crudest sort drew censure. Sidell recommended that blacks unwilling to volunteer be brought to headquarters nevertheless and be ordered to mark or sign the form to indicate that they *were* volunteers. After all, slaves were accustomed to doing as they were told.[40]

When the army had firmly established its power with respect to the recruitment of blacks, attention shifted to the tendency of many to enlist outside the state. As soon as the slaves learned that they could enlist without the consent of their masters, they came to headquarters in a steady stream.[41] But they quickly realized that it was safer to cross the border and enlist elsewhere, and by July 5, more than 12,000 had done so.[42] Other blacks left Kentucky to avoid being drafted. The largest number went to Tennessee, where the superintendent of black troops in June admitted having received 340 slaves from Southern Kentucky. Benjamin Bristow and others from Todd County urged the provost marshal of Tennessee to order all the Kentucky slaves camping around the post at Clarksville to be returned to their owners. Sidell estimated that there were 2,000 Kentucky blacks in Tennessee and 500 in and about Clarksville who had fled from Christian County, on the border between the two states. The commander of the Clarksville post claimed that there were 125 Kentucky slaves nearby, most of whom were unfit for military service. The issue became so bitter and controversial that Bramlette appointed an agent to take a census of the slaves who had enlisted outside the state. According to the provost marshal of Kentucky, proof existed that 594 slaves from Trigg, 210 from Todd, and 147 from Logan County had enlisted at Clarksville. Although these individuals had been enrolled in Kentucky, the records showed that they had enlisted in Tennessee,, and the provost marshal general permitted Kentucky to take credit for them. The War Department echoed Sidell, requesting that a complete tabulation of slaves enlisting in Tennessee be made for all Kentucky counties.[43]

On the northern border of Kentucky, Evansville and Cincinnati attracted fugitive slaves. Cincinnati offered a local bounty, and many whites as well as some blacks from Campbell and Kenton counties crossed the river to collect between $100 and $300. The provost marshal of Kentucky reported that Campbell County had not received credit for 542 men who had enlisted in other jurisdictions. The situation in Campbell and Kenton counties was made more difficult because they had very few blacks, and they, too, found it advisable to offer local bounties. Negroes began to rush from Central Kentucky. Eventually army officers from Northern Kentucky were authorized to recruit slaves in the larger slaveholding counties in the north and to enlist them in Campbell and Kenton counties. The non-slaveholding whites became entirely reconciled to the movement of Negroes to Covington to enlist; as more blacks enlisted, fewer whites would be needed.[44]

In July 1864 a second draft called for 16,805 men from Kentucky, and fewer than 4,000 met their obligation by personal service, substitution, or payment of commutation money. It would obviously be necessary to fill the quota with blacks, and the resistance of slaveholders and proslavery men was expected to intensify. On July 5, 1864, Lincoln issued a proclamation establishing martial law in Kentucky. He asserted that combinations had been forming in the state for "the purpose of inciting the rebel forces to renew" their operations in Kentucky.[45] Burbridge began making arrests which terminated the day after the November election with the apprehension of Wolford and Jacob, (Jacob had been making speeches advising armed resistance to the enlistment of blacks).[46]

By the end of July, Holt estimated that 10,000 black troops had enlisted for the July draft call. Slaves were coming in at the rate of about 100 per day despite the fact that they were often severely beaten when caught running away. Recruiting was particularly active in Henderson, where several hundred slaves were enlisted in August 1864. The adjutant general of Indiana had recruiting officers in Henderson and Owensboro, and Kentucky ultimately claimed 1,000 recruits in Evansville. Eventually the first flush of enthusiasm of the new recruiting drive began to fade away. Officers took blacks by force at a fair in Louisville and compelled the able-bodied to enlist. In some counties, including Shelby, public meetings were held by the citizens to build up support for filling the quota from black enlistments, and many counties did so. By the end of August, the editor of the *National Unionist* was sure that half the counties would ultimately take this course. Less than a month later, 14,000 blacks had enlisted in Kentucky. Lorenzo Thomas was sure their total number in Kentucky would reach 20,000.[47]

As the draft got under way in September, there was interference and resistance in many districts. After the first call, trained units had been removed from many districts, and no attempt was made to enforce the draft in many counties until armed protection was again furnished. In Southern and Western Kentucky the guerrillas intensified their efforts to sabotage recruitment, and because of the increased insecurity, many eligible blacks fled into Tennessee.[48]

On June 28, 1864, Lincoln had signed a law repealing the Fugitive Slave Law that had passed Congress after bitter opposition by Mallory, Davis, and Powell of Kentucky.[49] The repeal accelerated the decline of slavery and removed an important check on kidnapping. Bounty scalpers became numerous in Kentucky. They induced blacks to enlist for a small sum and carried them to the Northwest, where they were sold as substitutes for a large profit. Some of the provost marshals also provided slaves for the nefarious work of the substitute brokers.[50] To prevent brokers from the Northwest from operating in Kentucky, troops and gunboats had to be stationed along the Ohio.[51]

The order permitting blacks to be substituted for whites made it possible for the provost marshals to operate independently as bounty scalpers among Kentuckians who desired to avoid the draft.[52] To curb the substitute brokers coming from abroad, the Kentucky legislature made it a misdemeanor, punishable by a fine of $1,000 and one year of imprisonment, to remove a substitute from the state.[53] No such penalty was imposed on operations within the state. Seventeen counties ultimately offered bounties for substitutes, and blacks became the most available source of supply.[54] In September 1864, Gen. J. M. Schofield made an inspection of Kentucky and found instances of gross corruption in the administration of military affairs. "The provost marshal's department in Louisville and the military police of the District of Kentucky appeared to have been mainly engaged in trading Negro substitutes and extorting fines for violation of petty regulations," he reported.[55]

The attitude of the soldiers stationed in Kentucky was a more critical problem than was the trade in substitutes. New action taken by Colonel Wolford became the most serious incident relating to the arming of slaves. Wolford disbanded the First Kentucky Cavalry in February 1863 and promised in a speech to the regiment that if Lincoln did not modify his Emancipation Proclamation in twenty days, the colonel himself would fight for the South if forced to take up arms again. In an address at Lebanon in May 1864, Wolford expressed the belief that Lincoln's policy of enlisting Negroes had cost the Union army 200,000 white men. A Lexington correspondent for the *Knoxville Register* wrote that Wolford's regiment had been demoralized. The commander of another Kentucky outfit reported a "bad spirit" among his troops as well. The great fear was that low morale and resentment would spread to other regiments. The provost marshal of Kentucky believed that Kentucky soldiers were "indifferent to the question of enrolling Negroes, but they would conform to the opinion of the Civil leaders of Kentucky." Robert Breckinridge was sure there had been a scheme for "an *émeute* of the Kentucky troops in consequence of Wolford's arrest but it had been checked by Bramlette's pacific proclamation." The determined and energetic action of the army against Wolford made other Kentucky army officers hesitate. Their attitude contrasted with that of the regiments from the Northwest, which were generally in favor of using black troops. The officers of the Fourth Indiana Cavalry stationed near Henderson passed resolutions advocating a vigorous prosecution of the war. They declared that the president should use "every means in his power" to destroy the rebellion, and they pledged themselves to support all such measures undertaken.[56] Many northern regiments contained a few soldiers who were strongly committed to the arming of blacks and to the destruction of slavery, and the other members of the outfit identified with blacks, opposing the civilian population and the Kentucky units.[57]

The Thirteenth Kentucky Cavalry was stationed in Cumberland County to protect the provost marshal in the work of enlisting and drafting recruits. Col. J. W. Weatherford, commander of the regiment, informed the provost marshal that he "would furnish protection for any other purpose but the enrollment of Negroes," which he "would resist . . . to the last." The threats of the citizens and soldiers and the colonel's refusal to cooperate caused the provost marshal to flee the county under cover of night. Sidell conferred with Burbridge, who took the recalcitrant officer to task and made him promise to "do his whole duty." The officers and soldiers of the Thirteenth Cavalry, however, continued to interfere with the enlistment of blacks and on occasions used violence against the recruits and enrollment officers. A detachment of the Thirteenth was sent to Adair County to assist the provost marshal, and many of its members were active in preventing Negroes from enlisting.[58] A squad of the Thirteenth Kentucky Cavalry sent to Lebanon to protect the provost marshal in his work created so much disruption that the provost marshal had the men removed and placed charges against them. The climax came when the provost marshal was fired upon, supposedly by a soldier. Some of the officers and men of the Thirteenth Cavalry were court-martialed, and the colonel was temporarily placed under arrest, but the obstruction continued. In August soldiers of the Thirteenth Kentucky Cavalry stationed in Glasgow used threats of violence to prevent many blacks from enlisting. A. G. Hobson, commander of the third district of the provost marshal's office in Kentucky, contacted the colonel who promised to restore order within his command.[59] The resistance had now continued unabated for six months.

But although hostility to the enlistment of blacks was widespread, it was not universal. A soldier with the Nineteenth Kentucky Infantry in Louisiana was willing to come home and fight Kentucky rebels if an open rupture came on the Negro question. Col. Leonidas Metcalfe, another Kentucky soldier, was in favor of using black troops because they would be "a power and strength" in the struggle.[60] Albert Hodges reported to Lincoln that the Forty-ninth Kentucky Infantry gave him 417 votes to 20 for McClellan at the end of October, 1864. When the Fifty-seventh Kentucky Infantry passed through Frankfort early in October, it gave three cheers for Lincoln. The soldiers from Eastern Kentucky were strong for the Union.[61] In other units the story was plainly different. A recruit from a Northern state stationed in Kentucky accused Kentucky officers and troops of devoting most of their time to hunting for slaves and returning them to their owners,[62] and a colonel from a Tennessee artillery unit claimed that he knew many Kentucky citizens both in and out of the Union army who were acting in collusion with the rebels in arms.[63]

The great danger was the possibility of a clash between Kentucky outfits and regiments from outside the state. Several disputes broke out between the Sixth Kentucky Cavalry and the Eleventh Michigan Cavalry. On March 10, 1864, the Sixth Kentucky Cavalry left for the front, but not before a confrontation had occurred with the Eleventh Michigan Cavalry; shots were exchanged on the evening of March 9. Early in 1865 the white Kentucky cavalry that was on patrol near Camp Nelson came into conflict with the Eleventh Michigan Cavalry, and a Michigan soldier was shot in the head. The Kentucky cavalry fired several shots at the Sixth U.S. Colored Cavalry at Camp Nelson, and in Louisville an officer of a black regiment reported that hardly a day passed without violence to one or more of his men. Robert Terrill, who had helped organize the Eleventh Kentucky Cavalry but had resigned from it because of the Emancipation Proclamation and the enlistment of blacks, was "a boisterous opponent of the Government." He advocated "openly and noisily the cause of Southern independence" and agitated the question in Northern Kentucky. Conditions became so critical that the problem was made the subject of a special investigation, and near the end of 1864 an inspector general recommended to the War Department that regiments raised in Kentucky be transferred elsewhere so that they did not serve in the state.[64]

Kentucky's hostility to the enlistment of blacks never ceased throughout the war, finally emerging as "a general opposition to all Government measures" and to the enrollment of any class of citizens. Still, the pressure created by the draft of July was eased by the large number of Kentucky blacks who volunteered. In October 1864 a resident of Louisville wrote Joseph Holt that he had never seen "anything go on more smoothly than the draft" in Jefferson County, and the reports from some other counties revealed the same general circumstances. In at least some parts of the state, drafted men came in according to appointment or delivered their slaves without a murmur.

Lincoln's course of action with respect to Kentucky (and other border states) seems to warrant further explanation, however. After his March 1864 meeting with Bramlette the president explained his view in a letter to Hodges dated April 4. Lincoln claimed to have been controlled by events. As previously noted, when the border states rejected compensated emancipation, the chief executive felt forced to choose between surrendering the Union, and with it the Constitution, or recruiting blacks into the military.[65] Hodges showed the president's letter to various prominent Union men in Kentucky, only one of whom disagreed with Lincoln's reasoning. Indeed, the president's position was very close to that of the state's conservative Union men. As they saw it, the events of the war might terminate slavery, but intervention by the federal government for the explicit purpose of eliminating the institution was wrong. These men were convinced that Lincoln's actions were properly motivated.

Public opinion in Kentucky altered by degrees. In late October 1864 S. P. Chase spoke in Lexington, taking the position that slavery "must be abolished throughout the whole country." Chase's speech was received with earnest applause, and he was deeply impressed by the Unionism of Lexington. Chase spoke to the same effect in Louisville and Covington. He had almost been mobbed in Covington several years before, after making a speech which was much more moderate. Most noteworthy of all, however, is the fact that as public opinion was shifting along Kentucky's northern border, a drastic change was taking place in Kentucky's social structure. Since all slaves who enlisted were made free, 25,000 gained their freedom in 1864, and their families as well were legally free. By the end of 1864, the army was well on its way toward making emancipation a reality in Kentucky.[66]

CHAPTER SIX

From Soldier to Freedman

AFTER THE UNION victories at Vicksburg and Gettysburg in July 1863, attention was focused on the question of reconstruction. The most persistent topic of public discussion was the place of blacks in postwar society. Northern public opinion accepted the Emancipation Proclamation as permanently establishing the status of blacks as free men, and the proclamation recognized the right of emancipated slaves to defend their freedom. By the end of 1863, as we have seen, the policy of the army had been enlarged to include the arming of slaves as a necessary part of the program to increase the military strength of the Union army.

Although Seward rather than Lincoln was the architect of the modified policy the president gave guarded support to the changes that were taking place. Lincoln knew that the nation required the Negroes' help and that the freedmen needed to be treated honorably. "If they stake their lives for us, they must be prompted by the strongest motives—even the promise of freedom. And the promise must be kept."[1] By December 1864, Kentucky remained the only significant outpost of legal slavery in the nation.[2] But the institution lacked the ability to enforce measures necessary to give it reality. The action of the army in Kentucky was gradually modified to include provisions for the welfare of the blacks, and proposals for benevolence became an integral part of the military objectives. The army's role as the guardian of the slaves took shape as Congress slowly granted blacks a measure of equality and stamped out the remaining vestiges of bondage. After the Fugitive Slave Law had been repealed, slavery in Kentucky began to disappear because the surrounding free states would not return fugitives.[3]

By June 1864, the Republican party had committed itself to the abolition of slavery throughout the land. Lincoln accepted this policy and supported the Thirteenth Amendment with the hope that it would resolve the problems in Kentucky. While Lincoln was pursuing this course, Seward was covertly undertaking a military solution in Kentucky by using the army as an instrument to destroy slavery. Even after the draft quotas were filled, the army sought out new black recruits. The governor of Kentucky complained to Lincoln that such action was obstructing the restoration of the Union by committing the government to abolition as an objective of the war. The sentiment of the loyal masses of Kentucky, he said, was that the blacks should not enter into the settlement made at the end of the war. In January 1865 Bramlette informed the Kentucky legislature that since the adjournment of the last session of the General Assembly, the army had been sending out troops throughout the state to gather up blacks by force. "Wanton oppression of citizens, fraud, corruption, and imbecility, have too frequently charactized the military career of some officers in Kentucky during the time since your adjournment," Bramlette continued, but he firmly opposed all efforts, from every source, to make the Negro an issue in the struggle to maintain national life.[4]

The new aggressive program about which the governor complained was being conducted by Colonel Brisbin, who had been appointed by General Burbridge to be superintendent of colored troops in Kentucky. Brisbin was an antislavery man from Pennsylvania who kept closely in touch with the antislavery politicians. The colonel issued General Orders No. 6 early in 1865 to modify the provost marshal general's Orders No. 25 of July 25, 1864, which permitted owners to have their slaves who were fugitives drafted into military service without the blacks' consent. Brisbin's new order permitted his recruiting officers to arrest as vagrants and to enlist in military service all Negroes who had left their masters. The provost marshals were also asked to "encourge masters" to put their Negroes into the army and "to persuade" the blacks to enlist. In order to avoid conflict with General Orders No. 5, issued on August 3, which prohibited the use of force in recruiting slaves, Brisbin included a paragraph providing that "no officer will force, deceive, or inveigh any negro into the service of the United States."[5]

Complaints poured into Washington from Kentucky against Brisbin's recruiting officers. It was said that some blacks were seized by recruiters late at night while the slaves slept; others were reputedly tortured when they did not cooperate with the officers. Garret Davis complained on the floor of the Senate that the "entire negro military population" of Bourbon County had been "swept from their owners," leaving farms destitute. In the House, Brutus Clay also censured the army and Congress for robbing the farms in Kentucky of their labor. The provost marshal general ordered Sidell to investigate the complaints and see that the practice was stopped, and Sidell asked Burbridge to aid him in carrying out the order from Washington. J. B. Fry wanted to know under whose orders Brisbin was acting and specifically how he was forcing blacks into military service. Burbridge supplied the desired response. He directed his adjutant to inform Sidell that in all instances where recruiting officers had forced blacks to enlist, these officers had been "promptly called to account" for violating orders. Burbridge insisted that Brisbin's order was based on General Thomas's order of July 1864 and that vagrant runaway slaves were arrested and were told that they must either enlist or go home.

Nevertheless, with Brisbin's tacit consent, his recruiting officers were using force that lacked subtlety and often flagrantly violated the adjutant general's orders. Brisbin was convinced that many Kentuckians had sent their slaves away from home to prevent them from being drafted. When he issued his special order to seize these slaves, the owners became as busy hurrying the blacks back home as they had been sending the slaves away. Brisbin looked upon his order as having "hit the institution another powerful blow" in Kentucky and was convinced it would give the army 6,000 new black soldiers in the state. "I take every way I can to get the slaves," he confessed to Senator Wade. "I shall go on and if left alone will kill slavery in Kentucky. . . . The problem of freedom can be worked out under army rules and Kentucky is now nominally free."

The army's war against slavery in Kentucky caused Bramlette and General Burbridge to become bitter enemies. On November 14, 1864, Bramlette angrily informed the president: "I regret that General Burbridge is pursuing a course calculated to exasperate and infuriate, rather than pacify and conciliate. His whole course . . . has been such as was most calculated to inaugurate revolt, and produce collisions." Burbridge had added to his destructive measures against slavery a rigid and arbitrary control of commerce. By December 1864 Bramlette was charging that if Burbridge had followed the instructions from Washington concerning the enlistment of blacks and had consulted with chief executive of the state, harmony would have prevailed. For his part Burbridge questioned the governor's loyalty, and after he became aware that Bramlette was making efforts to secure his removal, Burbridge had army officers collect information about the governor calculated to prove that Bramlette sympathized with the Confederate cause. A radical Unionist of Kentucky informed Lincoln that the removal of Burbridge "would be a triumph" for the rebels and "the severest blow" that loyal people of Kentucky had ever received. Two delegations departed for Washington, the one to urge the general's removal and the other to argue for his retention. Seward supported Burbridge, and the general was retained—only to be eased out after he issued an order on February 6 disbanding all state troops under the command of Bramlette. Lincoln had considered taking this very action himself but had not authorized Burbridge to do so. Lincoln revoked the order, and on February 10 the *Louisville Journal* announced that Burbridge had been removed. A Union man of Lexington queried the president: "Are we to be sold to Governor Bramlette and the Copperheads of Kentucky? . . . General Burbridge is our leader, and we will not be led by Bramlette. . . . If Burbridge is sustained the Union party will be triumphant, if not the Copperheads will triumph and Kentucky is gone forever." Dr. Douglas L. Price, also a Union man from Lexington, wrote Lincoln: "Your enemies here are jubilant and your friends are despondent over the rumored removal of General Burbridge. With him in command we will quietly and peaceably eradicate slavery from the State." On February 23, a Union man reported to Henry Wilson from Frankfort, Kentucky: "Our friends [are] perfectly demoralized by reason of the recent action of the administration in regard to this military district. . . ." The *Frankfort Commonwealth* explained the president's action: "Mr. Lincoln had to change his commanders here, or give the whole of his time to the management of Kentucky affairs." The president had apparently decided to pacify Kentucky.[8]

The Thirteenth Amendment abolishing slavery throughout the United States seemed to Lincoln the best strategy calculated at once to pacify the state and to establish a national policy. An amendment to the Constitution would reaffirm the Emancipation Proclamation and would avoid the question of legality that would probably arise if slavery were abolished in the border states by a supplementary emancipation proclamation. The amendment would also place the freedom of the blacks beyond the reach of the whims of the changing legislative bodies. Congressional support for the proposal was growing. On December 14, 1863, a bill was introduced in the House of Representatives but was not brought up for debate until the last day of May 1864. In the meantime a similar bill was introduced in the Senate. When the Senate bill was reported from the judiciary committee, Davis of Kentucky deprecated all attempts to abolish slavery by federal measures. At the end of a long and fiery speech he predicted that mob violence would result from such legislation.[9]

In April, Reverdy Johnson of Maryland spoke on the bill to amend the Constitution, describing it as a worthy alternative to the destruction of slavery through a convulsive effort by the slaves themselves. Congress should act with "the mild though powerful influences of that higher and elevated morality which the Christian religion teaches."[10] The Reverend Robert Breckinridge wrote Johnson and commended him for his enlightened position. "It seems to me that the party now in possession of the Federal power would be justly chargeable with extreme recklessness or extreme folly," Breckinridge wrote, "if after destroying everything in the institution of slavery that made it endurable, they should now leave it in its present frightful condition—utterly demoralized."[11] The Senate passed the joint resolution to amend the Constitution, but it failed to receive the required two-thirds vote of the House.

In June 1864 the National Union Convention nominated Lincoln for reelection and included in the party platform a plank approving a constitutional amendment to abolish slavery "within the limits or the jurisdiction of the United States." Lincoln noted the resolution with approval.[12] In his

annual message on December 6, 1864, the president asked Congress to
reconsider the amendment to abolish slavery because "the voice of the
people" had been heard in the November election and the "will of the
majority" had "clearly declared in favor of such constitutional amendment."[13]

Proponents of the abolition of slavery by such federal means had become a more vocal minority in Kentucky by 1864. Since the opponents of
emancipation argued against the amendment on state's rights grounds,
however, many antislavery men outside of Kentucky urged that less tension would result if slavery were abolished by state action. Very few antislavery Kentuckians favored this procedure, because the Kentucky constitution
adopted in 1849 made such action difficult. First, as noted earlier, two
consecutive sessions of the Kentucky legislature were required to approve a
resolution calling a constitutional convention. The question then had to be
submitted to the people in an election, and only afterward could a convention measure be passed. It would therefore require six or seven years to
complete the process. Informed observers in Kentucky agreed that slavery
would be destroyed by the friction of the war before that time. Many Union
men agreed that state action would only result in dividing their party in
Kentucky.[14]

The Union party's victory in the November 1864 election brought a
change in the attitude in Kentucky concerning abolition. The altered tone of
the *Louisville Journal* after the election was obvious to even the least obser-
vant. The editor had become positively friendly to the emancipation policy
of the federal administration.[15] The governor of Kentucky had also radically
changed his position. In the election of 1864, Bramlette had supported
George McClellan and had opposed the administration's emancipation
policy. In his message to the Kentucky General Assembly, however, he
admitted that the rebellion had destroyed property in slaves and declared
that the last vestiges of slavery were burdensome.[16] On January 5, the
Union state convention met in Frankfort on the same day that the Kentucky
legislature convened in the capitol. The convention passed resolutions
asking the Kentucky senators and representatives in Congress to vote in
favor of an amendment to the Constitution abolishing slavery throughout
the United States.[17] The convention called on the Kentucky legislature to
cooperate in forwarding the request to Congress. Among the convention
members were many who had formerly voted for McClellan. A change of
sentiment of slavery was under way in the state.[18]

As a result of the election of November and in response to Lincoln's
message of December 1864, the Thirty-eighth Congress took up consideration of the proposed amendment. On January 6, 1864, a motion to
reconsider the antislavery amendment of the previous session was introduced in the House. George Yeaman of Owensboro, Kentucky, advocated

its adoption. He believed that if the people of the state continued to make a stand for slavery after it was overthrown, Kentucky would be hopelessly ruined. The state could and should move into a new era by cutting loose from the "dead carcass," he concluded. Anderson, also of Kentucky, favored the amendment, but Mallory condemned it because it was contrary to the demands of humanity and would "multiply and complicate the difficulties in relation to slavery."[19] Lincoln appealed for immediate adoption on January 6. On January 24 he sent a printed circular to all Republicans urging them to be present when the vote was taken. After many eloquent speeches, on February 1 the joint resolution was adopted by a two-thirds vote submitting the Thirteenth Amendment to the states for ratification.[20]

After the election of November 1864, Bramlette became aware of Lincoln's plan to place the Thirteenth Amendment once again before Congress. Both men sensed that the Thirteenth Amendment offered a solution to the turmoil in Kentucky. In addition, Lincoln knew of Bramlette's ambitions to run for a seat in the U.S. Senate. Lincoln was determined to use every political tool at his command to secure congressional approval and ratification of the Thirteenth Amendment, and Bramlette sent A. G. Hodges to Washington to confer with the president on affairs in Kentucky.[21]

When the General Assembly met, Bramlette asked for ratification of the Thirteenth Amendment with compensation. He suggested that it would be better to accept the amendment conditionally than to reject it entirely. In his subsequent message to the state legislature on March 1, he lamented the amendment's rejection and reminded the assembly that if they did not ratify they would simply be referring the question to the people in the August election and to the next session of the legislature. A. G. Hodges regularly reported to Lincoln on the progress of events in Kentucky, and Bramlette sent Lincoln a copy of his message. After the legislature adjourned, the governor canvassed the state urging the people to vote for representatives who would ratify the amendment. The radical journal the *National Unionist* of Lexington charged Lincoln and Bramlette with striking a bargain on the Thirteenth Amendment and the removal of Burbridge. The editor lamented that the administration had "given a stab to the Union cause in Kentucky." It was common knowledge in Kentucky that Bramlette had made overtures to Lincoln, suggesting through his agent, Hodges, that if the general were removed "he [the governor] would have the Amendment . . . ratified by the Legislature."[22]

Several factors had influenced voting on the amendment in the Kentucky legislature. Some legislators favored emancipation but thought it expedient to advocate state action. Others had been elected after pledging not to vote for any decided legislation upon the subject of emancipation. Still others marked time, hoping the question would be resolved by action outside Kentucky, that is, by ratification of three-fourths of the states. A strong timidity very much restrained the action of many legislators. Some politicians were afraid for their support among constituents, who might not be prepared for the amendment. Other legislators suffered from a disease that contemporaries recognized as all too common, which they called "nigger on the brain"—an extreme case of prejudice.

In the meantime the leadership of the governor had been compromised by the shift in his position on slavery. As recently as the presidential election of November 1864, after all, he had opposed the administration. The advocates of the amendment, not fully united among themselves, lacked outstanding, recognized leaders in the legislature as well. A friend of the amendment predicted its defeat in the state assembly because the "folly and ingratitude" of the legislative supporters of the amendment merited "such results as seem to be apprehended by them." Another supporter observed that there was "unfortunately . . . no master spirit to lead either body. And being in a woeful minority they hesitated to take a manly, firm stand upon principle and let policy follow in its wake."[23] Finally, the removal of General Burbridge demoralized the Union forces in the legislature. Before the removal of the general, the Unionists had mobilized forty-five votes in the legislature for Gen. L. H. Rousseau, the Unionist's candidate for the vacant seat in the U.S. Senate. After Burbridge's removal, they were able to muster only twenty-three votes in favor of the Thirteenth Amendment. "Many of our friends not feeling disposed to stand a fire both in front and rear have gone home and given up the contest," a disillusioned radical Unionist informed Sen. Henry Wilson.[24]

Burbridge was replaced by Gen. John Palmer, but the army in Kentucky continued to be an instrument for the destruction of slavery. Palmer was from Illinois, but he had been born in Christian County, Kentucky. He hated slavery, and as a young man he was convinced that he had been forced to leave Kentucky to seek employment because slavery had reduced the number of available jobs. Black recruitment had been discontinued, but on April 18 Palmer asked the War Department to permit the enlistment of blacks to continue in the state until the Kentucky regiments had been filled, or at least until May 15, when the March session of the legislature would adjourn. Palmer believed that the Kentucky General Assembly would pass the amendment abolishing slavery if black recruiting continued until that time. "We are recruiting as an argument forcible," Palmer explained. Stanton agreed and authorized Palmer to continue to enlist blacks even though orders had been issued to stop doing so elsewhere.[25]

One of the first acts performed by Palmer after he became commander in Kentucky was to issue General Orders No. 7 on March 4 instructing the post commander of Louisville to suppress all slave pens and other private establishments for confining blacks. The able-bodied slaves who were released were invited to enlist in the army and were given the $300 city bounty that had previously been pocketed by their owners. Slaves in municipal and county jails not charged with a misdemeanor or felony were also ordered released. Palmer addressed a letter to the judge of the police court in Louisville on May 15 informing him that blacks were not to be confined without being charged with a crime, and he sent an officer to make an investigation of the jail. Similar action was taken in reference to the Louisville workhouse. Palmer required post commanders to report on the enforcement of the order, and by March 8 a report had been submitted to him announcing that the slave pens had been suppressed and the jails cleared of blacks not guilty of wrongdoing. Palmer next acted to deal with one of the most visible marks of servitude. He authorized commanders to arrest any master who was charged with whipping the wife of a black soldier. Near the end of March, the general made himself even more disagreeable by attending a Negro church and telling the congregation that they were free, that their masters were no longer obligated to take care of their families, and that they must provide for their own households.[26]

One of the most decisive blows delivered to slavery was the act freeing the families of black soldiers. The army had urged Congress to pass it as a measure necessary to strengthen the morale of the black soldiers and to encourage recruiting by allowing the army to furnish security for the black soldier's family. The army claimed that the proposed legislation would reduce absenteeism and desertions. The measure was approved by Congress, Lincoln signed it, and Stanton issued an order to the army to enforce it. On March 10, 1865, the commander in Kentucky issued General Orders No. 10, which informed state authorities that he would declare a marriage to exist when two blacks recognized each other as husband and wife. Writing from Camp Nelson, Kentucky, where he could observe the effects of the law, John Fee reported to the *Louisville Press* that General Orders No. 10 had "really lain the axe at the root of the tree." Fee agreed with the army commanders in Kentucky who believed that the new act would encourage voluntary enlistment by slaves who had formerly remained at home. Since the wives and children of slaves would be protected by law, Fee believed, the men would enlist in great numbers, and those who were already in the army would "fight with more zeal and devotion." It was estimated that two-thirds of the remaining slaves in Kentucky were granted freedom by the act. Some army officers did all they could to enlarge the number freed by encouraging black single females to marry a black soldier.[27]

After the passage of the law granting freedom to the families of Negro soldiers, blacks in great numbers moved from the countryside to the towns and cities. Some masters drove the soldiers' families from their premises, and in some cases slaves sought to exercise their newly granted liberty by leaving the farms and plantations. Other slaves who were not legally free fled the countryside when their masters refused to pay them wages. The spirit of freedom was contagious, and insubordination became the order of the day as many slaves refused to be whipped or determined to take to the road because they had been beaten. Palmer later admitted that when he came to Kentucky in February, emancipation had been pretty well established by the blacks themselves. Slaves who moved to the towns and cities in 1865 joined the blacks who had arrived earlier, after fear of guerrilla raids drove them to leave rural areas. In the cities and towns many of these Negroes were seized and were confined to jails as vagrants. The pens and municipal and county jails became the last instrument by which the state sought to establish authority, control, and order over the institution of slavery. The patrol system had broken down, and slaves disregarded the regulations against going abroad in the city without a pass.[28]

When the slave left the master's service to take refuge in the city, the owner often advertised in the newspapers warning that anyone who hired his property would be prosecuted. Enough individuals were prosecuted to discourage farmers and entrepreneurs from hiring fugitives from service. The public also frowned on the hiring of slave labor without the consent of the owner. As a result most of the black refugees who gathered in the towns and cities were destitute and could not find employment. As early as April 9, the mayor of Louisville requested that Palmer rid the city of "vagrants (Negroes) who had left their masters."[29] On May 11 the mayor and a committee of the city council of Louisville complained to Palmer about the presence of large numbers of blacks in the city and again urged him to enforce the vagrancy law against them. Palmer observed that the state needed to adopt new laws which treated Negroes as free people; blacks should be allowed to migrate at their pleasure and to seek employment wherever it could be found. As matters stood, however, they congregated in Louisville but were forbidden to cross the Ohio River and to look for work in the Northwest. The state laws prohibited the captains of boats from transporting them. Vagrancy was voluntary idleness, Palmer explained, and the only crime of the refugees from slavery was poverty which came because even men seeking laborers dared not employ them.[30]

Palmer ordered that rations be provided for the refugees in Louisville and issued General Orders No. 32 to the effect that passes should be given to blacks who wanted to leave the city to seek work elsewhere. Steamboats and railroads were required to transport anyone having a pass from an army commander and the required fare. The slaves believed that Palmer could free them. On May 25 and 26, nearly 400 passes were issued to slaves to travel abroad to seek employment, and from May 18 to June 6, 2,571 were issued in Louisville. Many masters retained the labor of their servants by paying them wages of ten dollars or more per month. The general notified local authorities that he would protect the blacks "from forcible wrongs inflicted under the forms of law or otherwise." The pass system was Palmer's scheme to outflank the enemy, and the radical Unionist T. S. Bell was convinced that General Palmer's plans would "accomplish the object." The pass system was inaugurated after the state legislature had voted down the Thirteenth Amendment and became a more determined program after the amendment had been rejected during the adjourned session of May.[31]

By April the rural areas had been rapidly drained of labor, and the cities were so crowded that a plague was feared. Brisbin publicly called on Governor Bramlette to address critical social problems in Louisville and to correct the disturbed condition of the rural areas by working to secure the General Assembly's approval of the constitutional amendment. The moment the amendment had been ratified by the Kentucky legislature, the slaves would be quieter, Brisbin predicted; those still at home would remain there to till the soil, and those who had already left would return. He asserted that the alternative was emancipation by military measures. Brisbin warned Bramlette that he was in the process of recruiting seventeen additional black regiments. "From seventy to one hundred enlist daily," he noted, "freeing, under the law of March 3, 1865, an average of five women and children per man. Thus from 300 to 500 black people are daily made free through the instrumentality of the army." Brisbin agreed that the Negroes could be of more service in the cornfields than in the army, but if slaves were not freed at home, the army would absorb them. "Clearly it is the intention and policy of this Government to make every black person in it free," he observed, "and the sooner Kentucky makes up her mind to accept the new order of things . . . , the better it will be for her." Bramlette refused to accept Brisbin's proposal and insisted that the government's mission was not to destroy slavery but to preserve and restore the union.[32] Since the secretary of war had issued orders terminating recruiting and drafting, Brisbin's announcement that he was forming seventeen additional black regiments led some observers to believe that he was attempting to coerce Kentucky into ratifying the constitutional amendment. Should the people of Kentucky weakly yield to Brisbin's threat, "Negro suffrage and Negro equality would be the next sacrifice demanded," the editor of the *Lexington Observer and Reporter* predicted.[33]

On May 1, 1865, Lorenzo Thomas brought the recruitment of blacks to an end in all the departments in the West, but the secretary of war continued the recruitment of blacks in Kentucky until June 1. Kentucky and Delaware were the only states in which slavery still existed, and a well-organized and energetic recruiting program extending into June became an effective means of emancipation. Since the war had ended and the blacks were needed in the fields, the critics of the army policy in Kentucky were correct in their assessment of the purpose of the enlistment. The aim could only be to increase the number of free blacks in Kentucky.[34]

Throughout the month of May recruiting of blacks continued at a brisk pace in Central Kentucky. From 70 to 100 slaves were enlisted daily in May, and freedom for wives and children meant that at least 500 were liberated each day. A correspondent concluded that a few months of such recruiting would make the constitutional amendment purposeless. Many citizens complained; recruiting everywhere else had been discontinued, and large armies were being discharged because the war was over. The enlistment of blacks in peacetime was strongly resented, and near the end of May the lower house of the Kentucky legislature voted almost unanimously to ask the secretary of war the reason for it. Late in May two companies of black troops were sent from Camp Nelson to Garrard, where they created an uproar by pressing all of the black males in the neighborhood into service, disrupting the local economy. Agricultural stagnation was general throughout the state because of the upheaval and the shortage of labor. In the last year of the Civil War (1864–1865) tobacco crops dropped from 127 million pounds to 54 million; wheat from 8 million bushels to 3 million; hemp from 10 million pounds to 2 million; barley from 161,000 bushels to 137,000. But the harvest of corn, which was largely produced by white labor, increased from 39 million bushels to 58 million bushels.[35]

The secretary of war issued an order on June 1 through the office of the provost marshal general to bring all enlistments of black troops to an immediate halt throughout the country, but enlistments continued in Kentucky for a short time without any authorization. On June 2 there was a great stir in Madison County as squads of black troops forced slaves into military service.[36] At the end of May, Brisbin conceded that the army's strategy had failed to force the legislature to act. "The time has come," he declared, "when she [Kentucky] should be made to feel the strong arm of the Government."[37] Brisbin favored a program of congressional reconstruction. But Burbridge, the former commander of Kentucky, was convinced that the army had effectively performed its task. On July 20 he informed Stanton that slavery had been "practically destroyed" in the state "by the enlistment of Negroes." By the middle of May, not only every able-bodied man but also many old men had enlisted, since the war was over and the objective now was to free slaves. Although only 20,083 blacks between the ages of twenty and forty-five had been enrolled in Kentucky in 1864, 25,438 had been mustered by the end of the war. Thus color became the primary qualification for recruits, replacing age and physical fitness. Only Louisiana had enlisted more blacks than Kentucky by 1865 even though eight of the fifteen slave states had more slaves than Kentucky in 1860.[38]

Rumors spread across Kentucky that Palmer was going to issue freedom papers in Louisville on July 4. On July 3 a committee of blacks came to

Palmer's headquarters and inquired as to when and where he would declare their freedom. Although he told the committee that he had no authority to do so, on July 4 the city was full of expectant blacks. The general spoke to them. "My countrymen," he said, "you are substantially free!" A shout went up which could have been heard for a mile. Palmer thought his audience did not hear the word "substantially." As he recalled later, while standing there he decided to "drive the last nail in the coffin" of the institution of slavery even if it cost him the command of the department. When the noise subsided, he said: "My countrymen *you are free,* and while I command in this department the military forces of the United States will defend your right to freedom." Palmer believed that the events of July 4 practically ended slavery in Kentucky. Before the end of July, 5,000 blacks had crossed the Ohio River at Louisville. The general detailed six extra guards to patrol the streets of Louisville to protect the slaves in their new freedom of movement.[39]

By General Orders No. 49, on July 20, Palmer extended his policy of issuing passes throughout the state so that all slaves who applied for them could seek employment. Under the extended order, large crowds gathered at army posts in Camp Nelson, Lexington, Bowling Green, and Munfordville to secure passes. A correspondent for the *Colored Tennessean* in Nashville reported that the post at Camp Nelson was "actually besieged" by applicants. During the first three weeks in June, 671 received passes in Louisville, and in September, 2,230 more did so. By the middle of October it was reported that 10,000 had left Kentucky to go north of the Ohio River.[40]

The blacks treated the passes as freedom papers, and the military authorities in Kentucky did little to correct the misunderstanding. The passes were issued without regard to the status of the blacks, and the practical effect was to liberate the slaves, inasmuch as they were now free to move. When a group of slaves applying for passes at Camp Nelson were asked where they would seek employment, they replied: "We are going back to our home; master told us we could come and get our passes. He loaned us this carriage and these horses and promise to pay us wages." Palmer reasoned that when most blacks were slaves, color was a presumption of servitude. He calculated that fewer than 64,000 of the 230,000 who were slaves in Kentucky in 1860 still remained legally in servitude. To continue to presume slavery from color alone would be contrary to justice; to presume freedom without regard to color and to give protection accordingly, Palmer admitted, was to end slavery. As Palmer explained the matter to the editor of the *Louisville Press,* he was called on to extend protection to blacks where there was no proof at hand that they were free, and he had to presume that they were either free or slave. He chose to presume all blacks were free, which, he admitted, was to end slavery in Kentucky. The general informed the radical editor that all military authorities in all the defeated Confederate states were acting on the same policy. "It will of itself when enforced gradually but surely end slavery in Kentucky if it is not already dead," he prophesied.[41]

Palmer alerted the Secretary of War to the events of July 4 in Louisville, and the War Department issued General Orders No. 129 on July 25, which conferred upon the freedmen the same personal liberty that was enjoyed by other residents and inhabitants. No restrictions or restraints could be imposed on black freedmen that were not imposed on whites. The order provided that "neither whites or blacks" would "be restrained from seeking employment elsewhere" when they could not obtain it at a just compensation at their homes. Nor would they "be hindered from traveling from place to place on proper and legitimate business." The stated objective was "to secure equal justice." The War Department had placed itself squarely behind Palmer's new policy to confer freedom by military measures.[42]

Palmer's passes were not long in generating protests. A citizen of Lexington who was a former employee of Maj. Gen. G. H. Thomas, at the request of several citizens, complained to the general. D. L. Price, also of Lexington, sent a telegraph to President Johnson protesting against the provost marshal of Lexington, who was issuing "free papers indiscriminately" to blacks. Palmer denied that the passes being issued in Kentucky were free papers. After explaining his policy to the president, he concluded, "in short, slavery has no actual existence in Kentucky, and if the Constitutional amendment is defeated at the election, the whole active colored population will fly."[43]

Mayors of Frankfort, Paris, and Harrodsburg wrote Palmer asking him to deal with the massive numbers of unemployed blacks in these cities, who were alleged to be a nuisance. He suggested that if their freedom was acknowledged, the Negroes would become industrious and thrifty citizens. He sent the mayors a copy of the General Orders No. 129 of the War Department and warned them that its provisions would not permit him to tolerate special legislation for blacks. In one specific case Palmer set aside a Lexington ordinance forbidding Negro meetings on the grounds that it was an unconstitutional interference with religious meetings now that slavery no longer existed in Kentucky.[44]

When he spoke in public, the general lost no occasion to make his intentions clear in regard to slavery. On August 1 in Lexington he promised his audience that so far as he had the power, he would permit "no let up" on the "slavery question until the last shackle" was "struck from the wrists of the last slave." On August 16 in Louisville Palmer addressed a delegation of blacks from Lexington. "In my opinion slavery has no legal existence in any State or Territory of the United States," he told his audience. "I can assure you that my powers . . . will be employed for the advantage and protection of all the people of the department without distinction, according to their necessities and their rights."[45] In an interview at the end of August, Palmer again expressed the opinion that slavery had ceased in Kentucky. The question had, he said, entered the realm of federal rather than state jurisdiction; the United States would determine whether the institution was to continue or to cease. "The Government of the state of Kentucky, so far as [it] relates to . . . the African and mixed races, is subverted and overthrown," Palmer maintained.[46]

Palmer's policy alienated many Union men who felt that his revolutionary measures were destroying their party in Kentucky. The events growing out of the election were critical in the development of opposition to Palmer in the ranks of the Union party. In the election of August 7, the conservatives won by a close vote. They carried both houses of the legislature and also won five of the nine congressional seats. Palmer's slave pass system had offended many who might otherwise have voted for the Union party, and many party leaders believed Palmer's Negro policy had cost them the election.[47] Cong. Green Clay Smith and Governor Bramlette called on the president and Secretary of War Stanton and condemned the actions taken by General Palmer.[48]

In a memorandum written after the Washington meeting, Smith asked for the general's removal. "General Palmer's day of usefulness is past," he explained, and the Union party in Kentucky could not "recover under his command." Since slavery still legally existed in Kentucky, Smith claimed, Union men were opposed to Palmer's policy with regard to passes. Smith said that Union men had written dozens of letters in protest. The general had destroyed all hope of the adoption of the Thirteenth Amendment in Kentucky, Smith asserted; he advocated the appointment of another commander who would work with Bramlette to secure the amendment's passage.[49]

Palmer went to Washington to answer the criticism directed at him or, as one of the radical Unionists of Kentucky put it, "to get some more power for engineering Kentucky through with her dead carcass, slavery." After Smith's letter was published, Palmer replied that slavery was indeed being destroyed by his policy. "If slavery is to be recognized, protected, and defended in Kentucky, General Smith and other friends of the system do right in asking my removal." "Slavery cannot recover under my administration," he added. "It drove me from the State in my boyhood. It may do it again, but it will receive no protection, acknowledgement, support or countenance from me." He further explained that the pass system proceeded from the idea not that slavery absolutely did not exist but merely that other interests were of paramount importance. In a rebuttal Smith argued that it was a question not of whether slavery was to be reestablished but of whether it was to be eliminated according to law. Smith charged that Palmer's personal prejudice had overridden all law and government and had disrupted the quiet of the state. The general had distracted the community, had broken up the labor system, and had inflicted much injury upon industry and the prosperity of Kentucky—and he had aroused passion and prejudice toward the Negro.[50]

In a published rejoinder Bramlette explained the destructive effects of Palmer's pass system, which had gone into effect three weeks before the election and during the small grain harvests. Palmer's Negro policy had so incensed thousands, the governor claimed, that they had either voted against the amendment candidates or had refrained from voting. Bramlette stated that the objection to Palmer's course was based on a desire not to maintain the institution of slavery but to preserve and support government and the law. To the extent that he was referring to the Union party supporters, the governor was correct. Both Smith and Bramlette had campaigned vigorously in support of the adoption of the Thirteenth Amendment. The Kentucky correspondent for the *New York Herald* reported that Smith and his family had willingly surrendered nearly 200 slaves.[51]

Not all Union men condemned Palmer and his policy. On October 7, a group of radical Union men of Kentucky petitioned the secretary of war against the general's removal. They declared that Palmer was a tower of strength to the Union men in the state and had their unwavering support. The spokesmen also asserted that they were acting on behalf of 165,000 Negroes in Kentucky. Slavery, they insisted, was doomed; the amendment would be ratified in a short time. "The hue and cry over the pass system . . . is a part of the effort to grasp something from the dying throes of the slavery system."[52]

Maj. Gen. George H. Thomas approved of Palmer's administration and favored retaining him in command in Kentucky. Seward agreed, and Johnson refused to remove the general. More than a week before he received the vindication from the War Department, Palmer wrote his wife that he believed the president would sustain him, support that would be "equivalent to deciding that slavery is dead in the state." The anticipated official sanction arrived on October 23, 1865. "If I had been asked five or ten years ago what honor I would prefer as the highest which could have been conferred upon me, I would have said: 'Let me destroy slavery in my native state of Kentucky.,' " Palmer responded, and turned with renewed zeal to the work of forcing emancipation upon Kentucky. The provost marshal in Louisville issued from 150 to 300 passes each day. Palmer promised to carry out his policy by military force if necessary.[53]

Although Palmer and Brisbin failed to bring Kentucky to the point of abolishing slavery and created a more stubborn resistance to the prospect, Palmer undermined the institution to such an extent that its restoration was hopeless. Even if the Kentuckians and the federal government had agreed that slavery should have been nurtured and restored until it could be abolished under Kentucky's constitution, the blacks would not have submitted.[54] The Negroes were gradually taking their freedom into their own hands, furthering in their own way the ends sought by the army and the radical politicians.

The dominant, if not the sole, issue in the election of August 1865 for Congress and the state legislature was the ratification of the Thirteenth Amendment.[55] As early as March the parties began to prepare. The Union party state central committee appealed to the friends of the constitutional amendment to organize in every county in the state to enter the canvass on the question. A state convention meeting in Frankfort on May 23 adopted a platform "resolving to make a bold and straight-out fight." To the people of Kentucky the Union party announced that it would make ratification the single issue in the forthcoming election: "Slavery does not exist in Kentucky"; four years of war had "obliterated its substance and left nothing but its shadow among us." The Union party address promised a rapid increase in prosperity following ratification. Here, too, the Unionists maintained, lay the slaveholders' only hope of compensation from the federal government.[56] Adoption of the amendment would bring the state an influx of capital and white workers, dignifying free labor and improving the economic status of the white wage earner. It was also argued that elimination of slavery would promote education of the masses.[57]

The conservative party generally agreed that slavery had only a nominal existence in Kentucky, but conservatives viewed this fact as a reason for antagonism to the amendment. The federal government had destroyed slavery, and the opposition to the amendment expressed long-standing resentment of the enlistment of blacks and the slave pass system. The conservatives' attack was primarily directed against section 2, which stated: "Congress shall have power to enforce this article by appropriate legislation." It was claimed that the wording permitted Congress to grant blacks the right to vote and to testify in courts.[58] Some even insisted that the section would establish social equality.[59] To counter the claims of proponents that adoption of the amendment would dignify labor, opponents argued that the freedmen would drive out white workers accustomed to higher pay.[60]

The conservatives had the support of a substantial part of the politically active people of Kentucky. Southern sympathizers united with the party, and Palmer's magnanimity in dealing with the former Confederates as they drifted back to Kentucky in large numbers strengthened the hand of the conservatives. But the conservative party in Kentucky was "a house divided against itself." Members united against the Thirteenth Amendment but divided on the question of whether slavery should be abolished by state action or should be restored on a reduced but stronger scale. The Frankfort correspondent for the *Cincinnati Commercial* compared the conservative party with an English university society said to have numbered four members who represented five religious sects.[61]

The most important recruit to the support of the administration position was George D. Prentice, editor of the *Louisville Journal,* which had opposed Lincoln in 1864. The *Journal* put itself completely on the side of the advocates of the Thirteenth Amendment on May 16 by issuing "an Open Letter to the People of Kentucky." Prentice argued that the country was entering upon a new era of enlightened thought and action. "The wheels of progress are rapidly moving toward that magnificent destiny so clearly prefigured for the nation. Kentucky, with her numerous resources, cannot hesitate in the triumphant march of the Republic, else her glorious escutcheon will grow dim with decay." Until the day of the election hardly an issue of the *Journal* failed to carry an editorial in support of the Thirteenth Amendment. Yet not once did Prentice mention emancipation as it afforded justice to the slave. Of all the press in Kentucky, only the *Free South* discussed the humane treatment of blacks that would result from adoption of the amendment. In the slaveholding section of Kentucky, James Speed alone among the active political speakers took a forthright abolitionist position in the canvass. In Louisville early in October, Speed called slavery "legalized robbery" and noted that the amendment would ensure that the institution could not be reestablished anywhere in the nation.[62]

The election of August 7 was won by the conservatives in a closely contested race. The state legislature was carried with but few votes to spare. Of the ten strongest slaveholding counties in Kentucky, only Christian County gave a Union majority vote. In these ten counties, of a total population of 101,308, there were only 8,704 slaveholders, and only 25,400 nonslaveholders were voters. Even in 1865 when everything was against them, the slaveholders controlled three times their number at the polls. Their influence was exercised through social and economic control of the electorate by the use of *viva voce* system of voting and by the widespread prejudice against the blacks among the nonslaveholding whites. In the twenty weakest slaveholding counties, only Grayson cast a conservative majority vote. In these counties there were nearly 231,000 whites and 3,072 slaveholders.[63]

On December 7, the required number of states had ratified the Thirteenth Amendment and on December 18 the secretary of state announced that it had become a part of the Constitution.[64] On December 8, Governor Bramlette asked the new legislature to ratify the amendment so that Kentucky could "range herself with the mighty strides taken" on the road to progress. The power to enforce the freedom secured by the first section of the amendment, he said, was "aptly *limited* in the second to appropriate legislation for its enforcement." The adoption of the proposed amendment would "give us perpetual indemnity against the attempt to control the question of suffrage through the Federal power." A resolution was introduced in both houses of the legislature to ratify the amendment,[65] but the legislature stood "sullen and defiant," insisting that the action it had taken earlier was final. on January 17, 1866, the Union members of the legislature met in caucus and issued a public address declaring that Congress had no power "under the Second Section of the Thirteenth Amendment . . . to pass any law granting the right of suffrage in the States to persons of African descent."[66]

The opposition to the Thirteenth Amendment expressed antagonism toward the party that passed it even more than an objection to the amendment itself. The vote constituted a referendum on everything the Union party had done since it had refused to reaffirm the Crittenden Resolution in 1862.[67] It was the "stay-at-home rebels who carried the day." They came out in force because they no longer feared to reveal their sentiments under Kentucky's system of oral voting. The *Journal* was correct in assuming that many loyal citizens had stayed away from the polls. Many nonslaveholders who had resolutely sustained the Union during the war years no longer felt secure in Kentucky and were migrating to the Northwest now that the war had ended. Many of the nonslaveholding laborers did not feel comfortable revealing their sentiments by announcing their vote, and therefore they, too, stayed away from the polls. In addition, some skilled white workers were inclined to accept the conservatives' argument that blacks would make inroads on their jobs once freedom was recognized in Kentucky.[68]

The conservatives had won white voters by effectively playing on their fear that Congress would now use the amendment to legislate political and social equality. The party resorted to the grossest misrepresentations, and the question was sometimes asked: "Would you want a Negro to marry your daughter?"[69] Despite their organizational weaknesses, the conservatives were better organized than the Unionists and spent their money lavishly to promote unscrupulous prejudice and sometimes slander. The friends of the constitutional amendment lacked mutual confidence, suffered from their own organizational weaknesses, and were divided by the pretensions of certain individuals. (Early in 1865 Rousseau and Bramlette each operated separate political machines to secure election as U.S. senator from Kentucky.)[70]

In the summer of 1865, instead of resolving pressing problems that blocked progress, Kentucky was fighting a battle in a war that had already been settled. Before confirmation of the Emancipation Proclamation on January 1, 1863, Maryland and Missouri had begun to abolish slavery, but Kentucky failed to move along the path that was being cleared in the border states. It was true that the problem was not as great in Maryland and Missouri, which had 87,189 and 114,931 slaves in 1860, respectively, while Kentucky's slaves numbered 225,488. Still, Kentucky with no fewer than forty-one regiments had more men in the Union military service than either of the other two major border states. There was a lack not of loyalty to the Union but of leaders with vision. Robert J. Breckinridge represented the type of leader who was needed, but he was too old and too ill to become active. He had proven his temper in the dispute over slavery in 1849, but at sixty-five years of age and in poor health, he was not capable of rendering the service he had given at forty-nine. Kentucky had no prominent men of the caliber of Sen. John B. Henderson and Gratz Brown of Missouri. (Ironically, Brown had been born in Kentucky and had spent the early years of his maturity in the state.) Kentucky had no press with the consistency and determination of the *Missouri Democrat*[71] or the journalistic vision of Maryland's *Baltimore American* and *Cambridge Intelligencer,* which calmly advocated emancipation with ability and unflagging zeal. Instead Kentucky had the *Louisville Journal,* which vacillated on the issue of slavery. The *Journal* had tremendous prestige and influence, but George Prentice, editor and owner, in the crisis was not bold enough to take a forthright position. Instead he turned the editorship over to Paul R. Shipman, a brilliant but vain man who made no secret of his opposition to the federal administration, which eventually led to his arrest. After the death of John J. Crittenden in 1862, Kentucky had no one in Congress to compare with Reverdy Johnson of Maryland.[72] The rejection of the Thirteenth Amendment was not important in itself, but it indicated the sentiment, attitude, and policy that would dominate Kentucky's public life until 1872.

CHAPTER SEVEN

The Search for Work

SLAVERY HAD EXISTED as a viable institution to a large extent because the slave did not have freedom of movement, did not receive wages for his work, and could be subjected to corporal punishment at the will of the master. By December 1862, the Kentucky slaves were moving about in such numbers that it was almost impossible to exercise any control over them. A correspondent for the *Boston Journal* reported in December 1862 that the masters in parts of Kentucky had been "compelled to cease flogging, for it is very easy for slaves to run away now, and not easy to catch them."[1]

By the end of 1863, large numbers of slaves in Kentucky were refusing to labor without wages. They were abandoning the fields in favor of the villages, county seats, and cities or were crossing the Ohio River to look for work in the North. A planter in Lexington recalled in 1865 that he had summoned his servants in 1863 and told them they were free. He offered them fifteen dollars per month if they would stay, and all remained with him. Peter Bruner, a black residing in Estill County, fled from his owner in 1862 and worked for wages only when employers agreed to pay him by the day. In 1863, he made an agreement to work a farm for half of what he produced. Some few farmers accepted the changing circumstances and paid the slaves. Two years of contract with the army had taught the Negroes much about the wage system. Even when the earnings of slaves hired to the army were paid to the owner, as in the case of railroads in Kentucky, incentive payments were made to the blacks. Those who were contraband were permitted to work for private employers under a system that was controlled by the army. On March 11, 1864, Gen. Lorenzo Thomas issued a set of contract rules for contrabands throughout the Military Division of the Mississippi that provided minimum monthly wages of ten dollars for men and seven dollars for women. Housing, clothing, and medical care were also furnished by the employer, but he could "make deductions from wages for sick time, indolence, insolence, disobedience of orders and crime."[2] Contrabands who were brought from the war zone into Kentucky by the army hesitated to accept work from private employers because they feared reenslavement and the operations of guerrillas in the country, but to the whites who came to the contraband camps for employees, the refusal by the slaves to accept employment was additional proof that blacks would not work unless forced to do so.[3]

When plans were being made for the planting season of 1865, the farmers of Kentucky began to realize that they were faced with a critical shortage of labor. As the complaints of the farmers became more general, the newspapers took up the discussion of the problem. In December 1864 the *Louisville Journal* urged the Kentucky slaveholders to consent to the emancipation of their slaves through the state legislative action so that the flow of Kentucky slaves to the Northwest could be checked and the blacks could be retained in the state as free labor. The editor saw "universal demoralization and anarchy" as the only alternative. The editor of the *National Unionist* believed that the solution to the immediate problem of slavery in Kentucky was to force loafing blacks to join the army, to find work, or to return to their former owners. The Kentucky legislature considered several bills which proposed change in the slave code. A bill was introduced to abolish the fugitive slave law in Kentucky in hopes that the repeal of the law would check the flow of Kentucky slaves to the Northwest, where they were going to escape the authority of the slave codes. The bill was defeated because the legislature still contained many who hoped to restore slavery and others who did not want to offend proslavery constituents. Many who needed labor to cultivate their soil considered the defeat of the repeal of the fugitive law to be a heavy blow to the agricultural economy as well as a signal for many slaves to flee across the Ohio River. An informed correspondent pointed out the seriousness of desertion of the field by the agricultural laborers. He informed the editor of the *Louisville Journal* that a critical labor shortage already existed in Kentucky and predicted that not one-fourth of an adequate labor supply for the crops of 1865 could be found in the state.[4]

The slaves' departure to the Northwest as wage earners, movement to the towns and cities, and enlistment all combined to create the acute labor shortage. Many farmers who had never before done physical labor found it necessary to cultivate their own farms. Others in the country surrounding Louisville were sometimes more fortunate, being able to hire German immigrants. During the season of 1865, conditions became more desperate. A farmer in Jefferson County lost sixty-three slaves, and his wife and daughters were forced to work on the farm and as domestics. The *Louisville Journal* urged the property owners to hire their slaves. Many farmers decided to come to terms with their blacks with the assistance of the army. They asked Palmer for help, and he agreed to cooperate with them in redirecting the Negroes to agricultural pursuits, provided the farmers would declare in writing that the laborers would be compensated. The army recognized the blacks who returned to the soil as liberated slaves and agreed to furnish protection to them and to enforce wage payments. Although the military encouraged such agreements with humane masters, few slaves who had broken with their owners were willing to go back to them, no doubt preferring to avoid a new life so reminiscent of the old. The farmers had greater success in retaining blacks who had not yet decided to leave. A great number of slaveholders in Kentucky decided to acknowledge that slavery no longer existed. They made contracts and thereby checked the departure of the laborers from their farms. By September 1865 many farmers had reported that the wage system was beneficial to both white and black.[5]

As soon as the army adopted the policy of enlisting blacks in the service, the military authorities in Kentucky began to make efforts to coerce unemployed Negroes into joining. The policy of permitting slaveholders to authorize the enlistment of fugitive slaves soon became a policy of requiring the unemployed who had abandoned slavery either to enter the army or to return to their masters. This practice caused an uproar among the slaveholding farmers, who were not consulted in the matter, because most able-bodied blacks preferred military service to slavery, and enlistment made them free men.[6]

The number of blacks in the larger cities of Kentucky continued to increase. By the middle of 1865 it was not unusual for a farmer to go to bed at night with twenty or thirty able-bodied hands and to wake up the next morning alone. After March 3, 1865, when the families of Negro soldiers were freed, female fugitives soon outnumbered the black males in the cities. They could find no employment because prospective employers feared that they would be prosecuted under state law for contracting with a slave without the consent of the owner. Grand juries regularly indicted employers who for economic or humanitarian reasons employed the blacks who were available in this vast labor pool. Even if the danger of being indicted appeared unlikely, as in cases where the slaves had fled from remote parts of the state, most employers were discouraged from hiring because public opinion frowned on the practice. In the meantime slaveholders stubbornly sought to force Negroes to choose between renewed slavery and starvation.[7]

Thousands of blacks sought passes issued by General Palmer in 1865, in order to travel freely.[8] Both the pass system and the measures taken in the state courts to resist it tended to accelerate the disorganization and demoralization of the labor system in Kentucky.[9] During the period from May to August 1865, the status of black labor and the future of the state's labor system became the principal issue in the canvass for seats in the legislature that would sit in 1865–1866 to decide whether Kentucky would ratify the Thirteenth Amendment. The editor of the *Louisville Journal* and the governor of Kentucky tried to impress upon the electorate the importance to the state's agricultural interests of ratification so that the blacks would remain in the state and on the soil. As noted earlier, it was argued that the amendment would free white labor as well as black;[10] the labor question, unlike other issues relative to the Thirteenth Amendment, was debated on economic principles rather than by appeals to prejudice and emotion. The institution of slavery continued to deteriorate after the August election. By November 1865 the need to establish a wage system to replace slavery had become a topic of great interest.

In October the citizens of Christian County met in Hopkinsville and drew up a proposal to establish a wage system for slaves in the county. They fixed wages for seven classes of black laborers and set up a board of four members to enforce the scale which they considered fair to the Negroes. Former owners had prior claim on the labor of their former slaves. If the former owner did not want the services of a given individual, others could hire him, but no member of the association should employ a black without the written consent of the former owner. General Palmer expressed his disapproval of the plan and opposed the regulation preferring the former owner's claim. After the Thirteenth Amendment was ratified on December 30, a second convention, held in Franklin County, fixed the pay for six classes of laborers who were to be employed there under written contracts.[11]

Many antislavery men in Kentucky were convinced that any kind of wage system would ultimately reduce the blacks to a new form of servitude. They believed that the ownership of land afforded blacks their only hope for freedom. John Fee proposed that liberals in Ohio and elsewhere form a company to buy and sell land to blacks, by which means the freedmen might obtain economic security. With the help of other reformers, Fee organized an agency, purchased 130 acres of farmland in Central Kentucky, and resold it in small tracts. By 1891, there were forty-two free families who had established a farm village on the tract.[12] Although Fee's venture was significant and successful as a pilot experiment, it was not extensive enough to alter the economic position of blacks in Kentucky.

In December, when Bramlette delivered his message to the legislature of Kentucky, he suggested that the General Assembly take steps to create a new free labor system to replace slavery. The governor proposed that measures be adopted to attract a superior class of white laborers who had formerly shunned the state. The development of mineral resources would require a class of laborers superior to that which Kentucky possessed, Bramlette explained. He asked the legislature to develop a program to encourage immigration.[13] As it happened, a movement with this very purpose was already under way and was to continue sporadically for almost a decade. In September 1865, D. M. Bell, a brother of the radical Unionist T. S. Bell, was in Scotland advertising in the newspapers and soliciting laborers to migrate to Kentucky. In addition, a member of Louisville's German community departed for Switzerland and Belgium in December as a representative of an association of Kentuckians who were financing his trip to recruit laborers.[14]

In the autumn of 1865 the Kentucky Land Association was organized in Louisville to buy tracts and sell them as homesteads to immigrants. The Kentucky Immigration Society, which was predominantly a German organization, sought a charter from the legislature. The two organizations planned to work together to supply industry and agriculture with white labor. A Jefferson County representative in the lower house of the legislature introduced a bill to create a bureau of immigration in Kentucky, and a state agricultural convention convened in Frankfort in December and resolved to support the movement "to encourage the immigration of a desirable class of laborers."[15] But by the end of December 1865, the traditional time for hiring slave labor, the farmers throughout most of the state had taken steps to contract with blacks. As a result, the interest in securing white labor declined, and the bill to create a bureau of immigration as well as the bill to charter the Kentucky Immigration Society failed to pass.

From the beginning of the movement to import white labor, the rural areas of Kentucky had shown little interest. Only in Daviess County was the question of foreign workers brought before a county convention at a meeting called specifically for the purpose. Since the meeting was held on March 24, weeks after the annual contracts had been made with freedmen, it was probably inspired by the lack of an adequate labor supply.[16]

As soon as the Thirteenth Amendment had been ratified, the farmers in most agricultural regions took steps to call county gatherings to select delegates who would attend a state convention and would devise a local system to organize the freedmen as free laborers. Groups assembled on January 1, 1866, in a number of counties to decide on a common labor policy. Identical resolutions were adopted in many cases, and it was generally agreed that the former master or employer should be given the privilege of employing his former slaves if he desired. The conventions favored a written contract by the year. Such a contract had been used before and during the war years, and it had the advantage of guaranteeing a labor supply. The meeting in Spencer County resolved that it was "inexpedient and unwise to declare against the labor of freedmen," and other county meetings expressed similar sentiments.[17] The state agricultural convention met in Frankfort on January 11, recommended that farmers employ their former slaves as wage laborers, and asked the state legislature to pass laws to expedite the new system.[18]

The Kentucky state legislature repealed the laws that were a part of the slave code of Kentucky and passed new ones validating contracts between white and black persons. The contracts had to be written and witnessed by a white person, and if either party violated the agreement, the other party would be considered to have fulfilled it. The law tended to work to the disadvantage of blacks because no provision was made to protect the weaker party. This was particularly true, since the legislation conferring civil rights on the blacks prohibited blacks from testifying against whites. The act stipulated that the contract could be drawn up so the parties could be held to it "as entire." This arrangement permitted the employer to withdraw from the agreement near the end of the season if the tenant committed a petty infraction, and in such cases the freedman forfeited all of his labor. A new vagrancy law was also adopted, making it illegal for blacks to loiter or ramble without having means of support. Finally, the legislature passed a bill making it a misdemeanor to persuade, attempt to persuade, or entice a Negro to desert the place of employment before the expiration of his contract for service. This act gave the employer, usually the former master, greater control over the freedman, because other farmers tended to avoid employing the tenant even though the former owner considered the contract forfeited.[19]

Other farmers were not free to impose contracts upon the freedmen without regard for the interests of the laborers. In 1865 the Bureau of Refugees, Freedmen, and Abandoned Lands had been established by Congress as the guardian and protector of the blacks, and after the Thirteenth Amendment had been ratified, the bureau extended its work to Kentucky. Oliver O. Howard, commissioner of the bureau, in 1865 issued a circular informing the assistant commissioners in the slave states that one of the principal objectives should be to "introduce practicable systems of compensated labor." The agents of the bureau in the slave states were authorized to negotiate written labor contracts between the freedmen and their employers. The blacks were free to choose their own employers, but once the contract had been freely negotiated under the supervision of the bureau, it was enforced on both parties. The ultimate goal was to make the freedmen self-supporting, and if necessary the freedmen were to be compelled to work. The overseer system was prohibited, and Howard warned the agents "against any substitute whatever for slavery which would perpetuate the system." The price of labor was to be determined by supply and demand rather than being fixed at an established minimum rate.[20] These regulations served as the general policy of the bureau in Kentucky when it was established in December 1865.

Clinton B. Fisk, the assistant commissioner of Tennessee, was ordered to extend his authority into Kentucky in the autumn of 1865 on the ground that refugees from the Confederate states had migrated into Kentucky. His instructions were to close down the refugee camps in Tennessee and Kentucky as soon as practical and to return the blacks to regular employment. By October 6, 1865, Fisk had closed all but one in Tennessee and Kentucky and had ceased to issue rations. He reported that his program had forced "the idle to work or starve." In accordance with bureau policy, an intelligence office was set up in Louisville in January 1866 to help freedmen find jobs.[21]

The bureau did not begin full operations in Kentucky early enough to exert much influence in the negotiation of annual contracts in the rural areas for January 1866 except in the case of Western Kentucky, where it had been established in 1865 as a part of the District of West Tennessee. In the eastern half of the state, most farmers refused to make written contracts with the freedmen in 1866, and those who preferred to negotiate such agreements with laborers usually refused to hire blacks who insisted on registration with the bureau. The bureau district that included the north central counties of Harrison, Grant, and Pendleton was an exception to the general attitude in the eastern half of the state: more contracts were registered in the Harrison district than in most other counties despite the fact that the officers of Harrison County bitterly opposed the bureau. The freedmen sometimes hesitated to enter into contracts, particularly annual ones, because they feared being reduced to slavery. The bureau therefore negotiated many monthly agreements for freedmen in Kentucky even though the agents urged the blacks to sign annual contracts as the best insurance of full employment throughout the year.[22]

The annual wages contracted by the freedmen in 1866 were generally less than fair, particularly in view of the critical labor shortage still existing in Kentucky. Most contracts called for a sum well below the hiring price that had obtained for slaves. The bureau in Kentucky made no attempt to require that the pay equal that which the slaveholders had received for labor hired out before and during the war, but the superintendent used his authority to raise rates in counties where contracts in 1866 provided monthly wages well below the average for the state. For example, in Carroll and Cumberland counties the average wage in April was only eight dollars and ten dollars per month for adult male field hands, while the average for the state was fifteen dollars per month for men. The superintendent ordered the Carroll and Cumberland agents to "obtain a higher rate" for the freedmen in future contracts negotiated in their districts.[23] By the summer of 1866, most freedmen were gainfully employed for wages that averaged twenty-five dollars per month for adult male field hands in the tobacco region and twelve dollars in the rest of the farm belt of Kentucky. Some of the blacks, however, seem to have preferred a life "of vagrancy and idleness." Reports from all sections of the state led the superintendent to estimate that 95 percent of the freedmen were self-supporting. The able-bodied who had not entered into a contract were compelled by the bureau to go to work.[24]

The greatest hindrance to a smooth transition from slave to free labor was the existence of bands of white men, often disguised, who preyed upon the blacks in the rural areas and drove them from their agrarian pursuits.

These gangs, known as "Regulators" or Ku Klux Klan, often intimidated farmers or persuaded them not to hire blacks, particularly black soldiers who had recently returned from the war. Another difficulty was that many farmers still believed that force was needed to secure work from the freedmen and continued to whip, flog, and abuse the black workers as they had the slaves. The bureau investigated such mistreatment, issued warnings, and took strong measures against those found guilty.[25] The agents were instructed to make every effort to have all freedmen contract through the bureau offices, especially as the time approached for negotiating the contracts for 1867. Blacks were not forced to use the service of the bureau, however. In some regions the whites still refused to allow negotiation by bureau agents and resorted to an instrument drawn up by themselves or by a lawyer. In some cases the farmer and freedmen relied on an oral agreement or understanding.[26]

The Freedmen's Bureau Act of July 1866 included provisions for bureau courts which, in Kentucky, were composed of the agent and two citizens. The jurisdiction of the courts encompassed all suits relating to compensation of Negroes of as much as $300 and all other cases between whites and blacks as well as all criminal action against Negroes such that conviction would lead to a fine of not more than $100 or a jail term of thirty days. All testimony was taken under oath and was permanently recorded. During the first year the bureau courts chiefly heard disputes between farmers and freedmen arising from contracts. In that period the bureau found it necessary to take action in more than 1,000 cases in which employers attempted to take advantage of freedmen by driving them from the farms instead of settling their contracts in good faith. On the other hand, some black laborers showed a tendency, particularly if they worked under a monthly contract, to desert one employer during harvest time and to work for another who was short of labor for a higher wage at a daily or weekly rate.[27]

The tendency of freedmen to decline to contract by the year persisted in 1867 despite the bureau's efforts. During the Christmas holidays, the season for negotiating agreements for 1867, new problems arose and some old grievances persisted. In some sections of the state where blacks had had difficulty in collecting wages for 1866, the freedmen departed for the towns and villages without visible means of support. In Daviess, Marion, Henry, and Oldham counties, where Regulators had operated extensively during the Christmas season of 1866 against both freedmen and farmers who had built houses for laborers, the processing of contracts was interfered with and was greatly delayed by the burning of the laborers' cottages.[28] Elsewhere the transition from slave labor to free labor proceeded without any really traumatic developments.

By 1867 the wage system for hiring agricultural laborers in Kentucky had superseded the sharecropper system. In 1866, in a limited number of cases, contracts had called for a mixed system whereby wages would be paid for the grain crops, which many farmers generally used for livestock, and a money crop, such as tobacco, would be produced on shares. Only in Madison and adjoining Garrard counties did the sharecropping system survive on a large scale in 1867. In these areas a great many freedmen received one-third of the crops for their labor. But even here sharecropping gave way to the wage system as the decade wore on. In Kentucky the widespread shortage of agricultural laborers enabled the freedmen to demand wages, which they generally preferred. The wage system tended to give black laborers a feeling of greater security in their freedom. For its part the bureau in Kentucky consistently discouraged sharecropping, believing that it was only used by irresponsible employers.[29]

In the last half of 1867, the economic conditions of the freedmen deteriorated. The August election inflamed the prejudice of the Negrophobes, and the Regulators stepped up their operations. Throughout the month of August the blacks in Northern Kentucky, in Kenton, Boone, and Grant counties, were greatly agitated, and large numbers left the fields and congregated in Covington. After the August election the rumor spread among the freedmen that they were going to be reenslaved. In the region of Mason County and Maysville following the election there was an increase in the harassment of both white and black Unionists.[30]

The greatest threat to the economic security of the freedmen in 1867 came from an industrial recession in the eastern half of the state. During the war large numbers of slaves from western Virginia had settled in the northeastern part of Kentucky along the Big Sandy—the only region of the state that gained in black population during the war. The area's principal industry was the iron works, which closed down periodically after the war. In the autumn of 1867 the Sandy Valley furnaces stopped operation for the remainder of the year, and many blacks faced the winter without means. In the region of Lexington and Frankfort large numbers of freedmen were thrown out of work by the closing of the hemp and bagging factories. In Northern Kentucky, in the region of Covington, more blacks were unemployed than ever before. The low level of the Ohio River added to the numbers of the jobless.[31]

The situation became more critical as the recession reached its low level during the winter months. Prices had increased to such an extent that food, clothing, shoes, and fuel were beyond the means of most blacks. The congestion in the towns and villages had also reached a new high, and many who were unemployed were quartered with those who had some source of income. The overcrowding came about also because incorporated communities offered a freedom of movement and a social and fraternal life that were missing in the country. The towns offered the protection of numbers from the outrages of the Regulators and better opportunities for the education of black children.[32]

Early in 1868 the economic conditions improved considerably. The hemp and bagging factories resumed operation in Central Kentucky, and the iron works in the Eastern Kentucky piedmont fired up their furnaces. There had never been an oversupply of agricultural labor, although there was a seasonal decrease in the needs. By April 1868 large numbers of blacks had obtained employment in the country and left the towns.[33]

Not enough blacks left Lexington to satisfy the Negrophobes, however. Since Fayette County was the center of the Blue Grass region, which contained the largest concentration of Negroes during the antebellum period, Lexington became the chief center of concentration for rural blacks who left the soil in Central Kentucky. A census taken early in 1868 showed that Lexington's population numbered 10,745 blacks and 10,196 whites. In 1860 the U.S. census had listed the city's white population as 6,241 and the black population as 3,280. The Bureau of the Census reported the black population of Lexington for 1870 at 7,171, an increase of 218 percent since 1860. An extremely large number of the resident Negroes were unemployed. The *Lexington Observer and Reporter* carried on an intolerant campaign against the blacks, who were described at best as vagabonds and a grievous nuisance. Many citizens took up the cry, and the legislature was bombarded with demands that it pass laws to remedy the city's problems. In 1869 the Kentucky General Assembly gave Lexington jurisdiction over vagrancy within the town limits and authorized a penalty of six months at hard labor, with a double penalty for the second conviction. The law was drawn up in such general terms that it was a crime to be unemployed. Lexington's white population had increased by 22 percent since 1860, so that whites were also unemployed, but society was intolerant only of unemployed blacks. The leaders of the black community realized the seriousness of the repeated, stereotypical charge of vagrancy. To counteract it and to render a service for unemployed Negroes, black war veterans called a public meeting in Lexington. There the freedmen passed resolutions expressing their willingness to enter into labor contracts with the whites. The former soldiers set up a labor and employment agency which placed more than 3,000 Negroes in jobs during the first half of 1869. This office was said to have "sent a laborer into every cornfield and almost every occupation of trust in Kentucky."[34]

As attention began to focus on the question of political rights for freedmen, outrages against Negroes increased, and the control over black agricultural laborers became harsher. The bureau agent in Russellville reported that if a Negro asked for the same wage for the same work as a white man, he would never again be employed, even "for the most stingy pittance." The resentment of the Regulators against the participation of blacks in political meetings and demonstrations took the form of overt acts of violence. The Regulators often boldly told the freedmen that their object was to drive all Negroes from the farms and force them to leave the country. At the height of the ordeal, arsonists began to put the torch to rural property in Central Kentucky. Almost nightly for several weeks, barns, hay, and oat stacks went up in flames, and farm animals were turned into grain fields. In Woodford County the August election triggered disputes that led to arson. The Regulators murdered two blacks in retaliation. On the night of August 11, 1870, blacks assembled en masse on a hill near Versailles armed with a variety of weapons and closed all roads leading to Versailles. They dispersed only when a militia arrived from Midway.[35] In Fayette County the loss of small livestock, such as hogs and sheep, was a common occurrence. Although the editor of the *Kentucky Gazette* charged the crimes to unemployed blacks, Lexington had a considerable number of whites without visible means of support, but the editor of the *Gazette* seemed to think the blacks had a monopoly on such crime. Disguised Regulators operated against individuals suspected of wrongdoing.[36]

With the coming of cold weather the acts of lawlessness declined for two months only to be renewed in January 1871, during the hiring season, when the activities of the night riders reached a new high. On January 12 several Negroes were wounded and murdered in rural Scott County, which adjoined Fayette County. A few days later the night riders struck twice in Fayette and once in Franklin, whipping and killing individuals in both counties. The alleged reason for the outrages was thefts of hogs and sheep. Competition of black agricultural laborers with white tenants was the probable cause of at least some of the disturbance. A large number of white tenants had been displaced by freedmen who paid higher prices for the rent of cabins in the rural areas in the Blue Grass region. The violence caused many blacks to flock to the towns for protection, fearing they might be the next victims. Concerned farmers, apprehensive about losing their labor supply, denounced the violence. The editor of the *Lexington Observer and Reporter* became the advocate of law and order and denounced the masked riders in strong language. Calls were made for legislative action to check demoralization of society and to remove the fear and mistrust that were laying waste the economy of Central Kentucky.[37]

The problems confronting the employers in securing an adequate supply of labor revived public interest in the question of immigrants and led to an act chartering the Kentucky Immigration and Industrial Association in 1867. As its name suggests, this association, based in Louisville, was primarily concerned with industrial labor, but the critical need of the moment was for more agricultural labor. In July the editor of the *Observer and Reporter* reminded his readers that he had repeatedly sought to alert them to the vital importance of attracting white immigrants to Kentucky for work in the fields. Such labor would mean less dependence on the Negroes and would make the power of blacks less dangerous if they became voters, he noted. If the Negroes numbered only one in ten, the editor believed, unscrupulous demagogues would not be tempted to inspire hatred of whites in black breasts. He denied that the advocates of immigration wanted to drive the Negro out of Kentucky. A meeting of the friends of immigrant labor in Lexington in October went on record as favoring state action to promote immigration. Early in November the Woodford County Labor Association was organized to promote foreign labor for the county, and it raised funds to send a recruiting agent to New York.[38]

During 1868 the labor problems and the question of immigration were fully discussed in farmers' clubs and county agricultural societies, and by 1869 the question was ripe for consideration at a statewide level. In January 1869, in his message to the legislature, Gov. John Stevenson reported that the labor supply of the state was not sufficient to maintain prosperity and that white foreign immigration offered the only relief. The governor limited himself to recommending the establishment of a bureau of statistics or an agricultural bureau to disseminate information on the advantages that Kentucky offered new settlers.[39]

On January 20, while the General Assembly of Kentucky was in session, the Kentucky State Agricultural Society met in Frankfort. Robert Mallory, the president, suggested that members come prepared to talk about the "completely disorganized" state of agricultural and domestic labor in Kentucky. Anticipating the society's meeting, the editor of the *Frankfort Yeoman* on January 19 claimed that the labor of the blacks had proven "wholly inadequate for the agricultural wants of Kentucky." It was universally admitted, he continued, that Negro labor was not sufficient in quantity or quality to cultivate the land and develop the mineral resources of the state. The editor suggested that legislation was needed to encourage immigrants to work Kentucky, and he called for a board of immigration to be established by the state with power to send out agents.[40]

After the Agricultural Society convention had adjourned, the *Yeoman* prodded the legislature to take action. When it failed to do so, the *Observer and Reporter* suggested that farmers consider the possibility of reestablishing the overseer system. Young whites who were idle should be attracted to the farms to act as managers, receiving wages or a share of the crop. The *Kentucky Gazette* did not believe that Kentucky's agricultural problems could be solved by white labor, because the white man would not work in the hot sun. The editor suggested that Chinese labor might solve the problem.[41]

The Democratic party and conservative farmers were convinced that the Fifteenth Amendment would make the black agricultural laborers useless.

They believed their only recourse was to turn to white labor. The *Kentucky Gazette* condemned politicians who tried to produce discord between the races; the farmer needed the Negro's labor but also his forbearance and confidence. The editor of the *Maysville Bulletin* lectured the blacks on the resolutions of the Negro convention: "As long as they resolve to work, there is some hope of future accomplishment," he asserted, "but if they continue the practice of robbing meat-houses, despoiling gardens and borrowing corn at midnight, as they have been doing in this locality, there is little to expect of them in their capacity as voters and lawmakers."[42]

The Lexington Farmers' Club was divided on the question of immigrant labor. The proponents of white labor created a second, special-purpose organization rather than divide the club, which was in accord on every other question. Some Lexington members sent an agent to New York, where more than twenty immigrants were contracted to labor in Kentucky. As public support increased, the leaders of the movement called a meeting to promote the introduction of white labor in Central Kentucky. The leaders hoped the Lexington movement could be expanded,[43] and a meeting followed in Bourbon County, during the same month, to advance a scheme for a statewide program.[44] The German societies of Louisville most successfully promoted immigrant labor locally. In August the Louisville societies sent an agent to New York. Prospective employers directly requested from the agent a specified number of German families. Some of the employers built houses for the new laborers before they arrived.[45]

A correspondent for the *Louisville Courier-Journal* who visited the agricultural centers in Kentucky from Paducah to Lexington found the agricultural societies in the Blue Grass region representative of the opinion throughout the state. Everywhere, he reported, there was a call for intelligent reliable labor from abroad.[46] The demand of county groups was so great that the board of directors of the Agricultural Society of Kentucky met during the state fair in October 1870 and endorsed requests that the state legislature incorporate an association to promote immigration to Kentucky.[47] In his annual message to the Kentucky General Assembly, Gov. John Stevenson asked the legislature to establish an immigrant bureau. The labor shortage in the countryside was real: the white population had increased by 14 percent from 1860 to 1870 in Kentucky, while the black population in the state had decreased 7 percent. The situation was made more critical by the concentration of blacks in twenty-one large Kentucky towns; the black population in these towns increased by 133 percent, for a total increase of 20,567.[48] The legislature, however, once more failed to act on the governor's recommendation.

In 1872 Gov. P. H. Leslie asked the legislature to pass measures to promote progress. His emphasis was placed entirely on industrial growth, and he again called for foreign labor to fill the vacuum, this time as a part of a broader objective of improving the moral, social, and intellectual condition of the laboring class.[49] The senate added a committee on immigration and labor to its standing committees, and a bill was introduced to establish a bureau of immigration as a department of the government. The committee on immigration made an elaborate report on the needs for a bureau and recommended that the senate pass the bill, but it was defeated in the absence of a constitutional majority. Support for the bill had come from the Louisville senators and from the mineral-rich mountainous districts, where the land was sparsely settled, but except for the senators from Henderson and Christian counties, legislators from counties with a large black population voted against the bill or refrained from voting.[50] The same legislature which had refused to finance a bureau of immigration passed an act to exempt the wages of laborers from attachment or garnishment until they had earned fifty dollars. While this law helped all poor people in the same way that bankruptcy relieved the affluent, the blacks were the most common victims of the attachment of wages under a misuse of the contract.[51]

Despite all of the agitation to bring in foreign workers, only slightly more than 3,500 white immigrants arrived during the decade 1860–1870.[52] The interest in their labor had been cultivated by commercial and industrial entrepreneurs rather than farmers, who wanted labor at a price of fifteen dollars or less.[53] Europeans found more attractive opportunities elsewhere. The Chinese constituted the most available supply of cheap agricultural labor from abroad. Chinese labor was already being tried in Louisiana, and it was hoped by some that this group could be attracted to Kentucky. The Orientals would be more tractable than people of other nationalities, it was thought, and could be expected to work for low wages. Some farmers appeared to have joined the call for Chinese labor in order to be able to bargain more effectively with blacks. The *Lexington Observer and Reporter* warned the freedmen that it "would be well if Pompey and Sambo take warning by the march of events of this kind and abandon their suicidal habits, and go to work with a will. . . . The tune then will not be 'forty acres and a mule,' but it will be 'work nigger or starve!'"[54]

Many blacks became uneasy about the possibility that they might be at least partially replaced by Chinese. A Negro convention met in Louisville in July 1869 and advised "the young men and youth of our State" to "learn trades and engage in agricultural pursuits as a proper mode of supporting themselves and giving encouragement to mechanics and agriculture."[55] A meeting of blacks in 1870 in Frankfort expressed strong opposition to bringing Chinese into the state "for the purpose of supplanting us as a laboring class, and placing us in a false light before the world as unworthy." They looked "with distrust upon all parties who would thus supplant us, when our labor and that of our ancestors have made them rich and opulent." The meeting adopted resolutions to "earnestly recommend to our people industry, economy and a faithful observance of contracts when correctly and strictly made."[56] The general alarm proved unfounded; no steps were ever taken in Kentucky to secure Chinese labor.

In 1870, the black laborers still had no protection against the night riders and could still be victimized by dishonest employers. The legislature refused to repeal the law prohibiting blacks to testify in state courts against whites. In November 1866 the federal district court in Kentucky declared that the bureau courts had no legal existence in Kentucky. The only remaining court in which black laborers could receive relief was the federal distrcit court, but its docket was so overloaded that few cases had any hope of securing a hearing. The Ku Klux Klan remained active in Central Kentucky throughout 1871. A meeting of blacks living in Central Kentucky convened in Frankfort and drew up a list of 116 outrages by organized bands in Kentucky from November 1867 to February 1871, claiming that the lack of security for black families made federal legislation imperative. A watered-down bill to restrain the Ku Klux Klan passed the upper house of the Kentucky legislature but was defeated in the lower house in February 1871. Congress asked the president to report on the security of life and property in the South and specifically mentioned Kentucky; [57]

The situation became so critical that it was difficult for farmers to secure an adequate labor supply, and in January 1871 they met in Frankfort to deal with the problem of security. Resolutions were passed urging strict enforcement of the laws and calling on the legislature to pass new measures to deal with lawlessness. The blacks met during the same month in Lexington and expressed their disapproval of the violence committed against the property of the farmers. They also claimed the right of protection against the outrages of the Ku Klux Klan. On February 5, the farmers of Fayette County convened in Lexington with citizens from most of the neighboring counties in attendance. The meeting adopted measures calling on the legislature to pass laws "to secure equal protection and equal punishment to all persons in the state courts." Legislation was requested for the creation of additional courts for the speedy administration of justice in Fayette County, to authorize the county judge to offer rewards for the apprehension of criminals, and to permit justices of the peace to appoint police as necessary to enforce the laws. The farmers invited the black laborers "to seek homes in the country" and pledged "to use their best efforts to secure to them the protection, rights and privileges guaranteed to them by law." The legislature of 1871 responded by adopting measures that freed black laborers from terms of the contract law of 1866, which had left the Negro tenants at the mercy of their employers. The same terms now applied to both white and black tenants. A law was also passed which, except in the case of schools, prohibited taxing black citizens at a higher rate than white.[58]

The farmers continued to woo the black laborers back from the cities by promising security and petitioned the legislature to pass legislation that would assist them. In 1872, both the whites and blacks of Frankfort again held meetings and asked for legislation to suppress lawlessness. Late in 1872 the people of Shelby County held a similar meeting, and in 1873 a gathering in Owen County denounced the Regulators. Like their predecessors, these groups also sought laws to protect the blacks. The legislature of 1872 failed to enact the measure dealing with night riders, but homestead exemptions were extended to all, "irrespective of race or color." This tax relief, greatly needed by black tenants, had been applied to poor whites as early as 1866. In 1872, the Kentucky legislature also exempted housekeepers working for families from having their pay garnished until they had earned fifty dollars. The new contract law of 1871 that prohibited black tenants from being legally charged with breaking a labor contract because of a minor infraction became more significant in 1872, when the legislature voted down a bill which would have imposed a civil liability on anyone who hired a laborer or servant before the expiration of a contract. These laws greatly improved the economic condition of black tenants.[59] Another measure enacted in 1872 permitted blacks to testify against whites, so that the black laborers could return to the soil with a degree of security. After almost two years of pressure from the farmers, Democratic advocates of law and order, and Republicans, in 1873 the legislature passed a stringent act against lawbreakers. The law made it a crime for two or more persons to conspire to intimidate any person, to band together to commit a felony, or to "go forth armed and disguised."[60]

Before 1873, the blacks had suffered severe legal restrictions as they strove to improve their economic conditions. Some nevertheless succeeded, despite discrimination. By November 1867 taxable property in Kentucky owned by Negroes was valued at $976,956, which was taxed at the rate of $3,661. In November 1869 the value had increased to $2,016,784, an increase of $3,661 in one year. In 1869, for example, some black farmers in Kentucky owned as much as 112 acres of land. Others had thirty, forty, or fifty acres in Oldham County, and sixteen Negroes had become owners in Maysville by 1869.[61]

Yet the freedmen's gradual progress toward greater economic well-being did not necessarily bring greater social acceptance and tolerance. After blacks had been granted suffrage in 1870, the Regulators intensified their activities. The bitterness toward the Negro felt by some parts of the white community was greater because the blacks' newly won franchise was to be exercised through the printed, or secret, ballot, which became mandatory in federal elections after passage of a law in February 1871.[62] The freedmen petitioned and protested for relief from persecution, and when peaceful methods failed, some turned to arson in retaliation, while others fled from the countryside.

The blacks had secured their economic gains partly by political pressure but largely as a result of the demand for their labor. The farmers for whom they worked had become important advocates of legal relief for the harassed, particularly in Central Kentucky. The representatives from the Blue Grass section had eventually joined the ten Republicans and New Departure Democrats in passing through the lower house of the legislature, by a vote of 58 to 14, a law that dealt with lawlessness. Only two Blue Grass representatives voted against the Homestead Exemption Law, which passed 60 to 26.[63] These two laws had significantly improved conditions for black tenants, but the Negro Testimony Law was to be the most important step forward in securing the rights of the newly emancipated laborers.

CHAPTER EIGHT

Families in Transition

THROUGHOUT THE ANTEBELLUM period when society was swept with great excitement, slaves in Kentucky often fled from servitude in family groups. As a result of the great commotion brought on by the Mexican War, and the debates concerning the proposals for a plan for gradual emancipation in Kentucky in 1849, so many slave families left their owners that the phenomenon attracted much public discussion. Fugitives also took to the roads during the period that followed John Brown's Raid on Harpers Ferry and during the early months of the Civil War. These episodes foreshadowed events after the adoption of the Emancipation Proclamation.

As the war progressed, the occasions that usually triggered a mass exodus were reports of invasions of Confederate troops, causing slaves to fear that the family might fall under the control of Confederate forces. The withdrawal of Federal forces from an area frequently touched off a massive movement of black families from an endangered region. The fugitives feared that advancing Confederates would impress them, remove them to the deep South, or even kill them. Occasionally a slave family would be struck by a fear, either real or imaginary, that their master intended to send family members south for sale or for security from the Federals. Rumors went through the black community that certain white families planned to remove to areas behind Confederate lines and to take the slaves with them. Many Confederate sympathizers did in fact retreat as the Federals moved south. In their search for safety and security, the slaves often fled to the Union army camps.

Unlike the prewar fugitive slaves, who usually fled alone, when the black refugee families escaped from servitude, if circumstances permitted, they often took with them property of the slaveholder to facilitate their existence as a free family—horses or mules or money or other valuables. More often the refugees took enough grain to supply rations for several days while they sought shelter.

The army was initially unprepared to help the fugitives. General Rosecrans continued Buel's policy of excluding contraband families and unemployable men from the military camps, and General Boyle did the same in Western Kentucky. Everywhere in the state, however, the soldiers followed the dictates of humanitarian conscience and pragmatism on many occasions instead of heeding general orders. As one soldier recalled: "They [slaves] could not be kept out, for they came in spite of orders . . . . when they came our officers could no more find it in their hearts to drive the poor things away than a mother or father could drive children forth from their home into a driving storm."[1]

At Columbus, Kentucky, the commanding general issued an order in August 1862 which barred all women from the camp lines unless they were granted special permission. The purpose seemed to be the regulation of morals, but the primary consequence was hardship for the wives of many black employees. Because many male slaves had chosen to abandon their owners and to work for the army, their spouses were forced to seek refuge within the army lines.[2] General Boyle's order banning slaves from the camps was extended by Gen. H.M. Judah, commander at Bowling Green, in March 1863. Judah not only excluded black males and females from the camps under his command but also prohibited them from residing nearby.[3] The measures taken to enforce the regulations sometimes included whipping and other forms of violence, but in spite of such adversity the slave family persisted in maintaining its unity as it sought freedom.

As early as 1862, the army in Kentucky recognized that when the movements of soldiers unsettled the slaves, the refugees fled in family groups. Such groups also dominated the large refugee camps that sprang up spontaneously within the Union lines as blacks desperately sought food, shelter, clothing, and protection. The number of fugitives at Columbus and Paducah, Kentucky, and at Cairo, Illinois, became so large that the army was forced to view the refugee camps as inevitable in the war zone.

The American Missionary Association sent agents to assist the slaves. S.G. Wright, an antislavery missionary from Illinois, went to Columbus at the end of 1862 when refugees concentrated there following the Confederate invasion of Kentucky and the guerrilla raids of the same year. Wright secured a large stable hardly suitable for human occupation to house 500 blacks who were mostly family groups of women and children, and he succeeded in persuading the army to issue them rations.[4] Like other missionaries and paternalistic reformers, Wright believed the isolation of the refugee camps offered opportunities to instruct the Negroes regarding their new privileges and responsibilities, and he immediately undertook to start a school and a church. The blacks of Columbus later contributed funds to build a permanent church of rough hewed lumber that could also be used as a school.

In 1863, when the Emancipation Proclamation was in effect, the army accepted primary responsibility for feeding and housing the destitute blacks. Even so, the comfort of the uprooted families was scarcely assured. Ration issues constituted the military's greatest charitable contribution. Laborers usually received a generous portion equivalent to that of a soldier, but refugees were given a reduced allotment. The blacks depended on the benevolence of the commissary department for adequate supplies of food, which was provided on an emergency basis and not as a permanent service. The missionaries and benevolent societies exerted their influence in Washington, but not until January 1864 did Secretary of War Stanton set up shelters for refugees in the vicinity of all army camps in the Federal occupational zones. Even thereafter the ration offered at the shelters continued to be significantly smaller than the soldier's.[5]

Housing for refugees was usually improvised. Abandoned barns and stables near the army camp became makeshift facilities. The available tents were often those the soldiers had cast aside as worn out and were often so tattered that they provided little actual shelter. In time the camps acquired barracks which were built by the contraband themselves from lumber furnished by the army. The Freedmen's Aid Societies helped by donating supplies of clothing. Many of the fugitive slaves entered the Federal lines wearing rags. The army lacked legal authority to purchase clothes for contraband, so the refugees had to rely entirely on the benevolent societies. The adult males could be given uniforms discarded as worn out or taken from dead Federals or simply rejected by the quartermaster. The children often wore adult garments cut down to fit. Most of the apparel was furnished and distributed by the Western Freedman's Society.[6]

After the Emancipation Proclamation was issued in January 1863, the number of black refugees from Kentucky in the camps increased. In many cases married men fled alone and sought employment with the army, and their wives and children followed later. A woman whose family owned slaves in Bourbon County expressed her belief in the cohesion and solidarity of the black family when she wrote to her mother in March 1863: "For three or four days the Federals have been taking off the negroes from this county to work or fight at Lexington . . . . Upon the strength of the fright, one of ours has left. He has been gone two days . . . , but I think he will come back, as we have his wife and four children."[7]

At about the same time, Adj. Gen. Lorenzo Thomas authorized the recruiting of slaves in Western Kentucky. As soon as the blacks in Western Kentucky had assembled at Columbus, women and children followed the new recruits. Since emancipation had not freed the slaves in Kentucky, Thomas advised the commanders in the camps to send the dependents home to be cared for by the slaveholders. The women and children were removed but soon reappeared in greater numbers. On August 4, 1863, the adjutant of the camp at Columbus issued a new order which indicated that black women were causing much trouble among the enlisted men of the

Fourth Regiment, Heavy Artillery, U.S. Colored Troops. The adjutant did not indicate the source of the problem, but he pointed out that no provision had been made for supplying women and children with rations. Black women were ordered to be expelled unless they were employed as servants for officers, in which event, it may be assumed, they had access to food.[8]

When the Union army began to enlist slaves throughout Kentucky in March 1864, the black families behaved much as they had in the western part of the state. Wives, mothers, fathers, and children, and sometimes uncles, aunts, and even grandparents, followed the recruits when they went into military service. Sometimes the reason given was that their masters had driven them off. On other occasions the refugees claimed they feared guerrillas, and at times the soldier's family confessed that the recruit had sent for them. The slaveholder often resented the enlistment of the male slaves and vented his anger on the wife and children. The black soldiers showed great concern for the welfare of their families, and the greatest obstacle to the recruiting of slaves soon became the lack of security for the soldiers' dependents. As blacks became more informed concerning the circumstances of the war, they more frequently asked recruiting officers what would become of their wives and children during their own military service. In November 1864 the colonel of the Seventy-second U.S. Colored Infantry at Covington reported that a large number of slaves had "offered to enlist," provided that "they had assurances" that their families would be freed by the government or at least protected by the army. The provost marshal of the first district (Paducah) in Kentucky informed his superior in Louisville, *"Attend to their wives and families* and they will immediately rush to arms."[9]

The desire for a secure family life was unquestionably the first priority of the prospective black soldier. The slaves had lived in a crisis throughout the antebellum period, and they knew what it was like to live perpetually in danger of being separated, children from parents and husbands from wives. Not only did slave families often flee as a group from their masters, but occasionally the husband and wife traveled long distances at great risk to liberate and reunite members of their family who had been parted by sale. Since most of the camps in Kentucky where the black soldiers were received and trained were not far from their homes, the men frequently visited families which remained with their masters. The soldiers occasionally even went home when they were denied official permission to leave camp, and they often carried with them part of their rations, "moonlighted" at odd jobs if the family lived nearby, or even stole to sustain dependents.[10]

When distance prevented the black recruits from seeing their wives during a short furlough or from slipping away and returning without being missed, the soldiers persisted in their efforts to keep in touch by writing letters or, more commonly, since many could not write, by having letters written for them. Many of the noncommissioned officers could write and often helped the enlisted men in the evening. The demand for writers was so great that a fee was frequently charged for the service—until post commanders restricted the amount to the value of the material furnished.[11] While the Twelfth U.S. Colored Heavy Artillery Regiment was stationed at Bowling Green, it was not an uncommon sight to see Sgt. Elijah P. Marrs, a black soldier, sitting at a desk "surrounded by a number of the men" of the regiment, "each waiting his turn to have a letter written home." At Camp Nelson in July 1864, soldiers crowded around John Fee in the evening seeking help with their writing. Other blacks took advantage of the willingness of the Sanitary Commission officers to compose letters for them while they were stationed at Camp Nelson. The Camp Nelson Sanitary Commission superintendent estimated that he and his staff wrote at least 5,000 letters for black soldiers in less than a year.[12]

After the first flush of excitement about the opportunity to enlist, the recruiting officers frequently had to devise means to entice the slaves into military service. Since enlistment often meant that the slaveholder would refuse to support the enlisted man's family, the pay received by the recruit became important. During the summer of 1864, Congress raised the black private's monthly pay from $10, minus the cost of clothing, to $16 and gave the slave the Federal enlistment bounty of $300.[13] While the recruiters generally appealed to the prospective recruit's patriotism and racial pride, they found themselves also obliged to ease his anxiety by promising to provide for his family's subsistence and security within a contraband camp. Sometimes the recruiters tried to find jobs for the soldiers' wives.[14]

The controversy concerning the presence of the families of black soldiers in the military camps was fought out and settled at Camp Nelson in Jessamine County. The women and children were initially driven away but returned, usually before another day had passed. There was much suffering in the improvised camp, but when the dependents were given over to their masters, many of the slaves were terrified of the consequences. The agents of the American Missionary Association urged that the families be permitted to remain in camp. A "severe struggle" ensued between the supporters of the local white community and the friends of the blacks in Camp Nelson. Capt. T. E. Hall, a New Englander, was the chief of the Quartermaster Department and principal supporter of the Negroes among the officers stationed at the post. He worked with the missionaries, and by giving the problems of Camp Nelson his undivided attention, he triumphed in the end.[15]

In May 1864, Col. A. H. Clark, commander of the post, ordered the provost marshal to expel the women from the camp. The next day three had returned. The commander directed the provost marshal to send out a patrol to arrest them and to confine them to military prison until they were all in custody, at which time they were to be tied up and whipped before they were again driven out. All other women were also arrested and were sent beyond the lines with the warning that they, too, would be whipped if they returned.[16]

Speed Smith Fry, who replaced Clark as commander, also opposed the presence of the black families. He vigorously condemned the refugee shelters as places for "wholesale license . . . devoid of a sense of moral obligations." After consulting with his superiors, Fry continued to bar runaway women from camp. On June 20, 1864, Burbridge instructed Fry to establish quarters for the women and children so that they were not left to starve. When Fry inquired about a permanent policy, Burbridge referred the problem to Lorenzo Thomas and secured instructions that the post should "discourage as far as possible Negro women and children from coming into camp" but should provide for them when they came.[17] The problem was also becoming more chronic and critical in other places where black troops were stationed in Kentucky. At the end of June 1864, the commander at Munfordville reported that women and children arrived daily with the black recruits, and he asked General Burbridge for instructions. In September the same question came from the colonel of the Thirty-ninth Infantry, commanding at Louisa, on the Virginia border.[18]

On July 5, General Fry called Burbridge's attention to the status of the blacks at Camp Nelson. "I have examined the condition of the Negro women, children and old men at this post," he wrote, "and find them very destitute, a burden to themselves as well as ourselves. If some means are not soon devised to return them to their homes, we shall not only have war in the land but pestilence and famine in the camp. Many cases of disease are already making their appearance among both sexes," he warned, "and of such a nature as to demand their removal beyond the limits of [the] camp at once." Burbridge referred the matter to Thomas. The adjutant general had already consulted the War Department on July 3, following the query from the army post at Munfordville. Thomas declared that since slavery still existed in Kentucky, he would require that women and children return to their owners, as they could be made useful in harvesting the crops. Three days later, on July 6, Thomas issued General Orders No. 24, requiring recruiting officers to first encourage all women, children, and older men to remain at home and second to return home those currently in the camps. Thomas commented on the many cases of disease among refugees in the camps and noted that under the state law the master was obligated to care for the blacks.[19]

The families of the soldiers at Camp Nelson were to be placed beyond the lines at an early date, the exact time to be determined by General Burbridge, with sufficient rations to last until they could reach their homes. Thomas suggested that notice be given of the day the order would go into effect so that owners might be there to receive their slaves. The slaveholders were pleased, thinking they would now find it easier to reclaim their property.[20]

The adjutant general found his order simpler to issue than to enforce. When he visited Camp Nelson in mid-July, he found "a number of old men, women and children," whom he ordered to be sent home. Since the specific date for removing the slaves from Camp Nelson was to be set by General Burbridge, and the missionaries and some of the military personnel had insisted that the wives of all black soldiers were free, Thomas asked the War Department to clarify the status of the females who had fled to the military posts in Kentucky where their husbands were being trained. The War Department responded that nothing had changed: the law authorizing the enlistment of blacks made "no provision for their families" except freedom to such as were "owned by disloyal masters."[21]

On July 7, the day after Thomas issued his order to remove the women and children from the camp in Kentucky, Col. H. W. Barry, commander of Fort Anderson, Paducah, reported to Gen. A. L. Chetlain, who was in charge of the recruitment of black troops in Western Kentucky, that a large number of women and children belonging to the soldiers of the Eighth Regiment, U.S. Colored Heavy Artillery, had gathered in the vicinity of the fort. Since he could not issue rations to them, there was much suffering. He asked for instructions. "If any relief can be afforded them, I respectfully ask it may be done," he added. Colonel Barry was told to send the slaves home, but he refused to do so, maintaining that Order No. 24 conflicted with the articles of war prohibiting the rendition of fugitive slaves. Thomas instructed the colonel's commander to explain Order No. 24, and thereafter, if the colonel still persisted in his course, to arrest him for trial by a court-martial for disobedience.[22] Barry refused to yield and was arrested, but the slaves eventually won when the War Department decided late in July that the dependents at the fort in Paducah were not to be dispersed but should be dealt with as were all other fugitives in the Department of West Tennessee. Barry was subsequently released and restored to his command.[23]

Lt. Col. John Bishop also questioned the procedure for handling cases involving women who were fugitive slaves. After Thomas has issued Order No. 24, Bishop, who commanded the post at Owensboro and the 108th U.S. Colored Infantry, referred his query to General Burbridge. A response came from the adjutant general of the Department of Kentucky, who upheld Order No. 24, but Bishop persisted. "How can we return fugitives to their masters in the face of General Orders No. 27, War Department, 1862?" he asked. When he was referred to the revised army regulations for 1863 and again to Thomas's General Orders No. 24, he appeared to yield.[24]

On August 13, 1864, Burbridge placed the expulsion order for Camp Nelson "under the Acts of Congress and orders for the War Department."

Fry issued order No. 19 on August 23, driving from the camp all female slaves who were residents of Kentucky. He ordered all officers who had "negro women in their employment" to deliver them up to the patrol to be brought to headquarters and threatened to arrest any officer not complying.[25] The women and children were sent away, but hardly a day passed when new ones did not arrive or when some of the dispersed slaves did not return. Fry did not follow up on his order because he was temporarily sent to Paducah on public business, and after he returned, he received permission to campaign for Lincoln. In October, Captain Hall was relieved of duty, and the secretaries of the American Missionary Association learned that he had been replaced by one who "knows not Joseph." Through the month of November, rations were cut off from the refugee camp. The slaves existed on the limited supplies provided by the Sanitary Commission. Then, on November 14, the adjutant of Camp Nelson asked the headquarters of the Department of Kentucky to permit the removal of the Negro women and children from the camp, as they were "in a suffering condition."[26]

On November 23, without previous warning of the action that was to take place, under order of General Fry, some 400 women and children were carried from Camp Nelson in wagons and carts and were distributed along the wayside between Camp Nelson and Nicholasville. The refugee camp was leveled. Slaves wandered through the woods and languished on the highways, seeking out barns or mule sheds to shelter themselves from the weather in their half-starved, half-naked condition. The morning was bitter cold and the thermometer was below freezing all day. At least four people froze to death in the wintry blasts. Some made their way to Ohio, but most huddled in makeshift shelters in the neighborhood of Nicholasville, where they were found by the missionaries who sought them out in a wagon filled with bread that Hall had paid for out of his own pocket.[27]

General Burbridge was leading a military campaign in Eastern Kentucky and western Virginia, and his adjutant, J. B. Dickson, who was in charge at headquarters, was far more liberal than the general. Dickson was in a position to make decisions, and he immediately took action to assist the refugees. Since Hall happened to be back in camp, Dickson placed him in charge of the affairs concerning blacks there and telegraphed Burbridge to ask that Fry be ordered to take care of the slaves at the camp. Burbridge countermanded Fry's order, and Dickson instructed Hall to erect dwellings for the soldiers' families. Fry was ordered to assist Hall in every way possible, but Fry instead placed Hall under arrest. After a delay requested by Thomas, Dickson arranged to have Fry removed from command. By December 1, 1864, from 200 to 300 women and children were back in Camp Nelson, and during the next few weeks they continued to arrive daily in groups of from 2 to 20.[28]

Hall constructed a permanent refugee camp which was set apart from the soldiers' quarters. The quartermaster's department furnished the material, and the soldiers built barrackslike structures intended to house several families. The buildings were not ideal, but John Fee agreed that at least they offered women greater protection at night than a tent would. Fee from the beginning had urged the army to shelter the families. To his consternation, however, an epidemic broke out and quickly spread among the children. Although 250 to 400 refugees who had been expelled in November returned, 102 eventually died in the dormitory. Fee insisted that cottages would be better, since they would promote health as well as morals, and he was later able to secure approval to have units built for the families who had children.[29]

Hall wrote to a New England clergyman and explained how the friends of the slaves had won the victory at Camp Nelson. "The slave Oligarchy . . . put into my hands the most potent weapon I could use," he wrote, referring to the inhumane order issued during the coldest spell of the season. After Hall had persuaded Burbridge to revoke the order, he took affidavits from many of the sufferers and sent them to the leading newspapers. He also sent Sen. B. F. Wade of Ohio a strong letter to be presented to the secretary of war, who ordered that all women and children seeking refuge should be cared for in Camp Nelson. This document prevented the army in Kentucky from expelling the soldiers' dependents when warm weather returned in 1865.[30]

Similar problems were being encountered elsewhere. While the Twelfth U.S. Colored Heavy Artillery Regiment was stationed in Bowling Green, hundreds of blacks—the wives and families of recruits—came into camp seeking protection because the former masters of many had driven them from their homes. The group was composed entirely of women and children from six months to eighty years of age. Elijah Marrs, who was detailed to care for them, took over as his headquarters an old Methodist church that had been used by blacks. He distributed army rations to the refugees but had difficulty in clothing them. Many did not have a second garment, and within four weeks some were almost naked. The refugees remained there for more than six months until Marrs was ordered to transfer them to Camp Nelson, where permanent shelter was being made available.[31]

On December 15, 1864, Lorenzo Thomas issued Order No. 29, which required that the families of black soldiers be promptly sheltered in all camps in Kentucky. The order explained that without proper care of dependents, slaves would not enlist. Thomas made Burbridge responsible for seeing that the humane intentions of the federal government respecting the blacks were executed. Burbridge was ordered to have suitable buildings erected at Camp Nelson and at all other points in Kentucky where black recruits were received, and he authorized the Quartermaster Department at Camp Nelson to furnish transportation so that A. Scofield, an AMA agent, could go to

Syracuse to obtain clothing. Since the instructions from the surgeon general prohibited the issuance of medical supplies to refugees, Burbridge secured authority directly from the War Department to supply destitute families of black soldiers with medicine.[32]

By the end of December 1864 the new policy was in full effect, and Adjutant General Thomas admitted that there could be no other solution to the refugee problem. On December 25, a large new contingent arrived at Camp Nelson stating that they had been driven from their homes and, in some instances, that their masters had had the cabins pulled down over the slaves' heads. Thomas believed that the brutal masters were Confederate sympathizers and that the slaves of Union men had left home by choice rather than because of inhumanity.[33]

The missionaries and the antislavery military officers developed an effective program of voluntary benevolence in cooperation with the army, but the military personnel and the missionaries had their differences. The army officers who controlled the benevolent program after November 23, 1864, were motivated by anti-Southernism and the desire to secure black military power as expediently as possible. On February 15, 1865, James Brisbin wrote Fee that no additional homes could be erected at the time and that no further women and children should be encouraged to come to the camp. "Only those who are ill-treated and indigent should be received," he wrote; "only the worst case should be received."

The fugitive slaves who gathered at other posts in Kentucky where Negro soldiers were stationed never received the protection and security they received at Camp Nelson. In some places black soldiers' wives and children were suffering for the necessities of life as late as September 1865, long after they had been declared free. Even in Camp Nelson, Hall at times appeared to be more interested in putting down the slaveholding class than in helping the slave, but the sincerity of his good intentions could not be doubted. Lumber deals for his own profit often occupied his attention while he was serving as the chief of the Quartermaster Department and as superintendent of the refugees. Fee had reservations about Hall because he liked "his dram too much," but Fee admitted he had "sympathy for the poor and quick perception of the right." Still, Hall, like Brisbin, was primarily concerned with the physical needs of the dependent slaves. On February 24, "a good Union man" with a wife in New York came to Camp Nelson to reclaim a slave girl. "Capt. Hall said 'Yes' because she would be 'better off there than here.' " Lester William, a New England missionary, said no, and Fee said no. Captain Hall took Fee aside and gave him "a private chat." Fee said: "No—not for a moment!!! Her father is a soldier—Natural guardian. We must do for her *morally* what M. Barnes as a chattel owner will not do—this is more than 'hogs and hominy.' " The captain winced and retired.[34]

Thomas had originally insisted that the black women should be returned to the farms to plant and harvest the crops needed by the army; Fee wanted them to remain in the camps and plant crops there. By the end of December 1864 Fee had persuaded Thomas that the women could usefully be employed in the camp, though Thomas persisted in viewing it as a temporary measure until "other provisions" could be made for the black families. Both men probably overrated the importance of employing the women at Camp Nelson, but granting the women the opportunity to work did improve the family's sense of security and allayed the anxiety of recruits about the welfare of their dependents.

Fee testified to the fact that "the faith of the soldiers" had been injured by the army's callous disregard for their families. When the wives were driven from camp at the point of bayonets, "the husbands and fathers were very indignant. I did on more than one instance use my influence with such to induce them not to show resistance. They were angry. We could not blame them." In working to restore the morale of the soldiers at Camp Nelson, Thomas and Burbridge willingly followed the lead of Burbridge's adjutant J. Bates Dickson and committed themselves to making the greatest possible use of the slaves to strengthen the manpower of the army. In the words of a correspondent from Camp Nelson for the *New York Tribune,* no more effective plan "could be devised for arresting the progress of negro enlistments than that which visits upon their families a merciless persecution."[35]

In their conduct the black soldiers merely reflected the anxiety and concern of conscientious husbands and fathers, and commanders did well to heed such feelings in order to sustain morale. In one instance a soldier of the Twelfth U.S. Colored Heavy Artillery was furloughed at Bowling Green to visit his wife, who lived beyond the Barren River. When he learned that she had been treated very cruelly, partly because her husband was a soldier, the commander of the regiment sent Elijah Marrs with a detachment of ten black troops to bring the woman into camp. When this expedition failed, the commander sent twenty mounted soldiers to accomplish the task—only to learn that the wife had "fled to parts unknown."[36]

Not all commanders of black regiments showed such concern, however. A black serving with the Fifth U.S. Colored Cavalry in Lexington complained about the abuse of the soldiers' right to see their families. "Our wives and children are laying out doers *[sic]* and we have no chance to get a home for them. When our wives come to the camp to see us they are not allowed to come in camp and we are not allowed to go out to see them. They are drummed off, the officers say, go you damn bitches," he wrote. This soldier asked that black troops in the regiment be permitted to "go home to situate" their "familys *[sic]* for the winter."[37] It is not known whether this important request was granted.

The soldiers of the 109th U.S. Colored Infantry stationed at Louisa were not so submissive. In August 1864 a wife came into the camp with her husband but was ordered to leave because women were not employed in any capacity in the camp. She left but returned, only to be taken into custody by the sheriff of Lawrence County with a warrant issued by the county court. She was forcibly seized from the sheriff by fifteen or twenty men of the 109th Infantry. The commander, who was blamed for the incident, promised that the woman would be turned over to the sheriff and the men arrested.[38]

The controvesy concerning the dependents at Camp Nelson led directly to congressional legislation which freed the wives, children, and mothers of black soldiers. First, during the summer of 1864, Fee wrote a proposal for a program by which the army, with the help of the missionaries, would care for the refugees. The proposal was endorsed by Hall, and Fee sent a copy to both Secretary of the Treasury Chase and Senator Wilson, asking them to assist in securing its adoption, which they agreed to do. The crisis of the expulsion of November 23 provided the essential impetus, and on January 2, 1865, Fee received the necessary authorization. Since wives, mothers, and children were, as slaves, still subject to Kentucky's slave code, however, to circumvent the state's control it was necessary to free the soldiers' dependents by federal legislation. Shortly after Fry expelled the women and children from Camp Nelson, a great debate on the subject arose among the officers and missionaries at the camp. Many of the missionaries believed that the act of freeing the soldier necessarily extended freedom to his family.[39] Sidell, still the provost marshal general of Kentucky, thought that Congress should free all women and children who were supported by the U.S. government because they had been turned out of their homes by masters after their husbands joined the army.[40]

During the summer before the expulsion of November 1864, Sen. Benjamin F. Wade visited Camp Nelson and heard reports of the harsh treatment of black soldiers' families. The correspondence of T. E. Hall refreshed his memory on the condition of the fugitive slaves at the camp. Wade was an important advocate of legislation to protect the dependents of black soldiers. In the Senate he earnestly advocated the immediate adoption of a measure freeing these families, warning the lawmakers, "The Negro will not enlist unless you free his wife and children." He told of seeing a woman at Camp Nelson who had been brutally beaten before she reached the post, and he inserted into the record the affidavit of a black soldier whose wife and children had been threatened by a master seeking to prevent the man's enlistment. The soldier had enlisted and had taken his family to Camp Nelson only to have them suffer the harsh fate of the November expulsion.

During June 1864 one of the benevolent agents in Kentucky wrote Wilson a letter describing the cruel treatment of black women in Kentucky by the slaveholders, who acted with the consent and cooperation of the military officers of the state. The informer reported an incident that had taken place in a convalescent camp in Kentucky. The commandant of the post ordered the provost marshal to seize a slave girl working as a cook in the camp and to deliver her to her master outside the lines. When the girl was seized, she frantically appealed to everyone for protection and then begged the guards to shoot her on the spot rather than deliver her to her cruel master. The personnel of the camp were moved by her appeals and took her from the guards by force. They dressed her in men's clothing and secreted her away before a mounted patrol came to conduct a search.[41]

In introducing his resolution to free the wives, mothers, and children of black soldiers, Senator Wilson was undoubtedly moved by the events at Camp Nelson. Then, too, as Wilson later wrote, by January 8, 1865, "nearly one hundred thousand" blacks had entered military service, "mostly from the border states and the slaves of loyal masters." "While they were fighting the battles of the country, their masters, who were generally opposed to their enlistment, could sell into perpetual slavery their wives and children. To deter slaves from enlisting, or to punish them when they did enlist, slave-masters made merchandise of wives and children of colored soldiers and often sold them into a harsher bondage." Wilson's measure, entitled "a resolution to encourage enlistments, and to promote the efficiency of the military service," passed without serious opposition but was rejected by the lawmakers who represented Kentucky. Stanton regarded the measure as being "of the highest importance," however, commenting that it would add "to the numerical and efficient strength of the army,"[42] and Lincoln signed the bill without delay.

On March 12 Palmer issued an order informing the public that he would enforce the freedom of the dependents of black soldiers as a military measure. As he explained, the order offered "colored men not in the army . . . an opportunity to coin freedom for themselves and their posterity." In addition it was a social measure, however, as Kentucky's laws did not recognize the marriage of slaves and awarded the custody and guardianship of black children to the slaveholder rather than to the parents. When Gov. John L. Helm tried to reclaim two female slaves who had married two black soldiers in the camp at Elizabethtown, Palmer refused to return them even though Helm insisted that the two women already had husbands. The general told Helm that the army was compelled to recognize that black soldiers "could have wives and children"; after all, "marriage existed before laws were made, and children were the product of such marriages." In the absence of appropriate state laws, Palmer determined that blacks entering military service were married by "the mere fact that those persons recognized each other as husband and wife." He admitted that the law was greatly abused by some recruits for the sake of freedom; "there is no reason to doubt that polygamous alliances were very often formed for the sake of freedom under the laws of Congress."[43] Although its validity was to be challenged, the measure offered blacks an instrument by which they could prevent the continuance of hereditary slavery, and they were encouraged to use it by at least some army personnel.

The act freeing the families of Negro soldiers brought about the hoped-for increase in black recruits. In some cases female slaves encouraged their husbands to enlist in order to secure freedom for their children. On March 9, 1865, a Louisville family reported fairly typical circumstances: "On Thursday last, Eliza, our cook, prevailed on old Jesse to enlist and she is free and has left us. Kizzy's husband was drafted and she is free and has left us—so you see with cook and wash-woman both gone we are in a fix." Few other families may be supposed to have accepted the situation with such grace.[44]

There were signs, however, that controversy would surround the status of black soldiers' families until the Thirteenth Amendment abolished all slavery. In April, Judge L. Watson Andrews, in the Circuit Court of Nicholas County, ruled in two cases that the law freeing families of black soldiers was unconstitutional. The general expected similar rulings from all the circuit judges in Kentucky except three, and he was prepared to use military power to enforce the laws of Congress if he was so ordered. But Palmer did not wait for War Department authorization to disregard the ruling by Judge Andrews. After Palmer had informed Stanton of Andrew's ruling, he continued to enforce General Orders No. 10 with vigor by arresting all persons who mistreated, abused, or forcibly restrained the wives and children of enlisted blacks. He had two masters arrested and confined for trial before a military commission for beating wives of soldiers. One woman, whom Andrews ruled to be a slave though married to a soldier, was placed beyond Andrews's control. Palmer also ordered the provost marshal at Louisville to release from a slave pen a woman who was the wife of a deceased soldier.[45] The circuit court judges of Montgomery County and Fayette County followed Andrews's lead in ruling that the act of Congress was unconstitutional. General Brisbin placed the Fayette County judge under arrest. The Nicholas County case was taken to the Court of Appeals of Kentucky, and on December 15, 1865, the court upheld the decision of Judge Andrews.[46]

The adoption of the Thirteenth Amendment in December 1865 re-solved several questions pertaining to the black family's status. First, it gave the blacks a voice in determining the economic place that the husband and wife would occupy. To a great extent the women withdrew from field work, although they had never been used as extensively in Kentucky fields as their counterparts in the cotton kingdom had been.[47] Second, and more obvi-ously, the Thirteenth Amendment settled the controversy concerning the freedom of the families of black soldiers. On February 14, 1866, the General Assembly of Kentucky approved an act which legalized the marriages of freedmen and authorized black ministers in good standing in recognized Negro churches to solemnize marriages. Any couple who had lived together in slavery as husband and wife and intended to continue doing so was to be "held in Law as legally married." The children born while the parents were slaves were held to be legitimate for all purposes, provided the couple made a simple declaration of intent before the county court clerk and paid a fee of fifty cents. The law was not precisely drawn, and its real effects remained for the Court of Appeals to clarify.[48]

Since legal marriages certified by the state had been a privilege only of free people, many slaves welcomed the privilege of registering their marriages as a civil right. The fees required proved to be an obstacle, however. Although the fifty cents needed to register a marriage and the twenty-five cents required for a certificate of declaration did not amount to a great expense, many freedmen could not afford it. In addition, the commissioner of the Freedmen's Bureau authorized the ministers to charge a small fee.

There is no evidence that large numbers of blacks in Kentucky used their new privilege to change spouses. In some cases, however, freedmen broke off a relationship of cohabitation and traveled great distances to locate spouses from whom they had earlier been separated by sale. Such unions were then often registered. Commissioner Howard instructed the assistant commissioners to apply to freedmen in their jurisdictions existing laws pertaining to the marriage and divorce of white persons. Here, and in other areas, he declared, the same laws should apply to both races. Each assistant commissioner was to draw up regulations covering marriage and divorce procedures, and these were to be referred to state authorities to ensure that the bureau policy harmonized with the state constitution and state laws. The commissioner urged that the greatest care be taken to instruct the freed people as to the law's demands of them in regard to matrimony, and the magistrates and clergy who were certified to solemnize marriages were to "be earnestly solicited to aid the Bureau office in rectifying the existing evils" of cohabitation.[49]

Clinton B. Fisk had already drawn up Circular No. 5 on February 26, 1866, in accordance with the law of the Kentucky legislature, to regulate marriage of the freed people in the state. The bureau's policy in Kentucky was to refer freedmen to the county court for the marriage license. If the county court clerk refused to issue a license and certificate, the superintendent of the bureau in the district was authorized to do so and to solemnize the marriage. The superintendent was ordered to summon freed people who were living together so that they might take the necessary steps to become legally married. All persons who refused to comply were to be held guilty of a misdemeanor and were to be punished by a fine and imprisonment.[50]

When Jeff C. Davis replaced Fisk as the assistant commissioner of Kentucky, he supplemented the marriage regulations of the bureau in Kentucky by adding Special Orders No. 23, issued on June 26, 1866, which established procedures. Many agents reported on the status of marriage of the freedmen and submitted to county authorities a list of those who were living together in violation of bureau regulations. In counties where the authorities disregarded the status of the freed people's marriage, the agents licensed ministers and issued marriage licenses and certificates.[51] This was the circumstance in McCracken County, where the clerk of the county court initially refused to issue marriage licenses to freedmen. But in July 1866 the county judge of McCracken County took on the responsibility and the superintendent of the bureau ceased to be active in this work.[52] In other places when the agents referred the matter of marriage licenses and licensing ministers to the county court clerk, that officer assumed the entire responsibility, and the bureau agent limited his activity to furnishing the freedmen with information.[53]

Among the newly freed Negroes each party to the marital union was usually satisfied with one partner. Adultery was seldom reported,[54] although the superintendent in charge of the Maysville district observed that "the 'taking up system' is practiced by a very large majority of them." He recommended that the parties be arrested, brought before an agent, and compelled to take out certificates of marriage. The civil authorities of Mason County did not concern themselves with the marriage of blacks.[55]

In cases where a freedman deserted his wife and children, the bureau sent an agent to arrest the husband if he declined to support his dependents. In many districts freedmen who refused to secure a certificate of marriage because they would be compelled to live with the woman all the time were arrested and were made to choose between securing a certificate or being charged with adultery.[56] In some districts freedmen were said to have seduced black women with the promise of marriage. When the women gave birth to children, the bureau disposed of the cases "in the same manner as they would be by county judges in similar cases where both parties" were white.[57]

Both parties were not always black. In many cases which came before the bureau courts, black women brought paternity charges against white men. The charges against the men were hardly ever denied, and they were always settled by a small payment sufficient only to support the woman during her confinement.[58] In at least one interracial case, an infant of mixed parentage about eight months old was left on the doorstep of a black family. Investigation revealed that the white mother had fled to parts unknown, and the bureau paid an elderly black woman to keep the child until the matter was settled. The bureau insisted that the black father support the child, but he resisted on the grounds that "the woman made him do the devilment."[59] It is also recorded that the agent in Montgomery county persistently complained about casual cohabitation of blacks in his district, although he agreed that stable marriages in the black community were much more prevalent than during the slave days. The agent in Montgomery may not have been a disinterested witness, since serious charges were made against him of lacking devotion to his work among the freedmen.[60]

The Court of Appeals of Kentucky gave a very liberal and just interpretation to the marriage law of February 1866 and decisively modified the harshness of the decisions of the lower courts. Its opinion of December 14, 1866, limited the rights which a spouse in a customary marriage might claim. In one case, a slave claimed that a woman had been his wife by cohabitation; they had been recognized as a couple for more than fifteen years, until the woman's death in April 1866. The court held that since the two had not married as prescribed by the act of 1866, their union was not legally valid, and therefore the man's claim to be the dead woman's administrator was superseded by that of her brother. The court also held that following the adoption of the Revised Statutes, there could be no such thing as legal marriage by cohabitation and recognition alone; marriages not solemnized by contracts in the presence of an authorized person or society were void.[61]

The court took a humane position in cases involving children of slaves whose marriage had not been legalized by securing a certificate according to the law of 1866, ruling that children of such a union did not suffer a loss of inheritance. In 1868 the court of appeals ruled that if both parties were slaves at the time of birth, there could be no case for bastardy.[62] In 1874 the appellate court held that children were legitimate under a customary slave marriage even though the parents were not living together as man and wife at the time of the passage of the act of February 14, 1866.[63]

In the counties where the local authorities were not willing to legalize slave marriages and the bureau took charge of certifying them, the local authorities refused to recognize the bureau's action. In addition, some Negro preachers who received licenses from the bureau were not recognized by the state. In 1868, the court of appeals considered a case in which a black man had obtained regular marriage licenses under two different names, had married two women, and had lived with each for a short time. The defendant claimed the marriages were not legal because the first minister to solemnize his marriage had had no license, while the second minister had had only a license from the bureau, which was not recognized by the state. The court of appeals held that if the marriage ceremony was "pronounced by a person professing to have authority," and such was fully believed to be the case by either party, the marriage was consummated and was valid.[64] By this action the court of appeals legitimatized all that the bureau had done to secure freedmen legal marriages during its existence in the state. Concerning marriage rights and the rights of Negro children to inherit property, the interpretations of the court of appeals were completely free of any prejudice against the Negro, and the court went a long way toward rectifying the injustices of the lower courts.

A different set of problems related to custody. During the last year of the war, after the army had begun to recruit and draft slaves, some slave mothers left their children with slaveholders and followed husbands to military establishments. They returned later after the act of March 1865 to claim their offspring. In some cases children and parents were owned by different masters. In many cases the slaveholders resisted efforts of the parents to claim children who had been freed by the military service of the father. There was so much resistance to giving up custody of members of black soldiers' families that a post commander at Lebanon warned that troops would have to be deployed to force masters to acknowledge the freedom of soldiers' dependents.[65] The persistence of black parents in demanding custody of their children despite strong resistance is convincing evidence of the cohesiveness of the slave family in Kentucky and of its determination to secure total freedom. Since the father of a slave child was often viewed as having performed only a biological function, and as lacking paternal identity with the slave family, it is noteworthy that fathers of slave children in Kentucky made at least twice as many charges as mothers against whites who would not release slave children freed by the father's military service.[66]

When the father died in service and the mother was dead or had been sold out of the state, grandparents complained to the Freedmen's Bureau about the refusal of the white families to surrender the grandchildren to their nearest relatives. Grandparents often pressed a claim even when they had had no close contact with the grandchild. Occasionally the complaints were filed several years after the war, probably after a long search had been made to locate relatives. Many former slaves from Kentucky traveled long distances for weeks and months searching for members of their family who had been separated by sale or by the wartime upheaval. At eighty-four years of age, Will Oats recalled that after the war had ended, his aged grandmother had walked from Monticello in Wayne County to Camp Nelson to obtain the papers freeing her children, grandchildren, and herself.[67] Late in 1865, before the Freedmen's Bureau was established, General Brisbin ordered slaveholders not only to surrender custody of children freed by the act of March 1865 but also to pay children retained in slavery wages from March 3 to the date of delivery to their parents. Brisbin brought slaveholders who refused into court and forced them to pay. The black parents, however, were interested more in the first provision than in the second.

Parents who filed complaints to secure custody often claimed that they were able to support the children and sometimes urgently pressed the case because they wanted to send the children to school.[68] Education had become a matter for fresh concern. Before the bureau was in full operation in Kentucky, the state legislature passed a new apprenticeship law which required that white apprentices, but not black, be taught to read and write. When the bureau turned its attention to the matter, the commissioner issued an order that his agency would recognize state apprenticeship laws only if the laws made no distinction between the races.[69] The assistant commissioner of the bureau in Kentucky further instructed agents not to recognize any indentures which did not make provisions to teach the apprentice to read and write or did not secure the consent of the parents or proper guardian.[70]

The apprenticeship law of Kentucky required that preference be given to former slaveholders by the county courts in granting apprentice indentures.[71] Some masters used the law and their influence to force the apprentices into a form of slavery in disguise. Most judges of the county courts sympathized with and supported the former slaveholders under the authority of the Apprenticeship Act of February 16, 1866. There were even cases in which the apprenticed black was hired out for wages that were claimed by the master.[72]

Black parents not surprisingly viewed the apprentice indenture with distrust. Since most county courts did not consult them, many freedmen petitioned the bureau to break the indenture and restore their children to them. If there was evidence that the parent had been under duress at the time that consent was given to bind the child to an indenture under a white master, the bureau returned the child to the parent. After wage disputes under labor contracts, complaints involving apprenticeships were the most numerous type of case brought before the bureau courts.[73]

In areas where the county courts flagrantly disregarded the bureau's requirements that the master take the responsibility for educating black apprentices and that the parent's consent be secured before an apprentice indenture was valid, the assistant commissioner of Kentucky had the agents investigate every apprenticeship. The superintendent of the Maysville district of the bureau, which included fourteen counties in northeast Kentucky, had at least one county agent investigate all of the apprenticeships that were processed by the county court. The parties were then required to come into the bureau office and to agree to a new indenture providing that the apprentice "be taught to read, write and cipher." In January 1867 the assistant commissioner of Kentucky directed the agent of Warren County to investigate and report to the assistant commissioner's office "all cases where children" had been "apprenticed without the consent of their parents or guardians." Following such wholesale investigations hundreds of children were released from apprentice indenture.[74]

The bureau apprenticed the child of a black parent to a master over the parent's objections if the bureau court found that the parent was not morally fit to have custody of the child or that extreme poverty rendered the parent incapable of providing support. In January 1867 a black mother went before the Bourbon County Court and asked for a writ of habeas corpus to restore her child to her on the ground that the apprenticeship by the bureau restrained the child's liberty. The Bourbon court ruled in favor of the parent on the grounds that the bureau had no legal existence in Kentucky.[75] Two other decisions to the same effect were handed down by the Harrison County Court. The Harrison cases involved instances in which the bureau had canceled an apprenticeship because the consent of the parent had not been secured. Like the Bourbon court, the Harrison County Court had ruled against the black parents on the ground that the bureau was unconstitutional in Kentucky.[76]

The assistant commissioner was determined that these decisions would not stand as binding even if it was necessary to use U.S. troops to enforce the authority of the bureau.[77] In preparation to challenging the decision of the state judges in federal court, he consulted the wishes of each child's nearest blood relative. If neither parent was living, the relative might be a grandparent, a brother, an uncle, or a stepfather. Many individuals with such kinship ties petitioned the bureau for custody of black children because the county courts had refused to consider blood relatives at the time when the orphan was apprenticed. When apprentices fled from their masters, they almost always sought and joined a relative if their father and mother had not survived. In one such case, the bureau officers of Bowling Green took under consideration a freedman's petition for custody of his twelve-year-old sister, who had been bound to their former master until she was twenty years old.

The severe social upheaval that occurred in Kentucky after 1864 tested the strength of the slave family, which withstood trials of every description. Blacks who moved up from slavery suffered material hardships, starvation, exposure, and other adversity when they left behind the relative comfort and security of their masters' land. The depth of kinship ties manifested itself in a willingness to endure extreme deprivation; the family met the test by drawing on strength developed under the crisis conditions that had existed throughout most of the antebellum period. As slavery began to deteriorate with the progress of war, black families showed a determination suggestive of the mental anguish that they must have endured when they were separated by sales during the antebellum period. The argument of slaveholders and their apologists that the Negro's domestic ties were weak does not stand up to the test.[78]

Several factors strengthened the black family in Kentucky during Reconstruction. Although the county courts of Kentucky, under the pressure of influential whites, tended to fragment the households by apprenticing black children to white families, the state supreme court tended to unify them by its rulings on inheritance and the rights of parents. The act of Congress legalizing slave marriages in March 1865 also had a unifying influence, especially under the strict enforcement of the law by General Palmer and the bureau. Negro schools and the emerging black churches helped reinforce the family as a unit, but the principal element smoothing the transition from slavery to freedom was the blacks' inner resources. The hostile environment of Reconstruction bound family members together more closely. Slaves had created and maintained highly defined social relations and kinship ties in spite of white society. When they were free, blacks honored these traditions rather than the ideas and beliefs imposed during slavery by owners.

With the end of slavery the black family was able to exercise its freedom of choice for the first time without interference and without having others impose decisions concerning the most intimate affairs of daily life. This new freedom was reflected in many changes in the relationship of husband and wife. The male quickly assumed the role of the head of the house; his wife usually worked within the home or at other domestic pursuits. The gang system of labor was discontinued, and the family became tenant farmers, working a plot of land separated from those of other tenants. A cabin was built or was moved to the plot from the communal rows that had composed the slave community. Thus the family withdrew into privacy, and family life replaced communal life. At the same time black families moved swiftly to develop autonomous religious bodies by separating from the white churches.

A study of the bureau records for Kentucky shows substantial evidence of the black family's unity and solidarity as well as deep affection and concern for its members. The average freedman knew his family history and family tree and obviously valued blood relationships. The history of litigation relating to apprentices' indentures reveals the strength of the extended family as a powerful force in maintaining the identity and resilience of the black community.

John Fee's account of a Fourth of July celebration in 1865 at the refugee home in Camp Nelson suggests the blacks' patriotism as well as the depth of their family ties. On the morning of the Fourth, while the soldiers were detained for a grand review, the women, who had been free for fewer than six months, set up tables and brought out bread, meat, and pies that they had been preparing. After the military review had been dismissed, the soldiers, women, and children quietly assembled before the speaker's platform at the call of the chairman. A soldier was called on to offer up a prayer, and the schoolchildren entertained the audience singing songs. A noncommissioned officer read the Declaration of Independence, and a sergeant and another black soldier addressed the assembly. Not a single white participated in the program. The short addresses were followed by martial music, after which the audience marched in good order to the picnic tables, found places in family groups, and waited quietly for grace to be returned. "Not a drunken man was seen among all the thousands. . . . Not a single row, nor a single arrest of a single individual" was seen. Fee was sure that an equal number of whites anywhere in Kentucky would show less orderly conduct. The ease with which black men and women made the transition from slavery to freedom, when not prevented by forces beyond their control, demonstrates how well prepared they already were.[79]

CHAPTER NINE

The Testimony Question

REGARDLESS OF ANY ameliorating factors, blacks in the antebellum South were reduced to a helpless position by the denial of all civil rights. In his study *The Peculiar Institution,* Kenneth Stampp explained that the Negro was at the mercy of white society because he could not testify against whites. A second major problem that kept blacks exposed to the whims of the moment was the reluctance of white witnesses to testify against white offenders. The third reason for the Negro's vulnerability was the reluctance of the white jury to convict a white man of a crime against a black.[1]

When the Civil War broke out, five free states as well as all of the slave states limited the right of blacks to testify in the courts of law. By 1866 all of the Northern states recognized the right of testimony against whites,[2] and after reconstruction was imposed on the secession states, they submitted to radical reforms and acknowledged equal rights in the courts.[3] During the same period all of the border states except Kentucky came under the influence of the reform sentiment created by the war and granted blacks the right to testify against whites.[4]

The Freedmen's Bureau was established in March 1865, and Circular No. 5 was issued in May to authorize bureau courts to operate in all areas where the old codes still existed or where local laws or custom denied the freedmen the right to testify in state courts as free men.[5] These courts sought to guarantee the freedmen justice and civil rights. Wherever civil rights were secured without the interposition of the bureau, the courts were not established or were dissolved.[6]

On December 26, 1865, the bureau announced that it would operate in Kentucky, since the adoption of the Thirteenth Amendment had freed the slaves in the state. Clinton B. Fisk issued a circular informing the citizens of Kentucky that the bureau courts would sit in Kentucky until the state adopted and enforced laws which permitted blacks as well as whites to serve as witnesses and to testify in all cases; thereafter the courts would be removed.[7]

Fisk conferred with Bramlette as soon as he arrived in Kentucky. It was known that the governor favored the repeal of the provision in the slave code of Kentucky that forbade blacks to testify against whites in state courts. Like many able Kentucky jurists, Bramlette took the position that this provision had originally been put in the code, not because slaves were less truthful than whites, but because the slave's relations to a master made him incompetent, just as a wife's testimony was excluded in certain cases because of her relation to her husband. Since the reason for the law no longer existed, the governor favored abolishing it.[8]

Shortly after the legislative session of 1865–1866 convened, the radical Republican senator M. M. Benton from the Covington district offered a resolution directing the judiciary committee in the upper house to inquire into the policy of permitting blacks to testify in their own cases and authorizing state courts to receive the testimony of Negroes as witnesses in all cases. Benton's resolution was defeated by a large majority. Some legislators may have opposed the resolution because they considered it premature as long as the Thirteenth Amendment was unratified.[9]

The blacks of Kentucky kept themselves well informed concerning the issues which were shaping their future. They sought knowledge on public affairs from abroad, consulted leaders who read the journals, conferred with white friends, and kept in touch with the military commanders in Kentucky. Most blacks knew that the Thirteenth Amendment had been ratified within a few hours of the event. On December 28, 1865, both Fisk and Palmer addressed a meeting at the African Church in Louisville. Fisk doubtless informed the blacks of the fact that his circular had committed the bureau to guarantee them protection by the strong arm of the national government until the state enacted laws securing impartial justice to them.[10] The meeting of December 28 was used by Negro leaders to organize and promote a rally on January 1, 1866, in Louisville to celebrate the Emancipation Proclamation.

The New Year's celebration was attended by 4,000 or 5,000 blacks, who unanimously adopted resolutions petitioning the General Assembly of Kentucky for full equality. The convention resolved that among other "rights and privileges . . . , they were entitled to" the right "to appeal to and be heard in the courts as suitors and witnesses upon the same terms and conditions as others." General Palmer addressed the convention and expressed the hope that the state would remove "that remnant of barbarism" which meant that in Kentucky, crimes were committed against thousands of Negroes because they could not testify against whites. If the state did not take action, Palmer suggested, blacks could rely on the U.S. Congress to defend their freedom.[11] A similar New Year's convention was held at Frankfort. This meeting called on the Kentucky legislature to repeal all laws which failed to concede blacks' equal rights before the law. The petitions of the Louisville and Frankfort meetings were presented to the legislature but were referred to a committee from which they were not reported.[12]

It was agreed by all of the lawmakers in the Kentucky legislature that the old slave codes of the state had to be repealed, but there was no general agreement on new measures that should be adopted. The conservatives introduced bills abolishing most of the old slave codes in the state, which passed with little opposition. The General Assembly of Kentucky adopted an act conferring civil rights on blacks. This measure left much to be desired. Blacks could bring a charge for prosecution against anyone, but Negroes were not competent witnesses against whites, even when a crime had been committed against them by a white person.[13] The Kentucky act conferring civil rights on blacks gave Negroes a half-free status entitling them to little or no protection under the law. The fact that blacks made up only 16.8 percent of the total population in the state left them in a more critical position; as a largely impoverished minority they were economically parti-cularly dependent on contacts with the white majority.

Palmer maintained that the blacks, were "under no sort of restriction or disabilities" that were "not applicable to others." It was the duty of the bureau, he observed, "to exercise a general watchfulness and supervision over the interests of the colored population" to see that the nation's policy of racial equality was carried out.[14] The army would not interfere unduly in the lives and affairs of the freedmen but the bureau should not ignore a legitimate call for assistance. The general's reassurance did not satisfy the freedmen. The failure of the Kentucky legislature to grant Negroes equal rights had not passed unnoticed in the black community. A statewide convention met in Lexington on March 26. It was well attended and heard addresses by John Fee, C. B. Fisk, and John Ely, the superintendent of the bureau in Kentucky. The delegates adopted a "Declaration of Sentiments" and resolutions which expressed faith that the legislature would "ere long" grant the blacks their "just and natural rights"; Negroes were entitled to "each and every right and power guaranteed to every American citizen."[15]

The increased harassment suffered by freedmen led them to intensify their efforts to secure equality in the eyes of the courts. A special inspector sent to investigate the outrages in the bureau's eastern subdivision, which had headquarters in Lexington, documented sixty outrages as having been committed between the end of 1865 and March 1866. Lawlessness was encouraged, reported the inspector, by the denial of black testimony. If a crime were committed against the freedmen and there were no white witnesses willing to testify against whites, there was no evidence on which to base a prosecution.[16]

Information from other sources supported the inspector's findings. A Union member of Congress from Kentucky was informed by a constituent that the state courts had been turned "into engines of vengeance." A Kentucky farmer reported to his Cincinnati merchant that Kentucky freedmen had scarcely "any of the rights of human beings," and the state courts gave them no protection.[17] Fisk complained to Oliver Howard that in no Southern state that he had visited did "such a fiendish spirit prevail" as in some portions of Kentucky. "There are some of the meanest, unsubjugated, and unreconstructed rascally rebellious revolutionists in Kentucky that curse the soil of the country," Fisk charged.[18]

The lawlessness in Kentucky had a large number of related causes. After the adoption of the Thirteenth Amendment, the limited protection of the masters no longer existed. The failure of the state to extend the right of testimony to blacks, in all cases in the state courts, exposed the freedmen to the full effects of naked prejudice for the first time. Unskilled white laborers, fearful of competition from free blacks, expressed their insecurity in violence. Many slaveholders felt that they had gone into war on the side of the Union believing it pledged against abolition. Since they could not wreak their vengeance on the federal government, the freedmen became scapegoats. The extension of the bureau to Kentucky was a factor of great importance, and President Johnson's veto of the revised Freedmen's Bureau bill of February 1866 added fuel to a dispute that had already inflamed emotions to the boiling point. Finally, all of these elements were whipped into overt conflict by the encouragement of the proslavery press.[19]

On January 5, 1866, Senator Trumbull introduced a bill to protect the civil rights of freedmen. When the bill came up for debate in the Senate, James Guthrie of Kentucky asserted that the Civil Rights Act was "not warranted by the Constitution . . . by good policy and sound statesmanship." Most Republicans thought otherwise. The bill passed the Senate by a large majority after a brief debate. In the House the debate was more protracted, but the results were the same. The president vetoed the measure on January 27, and on April 9 it passed over his veto.[20]

The Civil Rights Act provided that "all persons born in the United States, and not subject to any foreign power" were "citizens of the United States without distinction of color." It guaranteed the blacks the same rights "to give evidence" that were "enjoyed by white citizens" and established a fine and imprisonment as punishment for any officer who denied blacks their rights under the law.[21] The new law strengthened the bureau's position as it worked to secure the right of freedmen to testify in all cases before Kentucky courts. In jurisdictions in which blacks were denied the right to testify against whites, federal agents were authorized to take the cases to federal courts.[22] With the Kentucky law of evidence obviously in conflict with the Civil Rights Act, the stage was set for a test of the constitutionality of the laws.

The War Department issued General Orders No. 44 in July 1866,

authorizing military enforcement of the Civil Rights Act by making troops
available for arrests where needed, and the bureau took the initiative in
resolving the conflict between state and federal law.[23] Since every circuit
court in Kentucky except the Lexington circuit denied black testimony
against whites, the bureau ceased to refer cases to the state courts and began
taking cases directly before a U.S. commissioner after affidavits had been
sworn. A writ of habeas corpus was secured to transfer to the federal court
cases involving blacks in state courts when black testimony was denied.
Where plaintiffs or witnesses did not have the means to appear before the
commissioner or the federal court, the bureau officers were authorized to
pay for the transportation. The bureau consulted Judge Bland Ballard of the
U.S. District Court of Kentucky, and he agreed to prosecute cases of
outrages by whites against blacks under state law when testimony was
denied by the state.[24]

As the federal marshals and the army made arrests of whites charged
with crimes against blacks and the prisoners were arraigned before U.S.
commissioners, many being held for trial in the federal court, bureau
officers noticed a decrease in the number of Negroes assaulted by whites. At
first prisoners who were taken in counties that were a great distance from
Louisville had to be moved to Jefferson County for a hearing before the
U.S. commissioner. The bureau gradually increased its number of judicial
officers until they had been placed in most counties that contained a large
number of blacks. The promptness with which arrests were made and the
speed with which the prisoners were processed seemed to deter undisguised
assaults on blacks, but federal court intervention in violations of state law
involving crimes of whites against Negroes had little effect in controlling
outrages committed by night riders and Regulators.[25]

During the October 1866 term of the federal court in Kentucky, Judge
Ballard ordered the grand jury to inquire into the offenses committed
against blacks under the Civil Rights Act. Ballard reminded the jury that it
must consider the act constitutional in spite of the president's veto, which
had been overridden, and despite public opinion; the law would be upheld
until the courts ruled otherwise. The jury should hear all evidence and make
indictments, if the facts warranted it, without fear, favor, or prejudice.[26]
Judge Ballard was in complete sympathy with federal efforts to protect civil
rights. Before the Civil Rights Act passed, he had written Lyman Trumbull:
"I have a strong desire that Congress shall pass the Civil Rights Bill over the
President's veto. . . . If this bill cannot be passed then some other bill must
be. It will not do to leave the civil rights of the Negroes unprotected."[27]
Ballard had also written the chief justice of the Supreme Court in an effort to
have an associate justice join him in hearing civil rights cases so that a ruling
on the constitutionality of the law could be determined, but since the
districts of the federal court system had recently been redrawn, it was not

possible for a member of the Supreme Court to sit with Ballard in the October 1866 session.[28]

In the autumn of 1866 the Civil Rights Act began to be enforced in Kentucky as a result of the failure of the state legislature to remove the restriction on black testimony. By the end of the October term, the federal court had heard several civil rights cases that would normally have fallen under state jurisdiction. All except one continued into the court's next session. The cases included *United States* v. *John Rhodes* and others involving defendants charged with a felony against a Negro. The jury brought in a verdict of guilty, and the defense challenged the constitutionality of the Civil Rights Act. The argument on the constitutionality of the act continued into the next session of the federal court in Kentucky, at which time an associate judge of the Supreme Court was to join Ballard in ruling.[29]

In the meantime federal protection of blacks had been strengthened by the new Freedmen's Bureau Bill that was passed in June 1866 by Congress. With new powers and a new lease on life, the bureau took a more aggressive stance in the enforcement of the Civil Rights Act. The agents of the bureau instructed and assisted the blacks in processing their cases in the federal courts. The more liberal Democratic and radical press, seeing that the federal government was increasingly interceding in the state's judicial affairs, urged the Kentucky legislature of 1867 to pass a law permitting Negroes to testify against whites.[30] In his message to the legislature in January 1867, Governor Bramlette asked the General Assembly to approve "wise and prudent legislation which would remove the flimsy pretense of an unreasoning fanaticism for any further disregard of the Constitution of our fathers through the Freedmen's Bureau and the Civil Rights bills."[31] But the legislature quickly defeated the bill that was introduced.[32]

The failure of the General Assembly to change the law was followed by efforts on the part of the state courts to check the encroachment of federal authority. In 1866, the Harrison and the Livingston County circuit courts declared the Freedmen's Bureau to be without authority in Kentucky, but the decisions were ignored by the bureau and both cases were transferred to the federal court. In January 1867[33] Commissioner Oliver Howard decided to determine the status of the bureau's judicial powers in states where civil courts existed. He asked all assistant commissioners to test the *Milligan* decision, which declared military trials null and void where civil courts were operating. Cases in Bourbon and in Harrison county courts in 1867 offered a ready-made opportunity, but the time was apparently not yet ripe. The lower courts' decisions against the bureau were upheld by the federal district court, and bureau courts ceased to sit in Kentucky.[34] As a result, after 1867 blacks were competent witnesses in all cases only in the federal district court and the circuit court of Fayette County under Republican judge William C. Goodloe.[35]

With bureau courts no longer operating in Kentucky and the federal district court appearing to make no progress, the superintendent of the bureau in the eastern district surveyed the status of the civil rights of blacks in the district. On May 16, 1867, he sent a questionnaire to all of the bureau agents in his district asking for a notarized report. In Northern Kentucky it was reported that civil rights were "only partially enforced." The agent in Maysville, who had authority over the counties to the east, reported that the act had not been enforced because the state courts had refused to uphold it and there was no U.S. commissioner in the district. Almost everywhere the reports were the same. Lawyers and county officials alike insisted that the Civil Rights Act was unconstitutional. Only in Fayette and Jessamine counties was the Civil Rights Act given any consideration. The agent of Jessamine County reported that after some "coaxing and threatening," the county court had "given freedmen some protection."[36]

The Kentucky Court of Appeals reversed a case from the Fayette County Circuit Court on June 15, 1867, disallowing the testimony of a black under the Civil Rights Act in a case of grand larceny. William J. Bowlin, the defendant, had been sentenced to five years in the penitentiary on the testimony of George Gardner, from whom Bowlin was charged with stealing money. The court of appeals reversed the decision and remanded the case to the circuit court for a new trial excluding the testimony of Gardner. The court declared in a unanimous decision that the Civil Rights Act was unconstitutional insofar as it applied to the jurisdiction of the state. The appellate court declared that each state had the unquestionable right to regulate its own domestic concerns, including the rules of evidence, and "Congress had no constitutional authority to repeal or essentially modify the law of Kentucky on the subject of negro testimony."[37]

The ruling in the *Bowlin* case marked a low point in the morale of Union men in Kentucky. General Howard saw the decision as retarding progress in the state, and he drew a connection between the appellate court decision and the 319 outrages committed by whites against blacks during the year.[38] The activity of the state judiciary stood in contrast to the apathy in the federal court. Benjamin Bristow, the district attorney for Kentucky, was responsible for bringing evidence before the federal grand jury. Since the Civil Rights Act had been adopted, more than 500 cases of murder and outrage against blacks by whites had been recorded, and it was often assumed that another 100 or 200 had not been reported. The bureau officers, as required by law, in effect served as a staff of agents for the prosecutor; during the first year after the passage of the Civil Rights Act, more than 200 affidavits of violations had been filed by the Freedmen's Bureau, and seventy-four outlaws and murderers had been arrested and examined by the bureau and commissioners and had been turned over to the federal court. When a particularly outrageous case was presented to Bristow fully supported by affidavits, he informed the assistant commissioner of the bureau that cases should be referred to him for prosecution in the federal court only after the state judges had refused to hear them. As early as 1866 Bristow dismissed a group of alleged Regulators after having them put under peace bonds, and in 1867, several other cases were disposed of by the same method. By July 1868 only nine convictions had been secured. The president had pardoned two, and another was waiting a new trial. In 1869 when it became obvious that there would be a test of the Civil Rights Act before the Supreme Court, possibly after a long delay, Bristow again dismissed many indictments pending before the federal court that involved the denial of testimony in the state courts. Such circumstances caused one correspondent for a Northern newspaper to observe that the Civil Rights Act was a dead letter in Kentucky.[39]

After the bureau courts had been abolished, the agents channeled cases involving misdemeanors to the federal court, since there was no other place where blacks could get a hearing when whites were defendants. The federal court authorities rebuked the bureau for cluttering the already overcrowded docket with trivial and petty offenses.[40] Andrew Jackson Ballard, the brother of Judge Ballard, was the U.S. court clerk in Jefferson County and was charged with screening. He was said to have dismissed many cases to lighten the federal court load. Judge Bland Ballard permitted Andrew Ballard to require every plaintiff in a civil suit to post bond to stand good for court costs if the ruling went against the plaintiff. The Civil Rights Act permitted a citizen to sue for damage suffered in a denial of his civil rights, and many blacks brought civil suits into the federal court against whites. Now, however, the clerk would not file a case unless a bond had been posted by the black or by his lawyer. As the plaintiffs were poor and the lawyers would not personally put up the money, few of these cases were heard. One lawyer placed thirty suits before the clerk to dispose of as he saw fit. In the state courts these cases were regularly handled for paupers without charge, but such civil matters were new in the federal court. It was common knowledge that the officials of the federal court frowned on civil suits brought by blacks against whites. Andrew Ballard had expressed opposition to federal interference with slavery during the war and was not considered to be in sympathy with emancipation.[41] Many observers believed the civil rights cases were not handled well in the federal court in Kentucky.

Judge Ballard was not without his critics. The Kentucky correspondent for the *Cincinnati Gazette* concluded that the state needed an upright judge, and "if the presiding judge would not permit the execution of the law, he ought to be promptly impeached." Yet even liberal Democrats severely criticized Ballard for his prosecution of testimony cases under the Civil Rights Act. The editor of the *Observer and Reporter,* who favored admitting black testimony, characterized Ballard's instructions to the grand jury on black testimony as a speech that could have been made by "an irresponsible and voluntary prosecuting attorney. . . . Is he a fanatic run crazy?"

During October 1867 the posture of federal authority changed in Kentucky. The case of *United States* v. *Rhodes* was adjudicated during the October term of the federal court. After the conviction of October 1866, the question of the constitutionality of the Civil Rights Act was argued in January 1867, but the judge deferred the decision until he could sit with Justice Noah H. Swayne, who presided over the sixth federal circuit.[43] In June 1867 the case was reargued, but not until October did Swayne rule that the federal district court had jurisdiction over the case and that the Civil Rights Act was constitutional.[44] The case involved a white defendant charged with burglary of a building owned by the black citizen, who was an eyewitness against the defendant. Swayne ruled that if the owner of the building was incompetent in state courts on account of color, the federal circuit court had jurisdiction.[45]

Immediately after the federal circuit court upheld the constitutionality of the Civil Rights Act, Benjamin P. Runkle, superintendent of the bureau in Kentucky, asked James Speed, who had been employed as the legal adviser and prosecutor for the bureau, to draw up a memorandum on the authority of the bureau in the enforcement of the Civil Rights Act. Speed's opinion was the basis for Circular No. 8, issued by the assistant commissioner of Kentucky to the bureau agents in the state, concerning the procedure for the protection of the civil rights of the freedmen. The agents were to instruct all freedmen to report any crime against themselves to a U.S. commissioner. Blacks were also to be advised to transfer all suits against them to federal courts when their personal and pecuniary interest would be advanced by such a change, and all state officers who violated the Civil Rights Act were to be reported to the bureau headquarters in Louisville.[46] As a result of the federal court's ruling on the Civil Rights Act and the new bureau instructions, bureau activity increased. The bureau became the most effective federal instrument in the enforcement of the Civil Rights Act in Kentucky.[47]

The Civil Rights Act provided for fines and imprisonment for any officer who denied blacks their rights under the law and made all judges in the state court system subject to prosecution in federal courts. In the eastern subdistrict of the bureau there was a strong sentiment for enforcing this provision of the law. On November 26, 1867, C. J. True of the Maysville office suggested to his superintendent, R. E. Johnston in Lexington, that in his opinion, "the best mode of procedure" in the civil rights cases was "to institute a suit in the United States Court against every judicial officer" who refused "to issue his warrant for the arrest and trial of every person so offending" or who refused "to receive Negro testimony in behalf of the party outraged." Four days later Johnson informed Ben P. Runkle, the

Kentucky superintendent of the bureau, that in his opinion the fourth section of the Civil Rights Act should be enforced against every judicial officer who refused to admit testimony of blacks against whites. There is no record that the Kentucky bureau suggested that Bristow take this action, but virtually every lawyer in the state was aware of the possibility. The attorney general of the United States could have ordered such a course, and the Kentucky district attorney could have initiated proceedings against the judges on his own authority, but no one took such a radical and swift solution to the problem.[48]

The black community did not merely observe the controversy which so vitally affected its interests. The fraternal societies of Louisville organized a celebration of the Emancipation Proclamation on January 1, 1867. The morning session of the convention, which primarily addressed civil rights, was followed by an evening session, which was given over to speeches. William F. Butler took the platform. "We asked no man for pity. We only ask you to take your hand off the black man's head and let him grow to manhood," said Butler as he scornfully rejected all paternalism.[49] After the Kentucky legislature of 1867 failed to grant equal rights in state courts, the blacks of Louisville met again on March 7 and organized the Law League to aid blacks in finding and compensating able counsel.[50]

The Colored Methodist Conference of Kentucky met in Lexington in April 1867. Speaker James Brisbin informed the delegates and their guests that they would soon have equal rights and urged them to persist in their demands for justice.[51] In June a group of blacks from Lexington petitioned Congress, demanding that they be allowed to testify as equals in the state courts.[52] During the same month James Fidler, a bureau agent, spoke to the blacks in Lebanon and encouraged them to persist in their efforts.[53] On July 4, in Lexington, a massive audience of blacks numbering from 6,000 to 10,000 heard speeches by John Fee, Brisbin, and William C. Goodloe. Goodloe condemned the inertia of the Kentucky legislature, declaring, "Your testimony must be admitted, otherwise you may be beaten and robbed nightly . . . , your ministers may be shot down every Sabbath in your pulpits, with impunity" in the absence of a white witness who would uphold justice.[54] From August to October 1867, blacks met in Frankfort, Mt. Sterling, Nicholasville, Paris, Winchester, and Maysville. The principal subject of oratory and resolutions was invariably the question of equality of testimony. Civil rights were also the subject of speeches at a gathering in Frankfort on August 1 sponsored by the African Methodist Episcopal Church.[55]

After the federal district court upheld the constitutionality of the Civil Rights Act, black leaders in Lexington formed the Colored State Central Committee and called a state convention in Lexington for November 26 to consider the steps necessary to secure the right of testimony in state courts and the right of suffrage. Local groups gathered to elect and instruct delegates to the November meeting.[56]

When the day came, at least forty-two counties were represented. The ninety-two delegates more fully represented the blacks of Kentucky than delegates at recent state political conventions had represented their party members. Only two whites were present. John Fee encouraged the audience in its determination to secure equality; Brisbin declined to speak. The black speakers devoted most of their time to discussions of the right of testimony and suffrage, and resolutions were passed dealing with both subjects. A petition to be sent to the state legislature demanded the right of testimony.[57]

Black conventions continued in commemoration of important occasions throughout 1868 and 1869. In October 1868 Benjamin P. Runkle, superintendent of the bureau, and Isaac S. Catlin, chief agent of the bureau's Louisville subdistrict, delivered addresses in Louisville. Both speakers stressed the rights and needs of freedmen. Catlin denounced the "unnatural inhuman and unjust ban" on their testimony in Kentucky and declared that the right to testify was "an inherent, God-given right." The speech was printed and circulated widely among the black leaders and clergy throughout the state to promote a statewide movement.[58]

By 1868 there was a coordinated black movement to secure equal rights in Kentucky. In January 1869 William H. Gibson, a black school-teacher, was sent to the National Convention of Colored People in Washington to represent Kentucky. Gibson persuaded the convention to lay the grievances of Kentucky blacks before the Judiciary Committee of the Senate and to petition the committee to draw up a bill increasing the number of circuits of the federal courts in Kentucky so that all blacks could be heard.[59] At a meeting in Louisville in July 1869 efforts were made to promote a state school system for blacks. The Colored State Education Convention did not limit its interest to education, however. Several orators addressed the need for equality in the courts of the state, and a resolution declared that the right to testify was guaranteed by the Constitution.[60]

By January 1869 the testimony question had given federal court in Kentucky a burden of cases so great as to be impossible to process. Besides the large number that went before the court directly, many cases were transferred before trial, and others were appealed from state courts. Democratic newspapers and politicians complained vigorously that prisoners were being taken from the custody of state authorities, but to no avail.[61] Numerous civil suits for damage were also prosecuted under the civil rights law against state officers and citizens.[62] The damages asked were often several thousand dollars, but the awards were usually nominal.[63]

Murder cases in Daviess and Lewis counties, however, greatly contributed to the revolution in public sentiment in Kentucky. In October 1866

William Bell, a white, murdered a freedman in the presence of two black witnesses. Bell was sentenced to death in a federal court in March 1868.[64] In August 1868 George Kennard and John Blyew, of Lewis County, murdered four of six members of a freed family because they would not house a black female kept by Kennard and Blyew. The only witnesses were the surviving members of the family. The defendants were tried in federal court and were sentenced to death in January 1869.[65] The extreme penalties handed down in these cases only aggravated public resentment of the role being played in Kentucky by agents of the national government.

The Democrats united in opposing federal intervention in the enforcement of state law but disagreed among themselves as to how to restore the state's authority. One group, the liberal Democrats, urged the General Assembly to establish equality of testimony in all state courts. On November 30, 1868, members of this group inserted a proposed bill in the *Courier-Journal* which was said to be supported by the Louisville Bar Association. The proposal was debated for the next two weeks.[66] Most of the lawyers and judges spoke in its favor. In January 1869 seven of the most esteemed lawyers and judges in the state petitioned the legislature in an open letter to change the law on the books. Many believed that a failure to enforce the Civil Rights Act would only invite stronger federal measures. Blacks meeting in Frankfort in February 1869 and in Lexington in March 1869 urged Senator Sumner to strengthen the Civil Rights Act to guarantee their rights in the courts.[67] The second group of Democrats, the conservatives, demanded that the state carry the Kennard-Blyew case to the Supreme Court. This plan could be carried out with less risk of alienating large numbers of constituents. Early in January 1869, Gov. John W. Stevenson called on the General Assembly to appropriate money to implement it. The legislature complied and thus committed Kentucky to two more years of bitter federal-state conflict.[68] Judge Ballard wrote the governor and expressed his satisfaction with the steps taken. Ballard had concurred with Judge Swayne in the case of *United States* v. *Rhodes,* but privately he was not satisfied with Swayne's opinion. "The doubts which I entertain respecting both the construction of the Act and its constitutionality render its administration pecularily unpleasant to me," he confessed to Stevenson.[69]

In 1866, William C. P. Breckinridge, the son of Rev. R. J. Breckinridge and a former Confederate officer, took over the editorship of the *Observer and Reporter.* His position was soon apparent: he advocated the repeal of the restrictions on Negro testimony. Breckinridge and other "New Departure" men believed that admitting the Negro to the full enjoyment of his civil rights, including the right to testify against whites was a prerequisite for progress. They proposed the Democratic party as the instrument to accomplish this end. In time, Breckinridge was forced to give up his editorship of the *Observer and Reporter.*

In 1869 Breckinridge ran for states attorney in Boyle County, and the testimony question was the central issue of his campaign. He intended to admit black testimony in all cases and upheld Fayette County as an example that should be followed by the whole state. He was supported by the *Courier-Journal* and the *Danville Advocate*. His greatest ally was Samuel B. Churchill, secretary of state, who wrote a series of letters in the *Courier-Journal* signing himself "Julius." Former Confederate J. Warren Grigsby, who had served in the state legislature, came into Boyle County and campaigned on Breckinridge's behalf. Breckinridge nevertheless lost the election and was for a time ostracized by the Democratic party. His bid for public office had unfortunately come at the high point in the tension between the federal government and Kentucky surrounding the Kennard-Blyew case.[70]

In 1870 the freedmen gained new leverage in their battle. Following the ratification of the Fifteenth Amendment the black conventions in 1870 sought primarily to organize their forces for political contests in which the right to testify would be an important issue. In February 1870 a convention in Lincoln County charged that the wives, daughters, mothers, and sisters of freedmen could be "debauched" and "outraged with impunity" because the state legislature denied blacks equality in the courts. This resolution struck at the heart of the controversy. Brisbin claimed that the right to testify in cases involving whites would enable many people of mixed blood to sue for a share of the white father's estate. Black women could not prosecute paternity cases against white men in state courts, but many such cases came before the bureau and the U.S. commissioners. These suits were almost always settled out of court for a nominal sum of money. Rape cases could not be brought into state courts when a black woman was the victim of a white man, and because of the heavy load of the federal court, federal authorities tended to give priority to crimes against the property of blacks and to cases in which bodily injury had been inflicted.[71]

A statewide Colored Republican Convention convened in Frankfort on February 23, 1870. Its resolution on testimony had obvious political over-tones: "We have seen and properly appreciate the proscriptive spirit man-ifested toward our race by the 'so-called' Democratic party of this State in denying us access to courts of law." Another resolution authorized the officials of the convention to petition Congress to set up additional federal courts in Kentucky.[72] The state gathering was followed on April 8 by a meeting in Louisville to celebrate the Fifteenth Amendment. "We have no terms to make with Kentucky Democracy," the assembly announced. "We demand . . . the complete and final abrogation of all laws now on our statute book which make distinction by reason of race, color, or previous condition of servitude."[73] In May and June meetings were held in Winchester, Paris, Lancaster, and Bardstown to celebrate the adoption of the Fifteenth

Amendment. In all of these meetings attention was directed to the failure of the state legislature to grant equality in state courts, and the Democratic party was usually held responsible and was condemned.[74]

After blacks secured the right to vote, many Democratic politicians felt it wise and expedient to respond to their petitions. Scattered Democratic county conventions took the Republican position and came out in favor of black testimony. The Republican party had consistently favored black testimony in state courts since 1866. The action of the assembled Democrats in some cases, was less a change of sentiment and an effort to win the black vote than an attempt to relieve white defendants and indicted state judges.[75] When the General Assembly convened in 1871, a delegation of blacks from Fayette County urged the legislators to address the testimony question and to relieve blacks from the outrages they were suffering. Governor Stevenson again expressed his support. The bills that were introduced in the General Assembly of Kentucky to change the law of evidence in the 1871 session, however, were defeated for the fifth time. As usual the Republicans supported the measures, but they were joined only by the New Departure Democrats.[76]

It became obvious as sentiment grew in favor of a change in the law that the defeat of the measure in 1871 merely served to postpone the question until the next session of the legislature, which would be composed of lawmakers with fresh instructions from the electorate. As the number of testimony cases on the federal court docket increased, white defendants increasingly complained about the expense of journeying far from home to appear in federal court and about the great cost of cases in the federal court. Since 1868 blacks had been able to transfer their cases to federal court whether or not a denial of black testimony was involved. Ballard had ruled that as long as a right was denied to any freedman, no citizen of that class was really free, and all blacks were therefore entitled to transfer their cases to the federal court.[77]

Probably the most significant force in bringing about a change in sentiment concerning black testimony was the delayed enforcement of the clause in the Civil Rights Act which provided for the prosecution of judges who denied the rights guaranteed by the law. In October 1870 Judge J. Hop Price of the Municipal Court of Louisville was indicted in federal court for failing to admit black testimony against whites. Early in February 1871, the Frankfort correspondent for the *Courier-Journal* reported that three circuit judges had been indicted on the same charge.[78] The *Kentucky Yeoman* expressed an opinion that had become common among Kentuckians by 1871: "If the Federal Government says that judges, who do not recognize certain laws, shall be punished and the State Government demands that they shall not obey them, every dictate of manhood requires that either these officers should be protected in the Administration of the State laws, or the

statute should be amended so as to prevent the conflict."[79] The consequences of the new developments were not long in materializing. In April a
circuit judge admitted black testimony in his court under the Civil Rights
Act,[80] and by August 9, other circuit judges had opened their courts.[81] In
May 1871, the *Louisville Ledger* remarked that Negro testimony could "now
be put aside as a *dead issue,* and one which need no longer be discussed with a
view to any action of the State Legislature for its adjustments."[82]

Before the legislature of 1872 met, new developments gave added
assurance that the law of evidence would be changed. The Fayette and
Kenton county bar associations as well as the Kentucky Bar Association
petititoned the legislature to enact a measure admitting blacks to testify
against whites.[83] All doubts that a new law of evidence would be adopted by
the next legislature were swept away when three youthful members of the
most powerful and prestigious families in Central Kentucky were indicted
in federal court on a charge of involvement in a lynch gang. Public sentiment
soon urged that state law be changed so that the defendants could be tried in
a state court. The case was laid over until late January 1872 to ensure action
by the legislature.[84]

The election of 1871 finally brought to the General Assembly of 1872 a
larger number of liberal Democrats,[85] and before the legislature had been in
session for a month, it had passed the long-sought law. The day after the
governor signed the bill, Ballard refused to accept any more black testimony
cases in his court.[86]

In April 1872, the Supreme Court of the United States, with two judges
dissenting, reversed the judgment of the federal circuit court of Kentucky in
the Kennard-Blyew case and required the case to be remanded to the state
court. The court ruled that in a criminal prosecution for a public offense, the
Civil Rights Act did not require that a state admit witnesses who were not
affected by the crime or were not parties to the cause.[87] The case, however,
had served a purpose. It had been added to pressure on the state legislature
to change the law of evidence, for it had pointed out to the people of
Kentucky in dramatic fashion that the federal government would press the
enforcement of the Civil Rights Act to the fullest extent. In October, 1872,
with the entrance of nolle prosequi in the *Bell* case, the federal court of
Kentucky cleared its docket of all suits growing out of the state's refusal to
admit black testimony. The conflict between the state and the federal
government had lasted six years.[88]

The resistance to black testimony had been strengthened by the abolition of slavery in Kentucky without compensation and by the establishment
of the bureau in the state.[89] The activities of the bureau kept the testimony
question before the public, however, and the conviction in the Kennard-
Blyew case in the federal court made the citizens of Kentucky aware of the
measures that federal authorities were willing to take to protect civil rights.

The farmers demanded that blacks be permitted to testify against night riders so that tenants would feel secure in returning to the farms. But the indictments brought against state judges secured the most rapid response. Finally, the steady agitation by radical Republicans and the black community brought a change in public opinion after adoption of the Fifteenth Amendment that made it expedient to consider the black voter. The law of 1872 marked the end of an era in Kentucky in which the state had served as a "legal testing ground" of civil rights.[90]

CHAPTER TEN

Black Suffrage

WITH THE RATIFICATION of the Thirteenth Amendment by three-fourths of the states, it was natural for the blacks to expect freedom to give them all the privileges and immunities of white citizens, particularly universal white male suffrage. Even before slavery was legally abolished in Kentucky, an organized movement had developed among the Negroes and their supporters to abolish all the incidental restrictions which antebellum society had imposed upon slaves and freedmen. Meeting in Louisville in June 1865, a convention of blacks sent a delegation "on a mission of liberty" to Washington to call the president's attention to the laws and other constraints which "bore . . . heavily" on the Negroes of Kentucky.[1] The delegation asked President Johnson for the protection of the federal government. They called his attention to the fact that Kentucky was the only state in the Union that gave blacks "no rights whatever in law or in fact." Negroes in Kentucky had "no oath, . . . right of domicile, or . . . right of locomotion." More than 30,000 black soldiers had fought under the nation's flag, and many had shed their blood for the nation. Did not the sacrifices of these citizens of Kentucky merit the recognition of their rights "in any political settlement" that was made in the state?[2]

On July 4, 1865, Negroes of Louisville organized a celebration of liberty. The correspondent for the *Anglo-African* summed up the sentiment of the 10,000 participants in a procession and an estimated 10,000 additional observers: "We can breathe the fresh pure air of heaven as men, now, not as chattels. . . . We have a right to 'life, liberty, and the pursuit of happiness.' " After several blacks had spoken, Maj. Gen. John Palmer addressed the gathering. "All of those intelligent white men were *rebels*— therefore *foolish;* and all of those senseless, ignorant niggers were loyal— therefore wise; and I am in favor of giving the right of suffrage to wise men," he declared. There is no slavery in Kentucky, he repeated over and over. James Brisbin, who followed Palmer on the platform, endorsed universal amnesty and universal suffrage. Brisbin believed that Negroes must have the vote if a loyal government was to be established in any slave state. A similar celebration was held on the same day by the Negroes of Camp Nelson, Kentucky. The blacks spoke in the morning, and in the afternoon the courageous abolitionist John G. Fee, who was just as enthusiastic a partisan of Negro suffrage as Brisbin, urged the blacks to organize churches and schools in order to prepare themselves for freedom.[3]

During the last half of 1865 Fee addressed Negro congregations in Louisville, Camp Nelson, Lexington, and Danville, always firmly supporting black suffrage and frankly encouraging the Negroes to anticipate the day when the vote would be theirs.[4] A liberal view of Negro suffrage was also taken by two of Kentucky's congressmen. William H. Randall of Laurel County represented the eastern district of Kentucky in the House of Representatives and favored full civil rights for the Negro. In the autumn of 1866 he traveled through his district while the county courts were in session and "strongly advocated negro suffrage." Cong. Sam McKee of Montgomery County spoke in favor of the Fourteenth Amendment, but he did not believe that granting blacks citizenship meant giving them the right to vote.[5]

When the Negroes of Louisville met in convention on January 1, 1866, to celebrate the anniversary of the adoption of the Emancipation Proclamation, they unanimously adopted a set of resolutions and petitioned the Kentucky legislature for full equality. A similar meeting was held in Frankfort on the same day.[6] On January 9, 1866, a convention of blacks from Central Kentucky met in the First African Baptist Church of Lexington for the purpose of considering their new status. The convention went on record as "favoring universal amnesty and universal enfranchisement."[7]

On January 15, a mass meeting of blacks in the First Colored Methodist Episcopal Church of Lexington considered the need to call a statewide black convention. A published address informed black readers that the state's "anomalous political condition" made action on the part of the blacks "much more imperative" in Kentucky than in any of the other former slave states. A convention was scheduled to meet on March 22 in Lexington.[8] When the day came, Fisk and John Ely, superintendent of the bureau in Kentucky, were present. Fisk "saw that negro suffrage was given a prominent place in the discussion."[9] The question of the freedman's right to vote was earnestly discussed by several blacks, including the Reverend George W. Dupree of Paducah and Horace Morris, cashier of the Freedmen's Bank in Louisville. A. H. Hubbard, the U.S. commissioner of the Lexington area, participated in the discussion. The convention adopted a resolution which claimed for the blacks "each and every right and power guaranteed to every American citizen, including even that of suffrage, as naturally and legally belonging" to them at once. A "Declaration of Sentiments" stated that while the blacks waived, for the time being, their right of access to the ballot box, they demanded the privilege of achieving "a well-ordered and dignified life."[10]

The sentiment in favor of Negro suffrage was not restricted to black leaders. The urge for political equality was also strong among the masses. During the August election of 1866 in Lexington, a correspondent for the *Louisville Daily Courier* wrote that "flocks of negroes . . . hung like a cloud around the polls, eager and solicitous" for the triumph of the Republican party. It was openly rumored, he claimed, after the defeat of the radicals, that blacks' right to vote was "a sine qua non—that at the next election, ballots of negroes would have to be accepted" in the service of the Republican party.[11]

Support for Negro suffrage among the rank and file of the Republican party was not widespread. On January 17, 1866, the Republican members of the Kentucky General Assembly met and passed resolutions favoring the right of each state to control the qualifications for voting within its bounds. On February 14, 1867, on the motion of Joshua F. Bell, the Kentucky House of Representatives by a vote of 81 to 1 resolved that the house and "the people of Kentucky" were unalterably opposed to Negro suffrage."[12] The action of the Republican legislators did not discourage the blacks. The celebration of the Emancipation Proclamation in Louisville on January 1, 1867, was primarily devoted to the question of political rights. William F. Butler, president of the convention, insisted that freedom was a mockery without the right to vote. "We claim . . . a position of political equality with whites as a matter of right, as a matter of justice," he declared.[13]

Although the Negro's desire for suffrage was not received with enthusiasm by the Republicans who controlled the Kentucky party, a change of attitude was under way. James Speed had earlier insisted that if the blacks were granted the right to vote, the state must accede. By the summer of 1866, however, Speed saw that Kentucky was falling completely under the domination of conservative Democrats. He realized that the Democrats were "likely to push" the Republicans from their "stools on the question of negro suffrage," yet he continued to believe in the importance of political equality for the freedmen.[14] In January 1867 Speed met in a secret caucus with the Republican legislators and urged them to take a stand in favor of universal suffrage. The debate was "decidedly acrimonious" and threatened to divide the party. The opponents of the black vote for the time being had their way.[15] In December 1866 radical Republicans under the leadership of Charles Sumner backed a bill in the U.S. Senate to grant Negro suffrage in the District of Columbia. Senator Davis of Kentucky denounced the measure in strong language. He dwelt upon the inconsistency of "a frenzied party . . . clamoring to have suffrage given to the negro" while they "frown [ed] upon" female suffrage. The bill passed through Congress, with all

Kentucky congressmen voting against it, and was vetoed by Johnson on January 7, 1867. On January 8, Congress passed the measure over the president's veto. In the House of Representatives no congressmen from Kentucky voted for the bill. Republican William H. Randall from Eastern Kentucky voted against it, and Republicans McKee and Rousseau refrained from voting at all. When the Republican state convention convened in February, the platform endorsed the national administration but resolved that Kentucky was unalterably opposed to Negro suffrage.[16]

The Republicans of the Sixth Congressional District came the closest of any Republican group to endorsing the Negro's right to vote. When they met in convention in March 1867, a resolution was introduced endorsing the national administration. A delegate objected because he believed the measure would commit the party to black suffrage. He introduced a substitute which declared that the matter rested under state authority. His version was voted down, and the original resolution passed with one dissenting vote.[17]

The Democrats were not willing to grant Negroes the ballot on any grounds and constantly exaggerated the strength of universal suffrage sentiment among the Republicans. In January 1867 the Democrats rejected the Fourteenth Amendment in the General Assembly of Kentucky because the majority claimed it could be used to give blacks the franchise. During February the Kentucky senate, which was decidedly controlled by the Democrats, passed a resolution with one dissenting vote, which asserted that the people of Kentucky were "unalterably opposed to negro suffrage."[18]

The determined advocacy of blacks' voting rights, however, could not be quelled. A Kentucky correspondent for the *Cincinnati Commercial* in April 1867 declared: "Negro suffrage is the vital issue of politics."[19] The drive to secure it centered around the Negro benevolent societies and a small group of radical Republicans who sustained and supported the blacks' interest in politics. Through the benevolent societies the leaders had contact with almost all freedmen in the cities and towns.[20] The Reconstruction Act of March 2, 1867, had assured the Negroes in the secession states of their right to vote, and the blacks in the border states were restless for a change in their own status. Although the freedmen were told by whites that they would never secure the ballot in Kentucky, according to one correspondent, blacks only laughed and replied: "It's a comin' massa."[21]

When the blacks of Louisville organized the Law League in 1867 to aid freedmen with legal problems, the association spent much of its time on the question of suffrage. The Law League's proceedings, published in March 1867, expressed hopes that the blacks would soon be "endowed with the elective franchise."[22] No Negro society or organization was able to avoid discussion and consideration of the question. In April the Colored Conference of the Methodist Church met in Lexington. Brisbin informed the congregation that they should have "a voice in the election of the country" which they had "helped to save." On August 1, blacks held celebrations at two different locations in Louisville to hear orators speak on the rights and duties of the freedmen. A meeting was held on the same day to raise funds for the African Methodist Zion Church in Frankfort. Speaker after speaker took the floor to discuss suffrage. Thomas H. Jackson, a Negro clergyman of Louisville, reminded the audience that blacks could vote in many parts of the country, and they needed the ballot in Kentucky to protect themselves from their enemies.[23]

On July 4, 1867, Brisbin, Fee, and radical Republican Judge William C. Goodloe of Fayette County spoke at a "Colored People's Barbecue" in Lexington. Fee advocated impartial suffrage as the most expedient course for blacks to pursue to secure the right to vote. "God was the author of the Emancipation Proclamation, the Civil Rights Bill, and would soon give suffrage" to the freedmen, he said, for Congress was in session at that time.[24] Goodloe informed the audience that, although they could not expect to secure suffrage from the state during their generation, Congress would grant them the right to vote before it adjourned.[25]

R. E. Johnston, superintendent of the eastern subdistrict of the Freedmen's Bureau, with headquarters in Lexington, sent a bundle of petition forms on May 30, 1867, to all of his agents in Central, Northern, and Eastern Kentucky. The agents were instructed to have the blacks sign the petitions that memorialized Congress to enfranchise them. Johnston instructed the agents to put the petitions "in the hands of the most influential" Negroes in the district and to secure the signature of every one who could be found. Some hesitated to sign because they feared that their houses and churches would be burned, but most did so after being assured that the government would protect them. (In at least one case in Mason County, a freedmen who signed the petition did suffer violence). The petitions were returned to Lexington, where they were bundled together and sent to Congress.[26]

The August election of 1867 for the state offices in Kentucky was an overwhelming victory for the Democrats. The Republicans retained only 7 of 38 seats in the senate and 10 of 100 in the house.[27] The party's need of Negro votes became obvious.[28] As early as October 1865, a small group of Union men, including Dr. Robert J. Breckinridge, Gen. Stephen A. Burbridge, Gen. James Brisbin, and others, had secretly met in Lexington to determine what action should be taken to protect the liberties of black and white Unionists. They decided to ask for troops and appealed to the radicals in Washington. Breckinridge's guidance was sought in military as well as civil matters.[29] Even with federal troops in Kentucky, conditions deteriorated. In March 1867, a group of "Loyal Kentuckians" called on Thaddeus

Stevens to use his influence in Congress to bring relief to the loyal whites and blacks in the state.[30]

Charles Sumner agreed with Brisbin in May 1867 that "nothing was more certain" than that Kentucky did not have "a republican form of government,"[31] and a radical correspondent for the *Cincinnati Commercial* called for reconstruction of Kentucky.[32] A contributor to *Harper's Weekly* in June wrote that the loyal Kentuckians had come to see that Negro votes were needed before loyal Kentucky could become a majority.[33]

The Union men in the counties bordering on Mason County were reportedly "constantly threatened and bullied" by the Democrats following the election of August 1867. The opinion was growing in the region "even among conservative Union men that the . . . black soldiers" were "much more entitled to vote than the men who went into the armies of the Rebellion and waged war to disrupt and destroy" the government.[34] James M. Fidler, a former bureau agent in Lebanon who had been defeated in his August bid for the Kentucky General Assembly, announced that "universal manhood suffrage" was "necessary and right," and Sam McKee also came out for Negro suffrage and the reconstruction of Kentucky.[35] In August the radical Union leaders of Kentucky considered meeting again for a secret consultation, but they delayed, hoping first to find out what action the congressional committee investigating conditions in Kentucky would take.[36]

The radical Republicans and the black leaders of Lexington met in July in closed session. There was no public statement on the proceedings of that session, but the black leaders organized a state central committee and called a state convention for blacks. It was rumored that after the August election, the Republicans would call a state convention in September, at which time they would declare in favor of Negro suffrage. The Republican convention did not take that stand, but a resolution was unanimously passed which opened the state convention to delegates without regard for color.[37]

During August the radical leaders held a series of meetings to organize the blacks for their future role in politics. In Mt. Sterling, Brisbin shared the platform with Sam McKee, and both strongly endorsed Negro suffrage. McKee predicted that by the next presidential election, the freedmen of Kentucky would be voting.[38] Following an appearance in Lexington, Brisbin journeyed on to Nicholasville and told the blacks of Jessamine County that there were only two ways to defend liberty—by the bayonet and by the ballot. "We must give you one or the other," he explained. "I know of no way of electing loyal men . . . in this or any other Southern state, except by extending the elective franchise to you black men."[39] At Paris on August 29, Brisbin and others promised a large audience of freedmen that Congress would meet during the winter of 1867 and would enfranchise them.[40]

The Benevolent Society of Winchester sponsored a meeting early in September which was primarily a political training program. A long parade of speakers instructed and advised the freedmen on their duties and responsibilities as voters.[41] During mid-October, Brisbin attended a similar rally in Maysville. "There are men in office now who will not give you your rights," Brisbin charged, "but when you get the right to vote you then can put men in office who will give you your rights." A letter was read at the meeting from John Ely: "You have earned your freedom and the privilege of the ballot, and . . . the day is not far distant when the right will be acceded."[42]

The Negro State Central Committee of Lexington issued a call on October 16 for a state convention to meet in Lexington on November 26. The chief purpose of the convention was to consider the steps necessary to secure Negro suffrage. All communities were urged to elect delegates.[43] A correspondent from Danville condemned the convention as a meeting gotten up by "foolish white men"; he urged the blacks to cultivate industry, good habits, and obedience to the law and not to snatch at the shadow like the dog in the fable.[44] Two Negro leaders in Danville published a circular also repudiating the convention which, they felt, was not calculated to promote the interest of the black community at that time.[45]

Local meetings were held throughout Kentucky to elect delegates and to instruct them.[46] A gathering at Mt. Sterling asked for suffrage for blacks in Kentucky because "they had given thirty thousand of their sons to the war for the Union."[47] Delegates in Clark County declared that "time had demonstrated that the liberties not only of colored people but the masses of the white people can only be preserved by clothing all the loyal part of the community with political privileges, and putting more restraint upon the rebels."[48] This convention took the most radical position that any Negro meeting had taken to date.[49]

At the state convention, Fee and Brisbin spoke on the subject of suffrage. Brisbin predicted that every black in the nation would be voting in a short time. R. T. James, a black clergyman from Louisville who was elected president of the convention, made the most important speech. James denied that the lack of education disqualified blacks for suffrage. "We claim the right to vote in the name of liberty that has been purchased by Colored soldiers," he declared. The convention drew up a petition to Congress, which Brisbin was commissioned to take to Washington.[50]

The opposition to the political activities of Negroes in 1867 was not limited to the Democrats and conservative Republicans. Not all black leaders agreed that the freedmen were following the correct course. On January 1, 1868, Horace Morris, a teller at the Freedmen's Bank in Louisville, spoke at the annual emancipation celebration in Louisville. He questioned the current political aspirations and activities of the blacks in Kentucky. "Politics is not our trade," he advised. The freedmen should not follow the radicals blindly, for these politicians were using them "for their own aggrandizement." He recommended hard work and education as the chief areas of concern to the Negroes.[51] Not all of the black community, nor all Republicans, entirely agreed that Negro participation in Republican politics was desirable.

When the Republican state convention met at Frankfort in 1868, it soon became clear that the conservative Republicans had not significantly changed their views concerning the political participation of blacks. The convention refused to permit Negro delegates to be seated. The radical Republicans offered a resolution in favor of black suffrage, but they had to settle for a measure expressing a commitment of equality before the law. In May, when the National Replication Convention met, it became clear that the national party was in harmony with the Kentucky Republicans. The national convention resolved, over the objections of some of the border-state delegates, that the suffrage question in the loyal states properly belonged to the people of those states.[52]

The radical Republicans and the mass of blacks in the towns and cities of Kentucky continued their efforts. By 1868, the bureau had become identified with radical Republicanism in Kentucky. As the successes of radicalism mounted at the national level, more hostility was directed toward the Freedmen's Bureau. The excitement increased as the canvass for the election of 1868 got under way. In Henderson, threats to burn down the bureau office multiplied. The superintendent of the Henderson bureau office feared a mob would attempt to destroy the office on election night. On July 4, 1868, political meetings of the Negroes abounded throughout Kentucky.[53] The blacks in the Blue Grass counties gathered near Lexington and heard Brisbin speak on black suffrage, which he said should be granted not because it helped the Republican party but because it was just.[54] At a picnic in Winchester later in the summer, Negroes enthusiastically heard Brisbin's "twenty commandments," the second of which was: "Never vote for a rebel or Democrat for office."[55]

When Congress met in December 1868, a number of suffrage amendments were introduced. In the debate in the Senate, Davis of Kentucky denounced the Fifteenth Amendment as a step to substitute barbarism for civilization. He viewed suffrage in the District of Columbia as setting a dangerous precedent for the rest of the country. When the Fifteenth Amendment came to a vote, both of Kentucky's senators opposed it, and only two of Kentucky's eight congressmen supported it. The radical Samuel McKee, who had voted against the enfranchisement of blacks in the District of Columbia, supported the amendment.[56] The movement in Congress to give blacks the vote stimulated a broader interest within the Negro community in Kentucky. On January 1, 1869, the Emancipation Day celebration in Louisville focused on the question. Henry J. Young, a Negro clergyman of

Louisville, spoke and urged his audience to "use every lawful means to obtain manhood suffrage" as a necessary tool for their defense.[57]

The usual Fourth of July celebrations were held by the blacks throughout the state. The largest celebration was held near Paris, and the franchise was the prominent topic of every orator.[58] On July 14, the Negro State Educational Convention met in Louisville to formulate a black school system for the entire state. The suffrage question vied with education for prominence, however. Thomas Jackson, a native black of Kentucky, declared that when suffrage was secured, the freedmen would give their vote to the men who would give them "equal rights before the law."[59] Echoing Brisbin's words, the convention resolved to uphold the "glorious union" with ballots as they had formerly upheld it with bayonets.[60]

Not all black leaders were optimistic about the political future of the Negro in Kentucky. Henry H. Trumbo, a successful businessman in Frankfort, saw the civil rights of blacks in the state as so precarious that he doubted that the Fifteenth Amendment would ever reach Kentucky. "The case seems dark," he observed, "but we are aware that the darkest hour is just before day."[61] J. W. Alvord, superintendent of schools of the Freedmen's Bureau, held a similar view. From his travels through Kentucky examining the conditions of the blacks in January 1870, he concluded, "At best, voting is the only thing which will save the negro."[62]

The black leaders of Kentucky met in Frankfort on January 27, 1870, to organize the freedmen for the anticipated ratification of the Fifteenth Amendment. The convention resolved "to resort to the most expedient means in organizing and educating" the people "on political issues and vital demands of the times." The convention agreed that when freedmen had the right to vote, they must use it "judiciously and with becoming dignity" in the interest of their race, but they pledged support to the Republican party.[63] A call was issued for a Colored Men's State Convention to meet in Frankfort on February 23, and once more the Negro communities met to select delegates.[64]

At a meeting held in Midway, it was agreed that all possible help should be given to maintain, uphold, and support the true principles of the Republican government. From Nicholas County came a report that the blacks had "thoroughly endorsed Republicans."[65] In Greensburg, Hardinsburg, Paris, and Lebanon, representatives from eighteen counties met. At Lebanon both the white and the black speakers urged the Negroes to "stand together" and to vote as a bloc. "They should vote as one man for the party that freed them." The meeting at Lexington resolved that the blacks would under no circumstances vote against their interest as a group. "We know our friends and will stand by them, provided they stand by us." In Louisville a black Republican club formed. "We know our friends," asserted the members, "and will testify our appreciation . . . at the polls as soon as they are open to our race."[66]

When the Colored Men's State Convention met in February, nearly a hundred counties were represented.[67] The delegates took steps to organize a Negro Republican party with local societies in every town and county. An address advised black citizens to maintain harmony within their ranks and urged them to ally with white Republicans.[68] A committee formed to canvass the state coordinating local plans. With ratification of the Fifteenth Amendment coming up to a vote in March, black lecturers went into the field. T. F. Boaz, a Negro clergyman from Frankfort, spoke in Shelbyville with great effect, and George Griffith of Owensboro addressed meetings in Daviess County at which blacks and whites sat on the same platform.[69]

In many counties the Negroes had a majority in the Republican party, and the black leaders demanded a voice in the party organization. The Republican committee of Boyle County had an equal number of blacks and whites, and the *Danville Advocate* reported that the Negroes exercised a veto over the nominations for county offices. In Fayette County, where the black voters greatly outnumbered the white Republicans, the Republican county committee scheduled precinct meetings in which each elected three white and three black delegates to attend the county nominating convention to select candidates for the August election. But the Negroes were not to be so easily satisfied. An all-black county meeting convened in Lexington, and the Negro orators made it clear that, since they held the balance of power, they should share the offices. The Scott County Republican party probably checked any movement for Negro officeholding by agreeing that in theory the blacks had a right to hold office.[70]

The Democrats encouraged the Negroes to demand offices as a means of dividing the Republican party,[71] but black leaders themselves did not agree on the question. Late in March, G. W. Dupree wrote a letter to the *Louisville Commercial* in which he declared: "It is not office and power that my people want, but it is simple justice. . . . My people has [sic] more cornfield common sense than to flatter themselves with the idea of stepping right out of two hundred years of slavery in political office, without a moment's reflection or preparation." Two days later his views were contested by M. E. Lynn of Frankfort. Lynn insisted that capable blacks did not need to wait until the masses were educated. "Mississippi did not wait until the next generation to send a Revels to Congress," he declared, and Kentucky had her Revels. Henry Marrs also disagreed with Dupree's position, expressing an argument similar to Lynn's. Marrs reminded the Paducah clergyman that the blacks held the balance of power in Kentucky and should use it to advance their people. Henry Bush of Bridgeport supported Dupree's position in the *Commercial,* and Marrs conceded that support of the Republican party was more important than holding office.[72]

With the announcement of the adoption of the Fifteenth Amendment, celebrations took place in black communities throughout Kentucky. The most spectacular was held in Louisville. During the festivities it was resolved to support and uphold the Republican party, which was said to have crushed the attempt to perpetuate human bondage. The adoption of the Fifteenth Amendment was declared "a victory of right over wrong, of liberty over slavery, of freedom over oppression." The convention agreed that blacks should make "no terms . . . with Kentucky Democracy."[73] Ratification celebrations were also held in Frankfort, Hopkinsville, Georgetown, and elsewhere.[74]

On May 4, 1870, the Republican state central committee met and selected two whites and Horace Morris to appoint a committee to canvass the state and explain to the blacks their newly acquired rights and duties. The Negroes appointed were George A. Griffith of Owensboro, J. B. Stansberry of Louisville, and Henry Marrs of Frankfort. They spoke throughout the state during the summer until election day.[75] The Republican state central committee also issued an address assuring the new voters that the Republican party, which alone was credited with securing black suffrage, would fearlessly and earnestly demand the rights and powers conferred by the new amendment. As the tempo of the campaign quickened, political meetings took place weekly in many communities.[76]

The Democrats charged that the Republicans were "making hobby-horses of the blacks" so as to ride into office, and the allegation may have had some effect. Democrats persuaded a Negro to announce for jailer in Shelby County, and there was fear that both a black and a white Republican ticket would appear in Fayette County. White Republicans in Fayette County generally agreed that some blacks should be on the ticket, since they numbered eight of every nine Republicans, but insisted that justice should bow to expediency because such a ticket would lose white votes. To check division in the ranks of the Republican party, prominent Negro leaders in central Kentucky issued an address to black citizens urging them to refrain from standing for office and to vote for reliable white Republicans. The candidacies of black Republicans or black independents were declared a Democratic trick "calculated to defeat the Republican party" and to keep the Negroes "hewers of wood and drawers of water."[77]

The Republican campaign did not falter. During July the picnics and barbecues in black communities took on the practical purpose of rallying support for specific Republican candidates. John C. Fee reached hundreds of black and white Unionists in Madison County with sermons and addresses, and Judge Goodloe spoke in most of the towns in Madison County and extended his campaign into Bourbon County, where Gen. John T. Croxton of Paris was urging the freedmen to use the Fifteenth Amendment to elect friends of blacks.[78] Sam McKee campaigned in the Negro communities in Fleming and neighboring counties, and Rev. G. W. Dupree lectured to his fellow freedmen in Western Kentucky. The black clergyman Elijah Marrs, like his brother, Henry Marrs, worked among the freedmen in opposition to the Democrats and solicited their votes for the Republicans through editorials in the press.[79]

The Democrats were divided as to the attitude they should take toward the new voters. Some wanted to compete with the Republicans and bid for black votes. Others felt they did not need the Negro votes to win the election and urged the party to refuse support from blacks. In order to prevent Republican victories in many cities, Democratic leaders managed to arrange for changes in charters so that Negro wards were placed beyond the city limits. Nicholasville and Paris avoided Republican control temporarily by this strategy.[80] In another piece of chicanery, Louisville, Lexington, Frankfort, and other cities blocked Republican dominance for a short time by having the legislature alter *their* charters so that the municipal elections could be held before the Fifteenth Amendment was ratified.[81]

The Democrats used other tactics to counteract Negro suffrage. Since most important landowners and farmers were Democrats, before the election the Negroes were threatened with a loss of employment. Militias were organized. As election day approached, they were drilled nightly in the Blue Grass region and became a subtle threat against black suffrage. On election day, blacks and whites often entered different doors or filed into the polling place in different lines, and in some areas the blacks were subjected to prolonged questioning so that all could not vote before the polls closed. In the rural precincts the viva voce voting kept many timid black agricultural workers away from the polling place; otherwise, their votes were cast for the Democratic ticket.[82]

After 1870, the Republican monopoly of the Negro votes began to erode. The blacks insisted that the right to vote implied the right to be voted for. As early as February 1870, in the "Address to the Colored People of Kentucky," the Negro convention advised the freedmen: "We demand the emoluments that the franchise has bequethed unto us." H. J. Young informed the same convention that when his race secured political and civil rights, the black man would "be like white men; some will be radical and some conservative."[83] The same position was taken by Horace Morris of Louisville. In April 1870 Edward A. Pollard of South Carolina wrote an article in *Lippincott's Magazine* in which he praised the progress of the freedmen. If the blacks were wise, he concluded, they would put native whites in office instead of carpetbagger Republicans. Horace Morris answered Pollard in a letter saying that Negroes were forced to identify with the radical Republicans as the only party that would give them anything. He agreed that the interests of the conservative whites and the Negro were identical.[84]

The resistance of the Republicans in Kentucky to Negro office seekers soon caused many black leaders to become disillusioned with the party, however. In 1871, three Lexington blacks bolted the Republican state convention and accepted seats in the Democratic convention. By June 1871 they had formed a black Democratic organization in Lexington, and a Negro from Lexington was soon canvassing central Kentucky for the Democrats.[85] The Democratic sentiment among the blacks began to spread to other districts.[86]

Still, a Democratic legislature had failed to pass a law permitting blacks to testify against whites and had also failed to deal with the problem of the Regulators and the Ku Klux Klan. The freedmen therefore found it difficult to overcome their strong antipathy to the Democrats. A new party, as suggested by Morris, soon took shape to overcome the repugnance to an alliance with the old enemy. In Kentucky, Cassius M. Clay led the way, and no white in the Bluegrass state was trusted more than he. Clay called a meeting of leading Democrats at his home to urge the launching of a new movement. On January 2, 1871, he informed a convention of blacks in Richmond that he would continue to advocate their claims until they had full equality, but he could not support Grant. If they would be prosperous and happy, they must stand by their old masters. On July 4, Clay spoke at a black barbecue in Lexington, made substantially the same speech, and proposed Horace Greeley for president.[87]

On February 29, 1872, the black Republicans of Covington, who had heard several speeches by the antislavery wing of the party in Northern Kentucky, met to decide their position in relation to the national administration. A resolution endorsing Grant's administration was defeated, and white and black radicals bitterly denounced the president.[88] When the state convention met in March, a radical Republican offered a resolution in favor of giving a "liberal share" of the subpositions within the gift of the Republican officeholders to Negroes. After bitter debate the resolution was referred to a committee of three whites and three blacks.[89] When a Negro delegate from Lexington suggested that the anti-Grant delegates from Northern Kentucky take a pledge to support the nominee of the Philadelphia convention, fourteen of the seventeen delegates from Kenton County, including the black delegates, bolted the convention and the party.[90]

After the Liberal Republicans and the Democrats had both nominated Horace Greeley, the Negro supporters of Greeley met in Louisville in a national Colored Liberal Convention and resolved that "equal human rights" had ceased to be an issue between the contending parties. The convention announced that it was necessary for the blacks to assume a "balance of power" position by freeing themselves of the dominance of the Republicans. Although the mass of black voters in the cities remained in the Republican camp, Negro stump speakers canvassed the state for the Liberal Republicans in competition with black orators of the regular Republican party.[91]

The election of 1872 marked the end of Republican dominance of the Negro vote. At a nonpartisan black educational convention in February 1873, a resolution was introduced expressing gratitude to the Democrat-dominated Kentucky legislature for granting blacks the right to testify in the state courts. Considerable opposition was expressed on the ground that the General Assembly had only submitted to federal pressure, but the resolution was adopted nevertheless. The legislature of 1873 also established a state system of Negro schools, although it did not provide equal per capita distribution of all school funds without regard to race. A resolution to return thanks to the legislature for this enactment was introduced in the February 1873 convention but was tabled.[92] The Democrats' failure to distribute school tax money equitably remained a strong grievance among the blacks. In a Negro state convention in November 1873, however, a resolution warned the Republicans that if blacks' claims to offices continued to be ignored, Negroes would feel no special obligation to the party.[93]

The division of black votes in the election of 1872 and the failure of the Republican party to reward blacks with offices contributed to the growth of the black Democratic movement, as did the passage of a state law in April 1873 to punish persons guilty of intimidating voters. The bill was sponsored by the Democrats and was supported by almost all of the party. This measure, however, passed partially because the election officers of Lexington had been indicted by federal authorities after the election of January 30, 1873. The officers had been charged with violating the Federal Enforcement Act of May 1870, which prohibited denying citizens the opportunity to vote because of race.[94] The Democrats hoped to stave off federal intervention similar to that experienced during the testimony controversy.

After the election of 1874, the *Frankfort Yeoman* could say without being challenged by the *Courier-Journal* that hereafter the Republican party could never "calculate with any certainty upon wielding the Negro vote as a unit."[95] The Republicans of Kentucky had lost their last claim to the bloc vote, and both parties now had to bid for a divided Negro vote. By 1882 the Democrats had removed the last of the postwar grievances of Kentucky blacks by passing an act to consolidate the state school fund and to distribute it on a per capita basis without regard to race or color.[96] The demand for equal education had stronger and broader backing from the black community than any of the other reforms that had been called for since 1866, as we shall see.

CHAPTER ELEVEN

Equal Education?

ON MARCH 16, 1863, Secretary of War Stanton appointed the American Freedmen's Inquiry Commission "to investigate the condition of the colored population . . . and to report what measures will best contribute to their protection and improvement, so that they may defend and support themselves." The representatives of the commission traveled extensively along the eastern seaboard before preparing their report. Their most striking observation was the interest of the contraband in education. The commission was much impressed with the high value that the refugees placed on schooling for their children and on religious instruction for themselves. Wherever the representatives went, they learned that one of the first acts of Negroes, when they found themselves free, had been to establish schools at their own expense.[1]

A principal goal of the Freedmen's Bureau was to assist in establishing schools for the freedmen. The bureau was not established in Kentucky until after the ratification of the Thirteenth Amendment, and nothing was done until 1866, but the progress of events during the war had opened way for blacks' demands for education. By October 1865 five black schools flourished in Lexington, and all were supported by blacks out of their own pockets. In addition, the blacks in Lexington and throughout the state paid taxes to support white schools.[2] A Kentucky contributor to the *Cincinnati Gazette* reported that there was "nothing connected with the liberation of slaves in Kentucky more remarkable than their thirst for learning." A special inspector of the bureau who was sent to investigate conditions in the eastern district of the bureau in Kentucky confirmed the "intense desire" for education that existed among the freedmen. In several towns and cities, the blacks had established their own schools, the correspondent for the *Gazette* stated, supported by tuition fees paid either by the parents or by the black people generally in the community. The state superintendent of the bureau in Kentucky received similar information from agents elsewhere in the state. Many schools had been established throughout Kentucky, especially in the

large towns, "all taught by black people and supported entirely by contribu-
tions from freedmen themselves."[3] By April 1866 thirty-three schools for
blacks had been reported by the bureau agents in different points of the
state, "all sustained by subscriptions from freed people" and taught by black
teachers.[4]

During the war, the antislavery American Missionary Association extended its religious and educational work to the freedmen in Kentucky.
John G. Fee, a pioneer in black education, organized a school for Negro
soldiers at Camp Nelson. Fee then traveled to adjacent counties and set up
county educational societies among the blacks. He also endeavored to
establish county aid societies among the benevolent whites in the counties
to assist the schools.[5]

Oliver O. Howard issued Circular No. 2 in May 1865 in which he
ordered the assistant commissioners in the slave states to work with benevolent and religious organizations to maintain good schools until a system of
free schools could be established by local governments. Howard planned to
work through the societies already in the field by helping to finance and
coordinate the work that was already under way.[6]

On December 26, 1865, Clinton Fisk, in a public circular informed
blacks that the bureau was prepared to protect them until the state enacted
and enforced the laws giving them full protection and equal justice. Fisk
urged the freedmen to take an interest in the education of their children.
They would, he said, find friends who would aid them "in the establishment
and support of schools."[7] Fisk's circular was quickly followed by a similarly
encouraging speech in Louisville by Gen. John Palmer.

After the ratification of the Thirteenth Amendment, the Kentucky
legislature passed a series of acts on February 16, 1866, which, among other
things, provided for the education of the freedmen. The law declared that all
taxes from Negroes would constitute a separate fund, one-half to be used to
care for Negro paupers and the remainder for the education of Negro
children. A capitation tax of two dollars was also levied on all black adult
males to be used for education.[8] A Negro convention held in Lexington on
March 26, 1866, met because the legislative enactments of February 16, for
reasons shortly to be explained, had failed to grant blacks equality before the
law. In the "Declaration of Sentiments" adopted by the Lexington convention, members pledged to labor to the utmost of their ability "to infuse into
the minds" of Kentucky's blacks the necessity of educating their children.[9]

According to an auditor's report, 41,804 black children in the state were
eligible for education in January 1866. The "Negro Fund" contained
$5,656.01 at the end of 1866, only one-half of which could be appropriated
for black education. If the fund had been apportioned in the same way that
money was apportioned for white schools, each black child in the state

would have been allotted six cents per year.[10] As long as the Negro, the poorest segment of the community, was forced to bear the full responsibility for the education of black children, the future did not seem very promising.

T. K. Noble, who was appointed superintendent of bureau schools in Kentucky, correctly interpreted the Kentucky law for the education of blacks as a dead letter from the beginning and felt that it was mere window dressing for Washington. Thirteen Negro schools with a total of 9,995 students were reported to have been administered under the law of 1866, but no money was appropriated from the Negro Fund because the law was repealed before the drafts could be honored. A new law of March 9, 1867, decentralized the system of Negro education by placing it under the control of the trustees of the common-school district and county courts, which were authorized to grant two dollars and fifty cents for each pupil taught.[11] The change in the law responded to local prejudice, which insisted that the whites in each county control black education even when it was sustained by taxes levied entirely on black citizens. In most counties, the general public was determined to have no black schools. Although some statesmen and civic-minded leaders saw the justice and advantage to themselves of establishing public schools for the blacks, Noble was largely correct when he observed that there was not "a prominent man in the state" who had "the moral courage to come out and openly advocate" Negro education.[12]

Kentucky, like all other Southern states, moved slowly to take responsibility for Negro education, and the Freedmen's Bureau acted to fill the vacuum. In most states the religious and benevolent societies of the North formed a partnership with the bureau: the society paid the teachers, and the bureau took responsibility for furnishing the building.[13] The black schools of Kentucky, however, received proportionally less from the benevolent societies than did schools in the secession states; the societies primarily lost sight of the fact that there were blacks who needed aid in states that had not seceded.[14] It was therefore necessary for the blacks in Kentucky to make up subscriptions, and they largely continued to sustain their own schools. Where churches were available in the black community, they doubled as schools, and the clergyman usually served as the teacher or exercised much control over the instructor.[15] Where no church existed, an abandoned or empty building was rented if prejudice in the white community did not prevent it. In spite of these hardships, freedmen both young and old continued to show great enthusiasm for education.[16]

By the end of 1866 the bureau had made $25,000 available in Kentucky for buildings, and a working relationship had been established with benevolent societies in a few of the larger towns and with black religious congregations throughout the state. Still, the money made available by the bureau was entirely inadequate, and efforts to secure more unfortunately failed. The assistant commissioner of Kentucky reported that the blacks in the state were bearing a large part of the burden of educating their children by paying, in 1866, at least $1,500 a month, in addition to the state school tax, to support their schools.[17]

The establishment of Negro schools by the black community and by the bureau met opposition throughout Kentucky, with the strongest resistance coming from the southern and western portions of the state. Even in Louisville, the rental of a building led to prolonged disturbance in the neighborhood. The bureau could rely on General Orders No. 44 to secure a detachment of troops to prevent Regulators from intimidating the teacher, students, and the black community into closing the school. By the end of 1866, physical violence aimed at suppressing the schools had practically ceased in the larger towns of Louisville, Lexington, Frankfort, and Danville, but outrages continued in the rural counties. As a result, Negro schools tended to cluster in areas where troops were stationed. As late as 1868, Noble reported that fifty places had been found where schools might have been established "but for hostility of white citizens."[18]

As it was almost impossible to secure a building for a Negro school in the small towns and county seats, and since the blacks were too poor to construct one, the system that gradually evolved was a joint effort of the black community and the Freedmen's Bureau. A religious congregation bought a lot for a church and the bureau furnished the money enabling a Negro board of trustees to construct a building that served as both a church and a school. The trustees of the school were always leaders in the religious congregation, which was often dominated by the minister of the church. If the teacher was not sustained by a benevolent society, the bureau required that the rent paid by the religious society for use of the school building and subscriptions from the students be used to support the teacher. The bureau also required that no child be denied education because of poverty.[19]

Shortly after the Kentucky legislature passed the act of February 1866 providing for the Negro Educational Fund, General Palmer spoke to the blacks and informed them that the Kentucky tax levied on them "was illegal and could not be collected" because it was contrary to the Constitution of the United States.[20] The two-dollar capitation tax had been bitterly condemned by Negroes throughout the state, and in some areas they had refused to pay it. In Mason County nearly all of the freedmen did so, and in some other counties, officers garnished blacks' pay. In still other counties officers assessed the freedmen more than the two-dollar tax, with some sheriffs levying four and even eight dollars. Some county sheriffs employed a black assistant to collect the tax. When the bureau became aware of the miscarriage of justice, the offending party was forced to return the money.[21] In some cases, the tax money collected from the blacks was put into the common fund and was used only for white schools.[22] In Owensboro in July 1867, the central committee of the United Brothers of Friendship met and formally entered a protest against the capitation tax. They informed the superintendent of the bureau that "More than twenty thousand free persons of color paid taxes annually into the state treasury, for a great number of years before emancipation," for the support of white schools. The committee insisted that the blacks had more than created a fund to educate their children. They protested against the school law of 1867, which authorized school commissioners to supervise black schools in each district, and they solemnly condemned the tendency to fill these offices with rebels.[23]

The revision of the school law of March 9, 1867, provided that all taxes collected from Negroes would be made available for the education of black children. The residue of the Negro Fund was to be used for the support of black paupers after the educational needs of Negro children had been met. The county government was given complete control of the black school fund. Although the law stipulated that two and one-half dollars were to be provided for each black child in school under a certified teacher for at least three months, two years after the provision was made for state funds for Negro education, only Fayette County had given any support at all to black schools. The provisions of the law were not imperative. The law read that the trustees of the common school district "may cause a school to be taught" instead of "shall cause a school to be taught." Because of the strong feeling against bureau control of Negro education, and because of prejudice against the blacks, the county officers refused to establish Negro schools. The state legislature abdicated its responsibility and leadership in the face of white prejudice, and the county officers were permitted to return to the legal situation that had existed before the Civil Rights Act of 1866. In some counties, bureau agents called meetings of county officials to urge them to appoint a receiver for Negro funds and to certify a teacher, but the bureau eventually concluded that the county authorities would do nothing unless "driven to it" by federal authorities. In Louisville, the friends of black education found all roads blocked. The city council resisted Negro education in any form, and a resolution presented to the Louisville Board of Education that favored carrying out the state law was brought to a stalemate because the sheriff and city assessor would not cooperate.[24]

The law of March 1867 was revised in January 1868 to provide that only excess funds were to be used to meet educational needs—funds remaining after the aid for black paupers had been met. With the exception of Fayette County, the Negro Fund was used entirely, if at all, to aid black paupers. Throughout the state much of the tax money was swallowed up by payments to whites, who received three or four dollars per week from the county court for caring for their elderly former slaves. In many cases these servants proved to be very useful around the house—to such an extent that they should have been paid a wage as employees. In Bourbon County the court awarded one claim of almost $800 for a pauper case, and after the county had met other claims, only enough remained from a total county fund of $2,500 to erect a few huts on the poor farm. Under these circumstances, I. S. Catlin, superintendent of the subdistrict of Louisville, viewed the Negro tax as "legalized robbery of the Freedmen."[25]

On November 1, 1867, Ben Runkle, the assistant superintendent of schools for Kentucky, took steps to have the law of 1867 declared unconstitutional or, alternatively, to have the funds distributed to the black community for the education of the black children. He asked Republican attorney James Speed for an opinion on the constitutionality of the poll tax that was levied on blacks in the state. Speed considered the law unconstitutional without reservations but suggested that the Kentucky legislature be petitioned to repeal it. Runkle then authorized Speed to draw up a petition, which was printed and circulated throughout the state by bureau officials. On January 15, 1868, 4,500 signed copies were ready to be presented to the legislature. The document respectfully asked that the legislature modify the law so that its implementation would not be at the discretion of county officials. The county judge or common-school commissioner could be made responsible for selecting one or more blacks in the county to report the number of Negro children taught at each school, and the court could assume responsibility for apportioning the money.[26] But the legislature utterly refused to take any action in the matter. Aware of the determination of the leadership in the bureau and uneasy about the possibility of federal intervention, the legislature moved rapidly to put the laws of Kentucky in harmony with the practices in the state. The bureau became more convinced that the great injury and injustice inflicted on the blacks would not be removed except by the intervention of federal power. James Speed was employed by the bureau to advise and implement federal action.[27]

Aware that the educational work of the bureau was soon to be terminated, Runkle and E. M. Crevath, secretary of the American Missionary Association's western branch in Cincinnati, and the leading black clergymen of Kentucky decided to set up a Negro state board of education in Kentucky with local boards throughout the state. An educational convention was to meet in Louisville from July 14 to July 17, 1869, to set up an organization through which blacks might regulate their own affairs after the bureau had been removed. The new organization would also be available to work with the state when officials had been persuaded to establish state schools for black children. The planning committee issued an address informing the black community about the use made of taxes levied to educate Negro children and reminded the freedmen that an amendment to the Constitution of the United States prohibited taxation without representation. The committee deemed taxation reasonable per se but expressed the belief that it was the will of God that blacks should be taxed as other men.[28] When the convention assembled, its 700 black delegates represented nearly every county. The sessions followed a program designed to explore the whole range of civil rights. On the third day, full attention was directed to the problem of education. A Negro board of education was established with plans for auxiliary societies in each county and town. A constitution for the educational society was adopted, with provisions for permanent headquarters at Louisville.[29]

The convention then petitioned the state legislature, asking that the taxes paid by blacks be used to educate Negro children. The convention informed the legislature that despite numerous applications, county judges and school commissioners had "invariably refused" to permit any of the tax money that blacks had paid to be used to sustain Negro schools. The petition also noted that the two-dollar poll tax was not assessed on white citizens. Finally, it advised the legislature that in nearly every state in the Union, the common schools were conducted upon the principle of equality without reference to race or color.[30] Unfortunately, however, the Kentucky legislature at this time reflected the strong sentiment against black education which was found in society at large. Although Kentucky had been one of the few Southern states which had not prohibited black education during the antebellum period, after the Civil War the public showed a determined resistance which was matched in few, if any, Southern states. The Reconstruction Act of 1867 had brought about the establishment of equal education in the Reconstruction states, but the state government in Kentucky was now controlled by those who, to a great degree, sympathized with the lost cause.

The reasons for the hostility were varied and complex. Not the least among them was the opposition resulting from the fact that the black educational system was dominated by the Freedmen's Bureau as an agency of the federal govenment,[31] although the bureau superintendent of schools of Kentucky, Rev. T. K. Noble, was a member of the Methodist Episcopal Church, South. The assistant superintendent for Kentucky, Rev. R. S. Gardinier, also a Methodist and a resident of Kentucky before the war, had been threatened with his life for preaching to blacks. He had nearly been drowned in Georgetown, Kentucky, and had had to flee the town because of his identification with the educational work of the bureau. A strong but dormant prejudice against the blacks had been activated by the federal measures and by the action of the army during the war and swept over the sections of the state that had been deeply committed to the institution of slavery.[32]

Since some of the teachers were white, the schools seemed to be promoting integration. In addition, the teachers were generally from the North. Yet the heart of the issue was that the Southern people regarded the blacks' teachers as persons unfamiliar with the customs and civilization of the South and believed that the Negro was being trained to accept social equality. The literature and text material used in the schools contained propaganda which was said to be hostile to the South. In addition, the pupils were taught to sing Northern war songs. The editor of the *Lexington Observer and Reporter* asserted that there would be few objections if Southern whites taught the blacks. Such a change in the teaching corps in Kentucky would restore confidence and remove suspicion, he suggested.[33]

Some farmers in Kentucky believed that the educated freedman would be worthless as a laborer and that he would waste his time if he were educated. They feared that eventually property owners would be burdened with increased taxes to sustain education for blacks.[34] In the final analysis, mass education implied a revolutionary transformation of blacks' traditional role. Even to Oliver Howard and other benevolent leaders in the bureau, black education was a social experiment with little historical precedent.[35]

A significant factor in the opposition to black education was politically motivated hostility. Education prepared the blacks to function as enlightened citizens, which implied training and an interest in politics. Education and suffrage were inseparable parts of the American ideal that the blacks readily accepted. The schoolhouse became the symbol of the Republican opposition in the minds of Democrats and conservatives. It was not only the educational center of the blacks but also the meeting place of the Union League, the politically conscious black benevolent societies, and the politically oriented Negro religious societies. The leadership of all of these was often vested in the same person, who served as teacher, minister, and political leader. Negro schoolhouses were often burned because they fostered political interests and ambitions.[36]

The blacks were encouraged to hold elections for the selection of their school officials, and straw votes were often taken on other matters on which they were not legally entitled to vote. As a result the instruments of education and suffrage became interwoven and interrelated. By 1868, when the franchise had become a more immediate objective, the adult night school served the dual purpose of promoting education and political awareness. The night school itself became the focus of special efforts by the bureau as the crusade for Negro suffrage seemed to be nearing its conclusion. Increased numbers of adults sought education in the night schools in 1868 and 1869.[37]

At the same time that the blacks in Kentucky were organizing to secure the right to equal education, they were also striving to secure the right to vote and to testify against whites in state courts. Schools for their children remained a paramount concern, however. As resistance to black educational objectives mounted, the freedmen saw that the ballot offered the means by which they could secure equal schooling, while the right to testify against whites could be the strongest deterrent to mobs and Regulators who interfered with the progress of Negro education. As early as 1867 some of the friends of the blacks began to see that suffrage was necessary to secure the goals of "universal liberty."[38] In July 1867, after informing the bureau commissioner of the extent of prejudice and hostility against Negro schools in Kentucky, T. K. Noble concluded that the only way to end the reign of terror was to arm the blacks with the vote. "Give the Freedmen the ballot, and you will hear no further complaints of an unfavorable public sentiment. In my judgment the education of the colored race will never rest on a permanent basis until they are invested with the right of suffrage and allowed to testify in all courts of justice," he declared.[39] With the removal of the army as the protective arm of the bureau schools, the freedmen were instructed to look more to the courts for protection. In meetings organized by bureau personnel, and in commemoration meetings organized by black citizens, more and more stress was put on securing the ballot and the right to testify in state courts against whites.[40] The Negro State Educational Convention of July 14, 1869, held in Louisville, was the great catalyst which enabled the blacks to understand the interrelations of the problems concerning education, suffrage, and the rights of testimony.[41]

The convention inspired a grass-roots movement that swept across the state. Many local meetings convened to discuss the importance of securing suffrage, equal rights in state courts, and equality of education. By August 1869, the assistant superintendent of the bureau for Kentucky could optimistically observe that the controlling class in the state would give Negroes their educational rights as soon as the blacks got the right to vote. "The day when they exercise the right of citizens at the ballot-box," equal education will be granted wherever they are a majority, he predicted.[42] Local initiative continued to develop in the black community. The blacks at Casey's Creek met in October 1869 and signed a protest petition which was sent to the bureau. The document complained about the heavy taxes that blacks were required to pay. "We want equal rights, with all men, and then we are willing to pay our tax like other men," the secretary of the meeting declared.[43] Three months later, at a mass meeting held in Lexington, the black citizens protested against the method the mayor and council were using to distribute the tax money collected from blacks for education. Since the school fund was small in relation to the number of students to be taught, the local government singled out a portion of the black children who were to benefit from the fund. Two-thirds of the children were left without public means of education. The mass meeting demanded that the city government make "an equal division of all money" among all black children. A committee of three was selected to confer with the council and mayor.[44]

The Freedmen's Bureau was closed in June 1872, but its educational work had come to a halt earlier in that year because no funds were available. In December 1869, the Kentucky superintendent of public instruction urged the state legislature to establish a state system of education for black children. He pointed out that the taxes levied on Negroes by the laws of 1866 and 1867 were being illegally used and were being misappropriated by blacks and whites in claims for care of paupers. In addition, because the law stated that local authorities "may" establish a school for Negro children rather than "shall," schools were not necessarily established at all. The superintendent correctly viewed the Kentucky law as unconstitutional and as placing the Commonwealth in an "attitude of acting dishonorably or unjustly toward the humblest and most ignoble of her children." He informed the governor and legislature that blacks were aware of the prejudicial nature of the law and were beginning to resist payment of the taxes. The state of black education was made even more unequal in 1870 by the passage of a law to levy on white citizens a tax of fifteen cents per $100 property to be used for white students only. Nothing was done to relieve the critical plight of Negro education.[45]

Agitation among the blacks increased. In August 1870, a state Negro teachers' convention met in Louisville and petitioned Congress and the state legislature, denouncing payment of a school tax in which the taxpayers could not share.[46] By 1871, it was obvious that the Kentucky school law would soon be challenged in the federal court, and the legislature was pressured to change the law. The legislature of 1871 responded by repealing the Negro Education Act of 1867 and established the same per capita tax rate for Negroes as was collected from the white population.[47] This measure did not answer the grievances of the Negro community, as it did not equalize educational benefits without regard for race. In the November 1872 term of the Jessamine County Circuit Court, a petition and affidavit were filed to transfer the criminal case of a black man to the federal courts. The petition asked for the transfer on the grounds that he was denied equal rights under Kentucky laws partly because his children were denied an equal share of the common-school fund. Disposition was delayed until it was known whether the federal judge would take the case, which apparently he did not. The auditor's report for 1873 showed that school taxes collected from Negroes were not spent to educate black children.[48]

After the legislature of 1873 convened, the black citizens of Kentucky called a Colored People's Educational Convention for February, 1873. The convention sent a memorial to the legislature earnestly requesting that there be "no special legislation . . . for colored people." They called for "equal school privileges" for Negro children. The convention resolved to establish the Colored Men's State Educational Union, and a meeting was called for July to organize it.[49]

The legislature of 1873 considered a bill to establish a state system for Negro schools; it was agreed that the Fourteenth Amendment required this much, at least. A bill was proposed to tax blacks at the rate of twenty cents on each hundred dollars of property, with a capitation tax of one dollar. The maintenance of Negro schools would still rely entirely on funds derived from Negro taxes, and the black children would have only a meager fraction of what was available for white children. Radical Republican William Brown amended the bill to provide for sharing of all school funds by all children whether they attended black or white schools. Schools were to be segregated according to race but were to receive equal tax support. The amendment was voted down, receiving only the affirmative votes of Brown and radical Republican William Goodloe. The other eighteen Republicans and all Democrats voted against the amendment.[50]

During the same session the legislature considered amendments to the common-school law (white) to permit school districts to tax themselves at a higher rate so that education might be improved. Goodloe offered an amendment to strike the word "white" from the section on the distribution of funds so that there would be an equalization of funds for black and white students. This amendment, too, was voted down, with only one Democrat and six Republicans favoring it.[51]

More determined than ever, the leaders of the Colored Men's State Educational Union called a convention to meet in Frankfort in November 1873. The convention expressed disappointment that its petition to the last legislature had not secured the educational advantages for blacks that accrued "to others upon the payment of school taxes." Members resolved that if the legislature of 1874 did not provide "such school advantages and facilities as are accorded to other citizens," they would empower their executive committee to take steps through the state and federal courts to do so.[52]

By 1874, it was clear to informed legislators that a uniform school system for blacks must be established if the state maintained a school system for whites. The supreme courts in several states had ruled that the Fourteenth Amendment required the establishment of Negro schools or the admission of blacks to a common school. In January in the case of *Ward* v. *Flood,* the California Supreme Court ruled that in the absence of the "same facilities for education," blacks must be admitted to white schools. This clear and concise ruling put the Kentucky legislature under pressure to do in 1874 what it had failed to do in 1873. The legislature passed a law on February 23, 1874, establishing a uniform school system for Negro children throughout the state to be financed by diverting the taxes from Negro-owned property entirely to the support of Negro education. The rate was forty-five cents on each hundred dollars of property owned by blacks, in addition to a capitation tax, fees, licenses, and forfeitures paid by the black citizens. The law remained unequal in both taxation and expenditures.[53]

Steps had been taken by Republicans and friends of the blacks to challenge Kentucky's educational system in the courts even before passage of the new law. In 1873, a white Republican in Bracken County refused to pay the common-school tax required by the school law of March 1873, because the law exempted blacks from sharing in the benefits of the common-school system. The circuit court ruled against the Bracken citizen, and when the ruling was appealed by James Speed, the attorney for the appellant, the Kentucky Court of Appeals upheld the decision in November 1874 by ruling that education was not one of the privileges and immunities protected by the federal government under the Fourteenth Amendment; the common-school election was not an election but merely an action of an agency of the state. The appellate court went so far as to declare that the Kentucky legislature had moved to equalize the burden and benefits of education by the adoption of the law of February 1874.[54]

The state superintendent of schools was authorized by the Education Act of 1874 to organize the Negro Teachers' State Educational Association. The organization was established in August 1877 and was to meet in August of each year. The meeting of 1878 in Danville adopted strong independent measures. A committee was selected to draw up a memorial to be presented to the next legislature of Kentucky setting forth the educational wants of the Negro citizens of the state.[55] When the legislature met the committee informed the lawmakers that the funds for black schools were wholly inadequate, and the legislature was asked to equalize the school funds on a per capita basis without regard to race and to establish a common age limit for all children. The committee selected by the Negro Teachers' Assocation met with the Joint Committee on Education of the legislature, which promised to give the proposal serious consideration. The legislature again failed to act, however, and the Negro Teachers' Educational Association adopted a resolution urging the blacks throughout the state to hold mass meetings and to call on the legislature to grant the relief sought by the memorial committee. Seeing a tax revolt of blacks on the horizon which would force a test of Kentucky's school law in federal court, the Democratic platform in 1879, without mentioning blacks, conceded that eventually "every child in the state" should be furnished with the "means of a fair English education." But the blacks were no longer satisfied with promises for the future, and the Negro Teachers' State Educational Association convention of 1879 again memorialized the legislature urging equal distribution of school funds.[56]

The convention which met in August 1881 sent a third memorial to the legislature asking for equal distribution of school funds. Steps were also taken to file a suit in the federal courts to secure the equal distribution of funds under the Fourteenth Amendment. Petitions and conventions having failed to secure revision of the school law of 1874, the blacks decided to take their grievance to the courts. On November 25, 1881, Emmet Bagby, a

Paducah Republican, filed suit in federal circuit court for Jesse Ellis, challenging the constitutionality of the poll tax because it was not imposed on whites.[57]

The memorials of the Negro Teachers' Association and of local Negro groups were presented on the floor of the senate by friends of the blacks, and a bill to equalize school funds was introduced in the legislature by the Republicans.[58] The bill provided for an additional tax of ten cents per hundred dollars of property owned by white citizens so that the tax on all citizens would be equal. The school funds were to be distributed on a per capita basis among the white and black students of the state.[59] The ratification of the new law would eliminate provisions under which, according to the state superintendent, the white per capita distribution in 1882 would be $1.40 and the Negro children's per capita allotment would be eleven cents.

The school bill was tabled on a motion by a Democratic opponent of the bill and was made a special order for April 19, 1882. Advocates of the legislation were sure that it was dead, since adjournment was scheduled for April 24, 1882. Development in the federal courts posed a dilemma. Judge John Baxter had ruled on the case of *United States* v. *Buntin* in the federal court at Cincinnati in February 1882, and the language of his ruling made it clear that Kentucky's school law was unconstitutional.[60] Informed whites declared in the press that the alternative to equal education was integration; and lawyers in the Kentucky legislature were aware that the supreme courts of Northern states had rendered decisions requiring compulsory integration of schools when the legislature had not clearly empowered school boards to establish separate school systems. These decisions had been based on the Fourteenth Amendment. The courts had ruled that Negro children could not be excluded from attending schools established exclusively for whites. Judge Baxter presided in the Paducah case, and the expected ruling from the circuit court of Paducah came on April 4, 1882. Judge Baxter's ruling in the case of *Commonwealth of Kentucky* v. *Jesse Ellis* was that the Fourteenth Amendment required any school funds created by the state to be equal and uniform in their collection and distribution, without discrimination on account of race or color.[61]

On April 11, in a speech in the house, Republican James Breathitt, who had introduced the Republican bill, made it clear to the Democrats that they faced a choice of abolishing the public schools, equalizing the school funds, or integrating the schools. On the same day, the ruling in the case of *Commonwealth* v. *Ellis* appeared in the Louisville papers. On April 19, a mass meeting of blacks in Paducah selected a committee to secure a lawyer to take their grievance back to the federal courts if the current legislature did not equalize school funds.[62]

The Democrats held a caucus on April 20, 1882, and the majority of the party agreed to submit to the requirements of the federal courts. Some conservative members of the Democrats walked out, but a majority of the regular Democrats decided to put forward a Democratic version of an equalization bill. The new law was adopted with the support of the New Departure men and the majority of Republicans, but the Democrats could have passed the law without Republican support. The adoption of the measure reflected not conviction but merely the recognition of expediency. Without the new law the black schools would cease to exist, as the court had declared the Negro capitation law unconstitutional, and black children had a legal right to demand admission to the white schools if no black schools existed. In the case of *Commonwealth* v. *Ellis* the court had stated that the legislature could undoubtedly "create" schools for black children distinct from those for white children,[63] and indeed the new law specifically provided for segregated schools, separate but equal. The Democrats had not primarily acted on principle or responded to public demands. They had merely yielded to federal force, as they had in the testimony law of 1872 and in the act to deal with lawlessness in 1873.[64] The New Departure men emerged from the controversy with new power and prestige.

The black community's persistent protest against unequal education had met only silence, and they eventually turned to the courts in the school case as they had with respect to the testimony question. In both cases the court had forced the legislature into a dilemma, and in both crises the Democratic party had divided. By providing that the tax provisions in the equalization bill be submitted to a referendum of the voters, the Democratic party abdicated its reponsbility and showed timidity, as it had in 1867. Although a decline in overt prejudice, due to the fear of federal intervention as well as to an interest in winning the Negro vote, was apparent in the changing attitude toward black education, the intervention of the federal court was crucial in enacting the law of 1882.[65] The courts, however, would not have ruled as they did without the persistent agitation of the black community.

Black and white schools were to operate under the same law, but the applications of that law were to diverge widely. The Supreme Court had already made its interpretation of the Fourteenth Amendment unmistakably clear. In 1880 the Supreme Court in *Stauder* v. *West Virginia* had broken down a state law that barred blacks from serving as jurors. The broad nature of the ruling made the decision's application to schools obvious. The court stated that the chief design of the Fourteenth Amendment "was to protect an emancipated race and to strike down all possible legal discrimination," which in essence declared "that the law in a State shall be the same for the blacks as well as for the white."[66] Kentucky officials understood that an attempt to enforce Kentucky's school laws, as they existed, against a federal court order would result in federal prosecution of state officials as had earlier been the case with respect to blacks' right to testify in state courts. Federal prosecution of state officials who violated equal rights of Negroes under the Fourteenth Amendment had only recently been upheld by the Supreme Court.[67]

The law of 1882 equalized the school funds and increased the money available for Negro education almost three times, but it was questionable whether the Negro community would be satisfied with the clause which stipulated that schools would be separate. The Negro Men's State Convention convened in Lexington in June 1882 to consider the new law, which would be put to a vote in August. On the first day of the convention, most of the speakers condemned the measure because of the segregation feature, but opinions were clearly divided.[68]

During the last weeks of July, Negroes throughout Kentucky held local meetings to determine how they would vote in August. The law assured them more educational funds without any increase in taxes and removed the special black capitation tax which had been so bitterly condemned. Still, many Negro leaders violently opposed the provision regarding segregated schools. Within the white community all responsible parties urged the people to ratify the new law. The voters were not deciding whether the school fund was to be equalized; the federal court had already decided that question. Citizens were simply deciding the amount involved. It was believed that if the state did not move to equalize the school fund, the federal courts would do so. Otherwise, the schools would be integrated, or the trustees of the common school would render themselves liable to penalties under the Fourteenth Amendment.[69]

The new school law was ratified by the voters in August 1882 by a majority of 1,700. The court mandate received scant publicity. When the schools opened in the autumn, very little had changed. Only Paducah and Louisville equalized the fund. All of the municipalities in the state except three maintained schools under special acts which placed the schools under municipal authority, and they continued the discriminatory special acts which, except in the case of Lexington, shut black schools off from public funds paid by white citizens.[70] Another legal challenge was necessary before the local municipalities would yield. On April 2, 1883, the federal district court at Paducah, in the case of *Claybrook* v. *City of Owensboro,* ordered the school board of Owensboro to distribute the school fund on a per capita basis equally among all children of school age without regard for race. An injunction was issued to prevent the continuation of the unconstitutional distribution, and the court ordered the consolidation of all school funds.[71]

The stage was set for a strong emotional reaction to the court ruling, but it did not materialize. A group of civic-minded, bipartisan citizens led by William Beckner, editor of the *Clark County Democrat,* called in April 1883, after the ruling in the Owensboro case, for a state conference to meet in Louisville to discuss ways and means of improving education of the state's children.[72] Attention was called to the fact that Kentucky's support of education fell at one of the lowest levels in the nation. Only one-third of the children of school age attended school.[73] The educational convention of April was unique in that it was integrated. The race issue was pushed into the background, and the central theme was the improvement of education. The convention issued an "Address to the People of Kentucky" urging a stronger commitment to public education by the local community. At another meeting in September 1883 delegates recommended an increase in the per capita allotment for state support from $1.30 to $3.00. A watchdog committee was to draw up a comprehensive common-school law for presentation to the educational committee of the legislature. The committee was instructed to be present in Frankfort while the legislature met and to keep in touch with its day-by-day proceedings.[74] The newspapers voiced almost unanimous support.

When the legislature of 1883–1884 convened, public opinion backed new reforms in the state school system. By May 1884, the legislature had passed a new law which provided for a tax of twenty-two cents to replace the tax of twenty cents levied in 1883.[75] The new law, however, included a provision that no tax paid by white citizens could be used to repair schools used by Negro children. Since the Judiciary Act of 1875 gave the state courts exclusive jurisdiction over all civil cases when the dispute did not exceed $500, the question of extending equalization to the cost of repairing schools was not likely to come before federal courts.[76]

The legislatures of 1882 and 1884 removed education from public attention as a controversial issue. At the same time, the segregation clause and the decisions in the cases of *Marshall* v. *Donovan* (1874) and *Claybrook* v. *Owensboro* (1883) set a legal pattern which could be used by other Southern states in charting a course to establish separate school systems for Negro children without the intervention of federal authority.[77]

Kentucky blacks were aware of their rights as Americans. They made full use of their freedom under the Fourteenth Amendment and the force bills to convene, petition, and agitate. They were conscious of their political power, and they exercised their suffrage to secure their rights. They insisted that the Republicans support the memorials of the Negro conventions, and when the party failed to respond, they renewed the agitation with more vigor. They urged the Democrats to support their goals by use of pressure-group tactics, and the New Departure Democrats responded. Blacks were cognizant of the legal instruments available to them under the Civil Rights Acts, the Equal Protection Clause of the Fourteenth Amendment, and the force bill, and when necessary they turned to the court for justice.

The freedmen were not satisfied with the equalization law. When the representatives of the black community assembled in the Lexington convention of June 1882, they declared that the equalization law was "cowardly,

Unamerican and infamous" because of the segregation provision. Their sentiments reflected the consensus of the black leadership throughout the state. Commonsense considerations and historical precedents, if not intuition, told them that a separate system could not be equal.[78]

The prolonged controversy over Negro education in Kentucky revealed a lack of leadership in the state legislature. The willingness of the legislature to turn the control of black education over to the rule of the archaic and prejudiced county government and municipalities showed a complete neglect of responsibility. The legislature was unwilling to lead the state out of the past and into the future. Although two farsighted superintendents of schools gave sound advice, the legislature remained unmoved until coerced by the federal courts.

On the national scene the Kentucky experience set a pattern of action that led directly to the judgment in the case of *Plessy* v. *Ferguson* in 1896, giving the Supreme Court's stamp of approval to the ruling of the lower courts, which had already become deeply entrenched in the Southern schools for more than a decade. The decision of 1896 served as a massive roadblock to the rights of black Americans.[79] It took the Negro's rights to education out of the legal realm and into a moral sphere. Once they had lost the protection of basic constitutional law, Negro schools were exposed to the fragile doctrine of "separate but equal," an ambiguous phrase sheltered by a moral system that was weak and pragmatic. The Negro's rights were subjected to a seemingly endless ordeal in the wake of *Plessy* v. *Ferguson,* and the balance did not begin to be righted until 1954.

Epilogue

THE NEGROES were enabled to secure their rights under the Fourteenth and Fifteenth Amendments by the consistent support of the Republican party of Kentucky, which gave them a channel of communication with the federal administration in Washington. The Democratic party was divided on critical issues, and sometimes the split offered an opportunity for dialogue within the dominant party even though the majority considered the Negro question as settled after the enactment of the legislation of 1866. The conservative Democrats, who were completely in control by 1867, were unwilling to concede anything to the blacks except that slavery was no longer supported by law. They hoped to keep the Negro in bondage by social pressure and unfriendly state legislation, but the rapid pace of events during the war had destroyed the effectiveness of their organizational structure. The county and city organizations were weak, and the inefficiency of the state's lawmakers was notorious.[1] The New Departure Democrats represented a small minority of the party, but their strength was greater than their number. They wanted to bury the past and to modernize Kentucky. They realized that since Negroes were a significant labor force, it was necessary to give them equality in the courts of law. They favored suppressing the lawlessness and violence of the Regulators. New Departure men included businessmen, former Confederate officers who were educated, and progressive lawyers. The Republican party was so small that it remained primarily a gadfly at the state level, although the party was able to control several cities. In the twenty years after the Civil War, no significant civil rights legislation was passed to improve the lot of the blacks that could not have passed without their votes. Yet Republican agitation had educational value, and Republicans gave the blacks important aid at the bar and on the bench. The Democrats, however, conceded little except under threats of federal intervention.

The three most significant civil rights laws passed in Kentucky during the Reconstruction era—the equalization law for education, the law granting equality in testimony, and the act to control lawlessness—came as a result of the intervention of the federal courts. In supporting these laws the Democrats reversed their position during previous sessions, and with federal court pressure the laws would have been enacted without the support of the Republican delegation in the legislature.

Kentucky was the only state outside the Confederacy in which Ku Klux Klan activities were significant. Since Kentucky did not undergo radical reconstruction, and Negroes did not vote in the state until 1870 and could not testify in cases involving whites until 1872, there was little or no political reason for the Klan's existence in the state. For this reason there was no statewide organization of the Klan.

The outrages of the Regulators in Kentucky equaled those elsewhere in frequency and brutality, but the Regulators were at no time able to accomplish their objective. No considerable number of black agricultural workers left the state despite the violence and brutality of the Klan's forays. Black education survived, and schools destroyed by arson were rebuilt. The blacks continued to hold protest meetings and petitioned the state and federal government to suppress lawlessness. The protests of the black community culminated in the meeting in Frankfort in February 1871, when blacks called on Congress for protection, demanding federal action.[2] With the Klan in Kentucky particularly in mind, Congress passed the force bill of April 20, 1871,[3] and the outrages diminished, although they did not disappear.[4]

Klan activities chiefly aimed at destroying the Negro's political status in the Confederate states but were checked and weakened by the Reconstruction regimes. Although the original Klan disappeared after the passage of the enforcement acts, the nightriders that succeeded the Klan became one of the principal forces in overthrowing the radical government in the deep South.[5] In Kentucky, violence was primarily the cause of the black community's unity and solidarity in demanding the right to vote and to testify in the courts.

The Liberal Republican party espoused many of the same principles that the New Departure Democrats had promoted since 1868. When the Democrats supported Horace Greeley, the nominee of the Liberal Republicans, the Democrats accepted the position of the New Departure wing of the party and thereby weakened the conservative tradition. The die-hard conservative Democrats supported a separate ticket, but many conservatives went with the faction supporting Greeley.

The conservative Democrats were nurtured by federal intervention in Kentucky. In 1876, the Supreme Court set out on a course that checked intervention when it handed down its ruling in the case of *United States* v. *Reese*. The Court declared that the Lexington election inspectors were not guilty of violating the Fifteenth Amendment because the amendment did not confer the right of suffrage upon anyone and only prohibited denial of suffrage because of race or color. The court pursued this view and in 1883 annulled the Civil Rights Act of 1875. As a result, the conservative Democrat faction lost its appeal as a rallying point for the states' rights doctrine. The passage of the equalization bill in 1882 by a majority of Democrats marked the end of conservative Democrat dominance; the electorate in the referendum of August 1882 ratified a measure that most Republicans had supported since 1873.

With the threat of federal intervention removed, the New Departure philosophy was accepted by a new generation of Kentuckians. They wrote the reform constitution of 1891, which included a clause prohibiting slavery and contained no racial provisions, so that the section of the bill of rights that proclaimed "All men are by nature free and equal" was a reality instead of a goal. The incorporation of the Australian (secret) ballot in the new constitution as a democratic provision was a greater gain for black citizens than for white. In addition, by prohibiting convict labor outside the penitentiaries, the constitution of 1891 eliminated one of the most brutal abuses of blacks. While equal justice was sometimes difficult for the black man to secure as he entered the new century, the perseverance of the blacks in the two decades after the Civil War gave assurance that there would never be a return to the ordeal of the 1870s.

Notes

ABBREVIATIONS AND SHORT FORMS USED IN NOTES

Acts of Kentucky	*Acts of the General Assembly of the Commonwealth of Kentucky*
AMA Correspondence	American Missionary Association Correspondence, Dillard University
Basler	Roy P. Basler, ed., *The Collected Works of Abraham Lincoln,* 9 vols. (New Brunswick, N. J.: Rutgers University Press, 1953)
BFP	Blair Family Papers, Library of Congress
BP	Breckinridge Family Papers, Library of Congress
BRFAL	Bureau of Refugees, Freedmen, and Abandoned Lands
CSP	Charles Sumner Papers, Harvard University
EFP	Evans Family Papers, University of Kentucky
ESP	Edwin M. Stanton Papers, Library of Congress
HJ	*Journal of the House of Representatives of the Commonwealth of Kentucky*
HWP	Herndon-Weik Papers, Library of Congress
JCP	John J. Crittenden Papers, Library of Congress
JHP	Joseph Holt Papers, Library of Congress
JJP	John Jones Papers, University of Kentucky
LC	Library of Congress
NA	National Archives
NMSUS	Elon A. Woodward, ed., "The Negro in the Military Service of the United States: A Compilation of Official Records," 7 vols. (National Archives, 1888), Typescript.
OR	*The War of the Rebellion: A Compilation of the Official Records of the Union and Confederate Armies,* vol. 69 (Washington, D.C.: GPO, 1898)
PMGB	Provost Marshal General Bureau
RG	Record Group
RLP	Robert Todd Lincoln Papers, Library of Congress
SJ	*Journal of the Senate of the Commonwealth of Kentucky*
SPCP	Salmon P. Chase Papers, Library of Congress
USAMHRC	U. S. Army Military History Research Collection, Carlisle Barracks, Penna.
U.S. Statutes	*The Statutes At Large, Treaties, and Proclamations of the United States of America.*
WGP	William C. Goodloe Papers, University of Kentucky
WP	B. F. Wade Papers, Library of Congress

INTRODUCTION

1. Asa E. Martin, *The Anti-Slavery Movement in Kntucky Prior to 1850* (Louisville: Standard Printing, 1918), 18-48; Victor B. Howard, "The Kentucky Presbyterians in 1849: Slavery and the Kentucky Constitution," *Register of the Kentucky Historical Society*, vol. 73 (July 1975), 237-38; Victor B. Howard, "James Madison Pendleton: A Southern Crusader against Slavery," *Register of the Kentucky Historical Society*, vol. 74 (July 1976), 199-200. 2. Victor B. Howard, "Robert J. Breckinridge and the Slavery Controversy in Kentucky in 1849," *Filson Club History Quarterly*, vol. 53 (October 1979), 337-38. 3. Frank Mathias, "Kentucky's Third Constitution: A Restriction on Majority Rule," *Register of the Kentucky Historical Society*, vol. 75 (January 1977), 18. 4. *Debates and Proceedings of the Convention for the Revision of the Constitution of the State of Kentucky* (Frankfort, 1849), 857-58. 5. Victor B. Howard, "Lincoln's Slave Policy in Kentucky: A Study of Pragmatic Strategy," *Register of the Kentucky Historical Society*, vol. 80 (Summer 1982), 281-308.

6. Thomas Crittenden left Kentucky and settled in Missouri, becoming governor of that state in 1881. B. Gratz Brown left Kentucky and became one of the leaders in the movement for Negro suffrage in Missouri. John Palmer, Richard Yates, and Richard Oglesby left Kentucky and later served as governors of Illinois. Brown, Palmer, Yates, and Oglesby played important roles in the crusade for Negro rights during Reconstruction. 7. *U.S. Census, 1860: Agriculture of the United States in 1860, Eighth Census,* (Washington, D.C.: U.S. Government Printing Office, 1864), 227-45. 8. H. A. Thomas, Jr., "Victims of Circumstances: Negroes in a Southern Town, 1865-1880," *Register of the Kentucky Historical Society*, vol. 71 (July 1973), 266-68. 9. W. E. Woodward, *Meet General Grant* (New York: Liveright, 1928), 237.

CHAPTER ONE

1. Ulrich B. Phillips, "Racial Problems, Adjustments, and Disturbances," in Eugene Genovese, ed., *The Slave Economy of the Old South* (Baton Rouge: Louisiana State University Press, 1968), 60-61; Victor B. Howard, "John Brown's Raid on Harper's Ferry and the Sectional Crisis," *North Carolina Historical Review* (fall 1978), 397. 2. *American Missionary*, vol. 4 (February 1860), 32-33, 34, 37-43; [William L. Garrison], *The New "Reign of Terror" in the Slaveholding States, 1859-1860* (New York: American Anti-Slavery Society, 1860), 9. 3. Lewis Collins and Richard H. Collins, *History of Kentucky*, 2 vols. (Covington, Ky.: Collins, 1882), 1:84. 4. Amstead L. Robinson, "Day of Jubilo: Civil War and the Demise of Slavery" (Ph.D. diss., University of Rochester, 1976), 351. 5. James D. Richardson, ed., *A Compilation of the Messages and Papers of the Presidents, 1789-1908*, 11 vols. (Washington, D.C.: Bureau of National Literature and Art, 1909), 6:5.

6. Elijah P. Marrs, *The Life and History of the Reverend Elijah P. Marrs* (Louisville: Bradley and Gilbert, 1885), 16-17. 7. Allan Pinkerton, *Spy of the Rebellion, Being A True History of the Spy System of the United States Army* (New York: G. W. Carleton, 1883), 187; Letitia P. Wallace to Nelson Furnace, April 1, 1861, Edmund T. Halsey Collection, Filson Club Historical Society. 8. *Cincinnati Commercial*, October 2, 1861; *Louisville Democrat*, January 10, 1861. 9. *Cincinnati Gazette*, November 23, 1861; *Frankfort Yeoman*, January 17, 1862. 10. T. J. Wright, *History of the Eighth Regiment Kentucky Volunteer Infantry* (St. Joseph, Mo.: n.p., 1880), 42.

11. Chauncey Cook to Mother, April 10, 1863, "Letters of a Badger Boy in Blue," *Wisconsin Magazine of History*, vol. 4 (1920-21), 332; *Northwestern Christian Advocate*, May 27, 1863. 12. B. F. McGee, *History of the Seventy-second Indiana Volunteer Infantry of the Mounted Light Brigade* (Lafayette, Ind.: S. Water, 1882), 33; *Louisville Democrat*, November 17, 1861. 13. Alfred Pirtle, "My Early Soldiering Days," pp. 6-7, Alfred Pirtle Manuscripts, Filson Club Historical Society; P. S. Fall to Betty Fall, February 26, 1862, Philip S. Fall Manuscripts,

Kentucky Historical Society. 14. *Cincinnati Gazette,* November 9, 23, December 17, 1861; *Cincinnati Times,* January 18, 1862. 15. *Lexington Observer and Reporter,* December 25, 1861; Joseph W. Keifer, *Slavery and Four Years of War: A Political History of Slavery in the United States,* 2 vols. (New York: Putnam's, 1900), 1:241-43.

16. Benjamin P. Thomas, *Abraham Lincoln: A Biography* (New York: Random House, 1968), 275. 17. *New York Times,* September 28, 1861; Col. H. Engerud, "General Grant, Fort Donelson, and 'Old Brains,' " *Filson Club Historical Quarterly,* vol. 39 (July 1965), 201-202. 18. *Louisville Journal,* September 3, 1861; *New York Times,* September 7, 1861. 19. Garret Davis to S. P. Chase, September 3, 1861, SPCP; E. T. Bainbridge to Joseph Holt, September 10, 1861, JHP. 20. Gary Lee Williams, "James and Joshua Speed, Lincoln's Kentucky Friends" (Ph.D. diss., Duke University, 1971), p. 15; Joshua Speed to Abraham Lincoln, September 1, 3, 1861, RLP.

21. Joshua Speed to Joseph Holt, September 7, 1861, JHP. 22. Robert Anderson to Abraham Lincoln, September 13, 1861, in Basler, 4:532. 23. Abraham Lincoln to Beriah Magoffin, August 24, 1861, Lincoln to John Frémont, September 2, 11, 1861, Lincoln to O. H. Browning, September 22, 1861, in Basler, 4:497, 506, 531-33. 24. *Louisville Democrat,* September 10, 1861. 25. Lincoln to Frémont, September 11, 1861, in Frank Moore, *Rebellion Record* (New York: G. P. Putnam, 1864), 3:126.

26. Joseph Holt to Lincoln, September 12, 1861, Lincoln to Holt, September 12, 1861, Holt to James Speed, September 12, 1861, in *Cincinnati Gazette,* September 18, 1861. 27. Lincoln to O. H. Browning, September 22, 1866, in John Nicolay and John Hay, *Complete Works of Abraham Lincoln,* 12 vols. (Cumberland Gap, Tenn: Lincoln Memorial University, 1893-1894), 6:359. 28. *HJ* (September-October, 1861), September 13, 1861, pp. 101-102; T. S. Bell to Joseph Holt, September 19, 1861, JHP. 29. Victor B. Howard, "Lincoln's Slave Policy in Kentucky," in *Papers of the American Historical Association Convention, 1979* (Ann Arbor, Mich.: University Microfilms, 1980), p. 4. 30. Theodore C. Pease and James G. Randall, eds., *The Diary of Orville H. Browning,* 2 vols. (Springfield, Ill.: State Historical Library, 1925-33), 1:502 (September 24, 1861); O. H. Browning to Lincoln, September 17, 1861, RLP; Allan Nevins, *Frémont,* 2 vols. (New York: Harper, 1928), 2:574.

31. George Hoadley to S. P. Chase, September 18, 1861, SPCP. 32. Wilson P. Shortridge, "Kentucky Neutrality in 1861," *Mississippi Valley Historical Review* (March 1923), 298. 33. J. G. Randall, *Lincoln the President,* 4 vols. (New York: Dodd, Mead, 1945), 2:7. 34. Victor B. Howard, "The Civil War in Kentucky: The Slave Claims His Freedom," (Paper delivered at the annual meeting of the Association for the Study of Negro Life and History, New York, October, 1979), pp. 7-9, 12-15. 35. *New York Evening Post* (supplement), October 4, 1864; James R. Chumney, Jr., "Don Carlos Buell, Gentleman General" (Ph.D. diss., Rice University, 1964), 130.

36. *Frankfort Commonwealth,* November 22, 1861. 37. *Cincinnati Commercial,* December 10, 1861; *Boston Courier,* cited by *Louisville Journal,* December 18, 1861. 38. HJ (1861-63), 401. 39. *Cincinnati Gazette,* January 22, 1862. 40. *Kentucky Statesman,* August 9, 1861; speech of Robert Mallory, June 15, 1864, *Congressional Globe,* 38th Cong., 1st sess., 2981-82. 41. *U.S. Statutes* (1862) vol. 12, pp. 592, 599. 42. Basler, 4:332, 439; 5:49. 43. Herman Belz, *Emancipation and Equal Rights* (New York: Norton, 1978), 26; Basler, 5:144-46. 44. James G. Blaine, *Twenty Years of Congress: From Lincoln to Garfield,* 2 vols. (Norwich, Conn.: Henry Bill, 1884), 1:372-73. 45. *Louisville Journal,* cited by *Covington Journal,* March 1, 22, 1862; "Uncle Tom" to John Crittenden, May 8, 1862, JCP.

46. Nicolay and Hay, *Works of Lincoln,* 6:120-22. 47. Basler, 5:192. 48. Basler, 5:49, 145; Pease and Randall, eds., *Diary of Browning,* 1:541 (April 14, 1862); *Cincinnati Gazette,* April 23, 1862. 49. Basler, 5:222-23. 50. Basler, 5:318.

51. Basler, 5:357.

CHAPTER TWO

1. John H. Rerick, *The Forty-fourth Indiana Volunteer Infantry: History of Its Service* (La Grange, Ind.: By the author, 1880), 26.   2. F. W. Keil, *Thirty-fifth Ohio: A Narrative of Service from August 1861 to 1864* (Fort Wayne, Ind.: Archer, Housh, 1894), 3.   3. See: "L. H. Rousseau's Speech at Louisville Banquet," *Evansville Journal,* June 27, 1862; Rev. W. W. Lyle, *Lights and Shadows of Army Life* (Cincinnati: R. W. Carroll, 1865), 230; Keil, *Thirty-fifth Ohio,* 3.   4. Theodore C. Tracie, *Annals of the Nineteenth Ohio Battery Volunteer Artillery; Second Division, Twenty-third Army Corps* (Cleveland: J. B. Savage, 1878), 73.   5. Keil, *Thirty-fifth Ohio,* 3; Col. H. B. Reed, "Personal Recollections," in Rerick, ed., *Forty-fourth Indiana,* 217. For a good description of how curiosity drew the slaves to the army camps when the camps were established, see Albion W. Tourgee, *The Story of a Thousand, Being a History of the Service of the 105th Ohio Volunteer Infantry Regiment* (Buffalo: S. McGerald, 1865), 72.
6. Gen. Gordon Granger to Gov. James F. Robinson, November 22, 1862, RG 393, Ky., NA.   7. Cited in *National Anti-Slavery Standard,* January 18, March 1, 1862.   8. Diary of Capt. Oliver Lyman Spaulding, December 25, 1862, University of Michigan Historical Collection. A correspondent for the *Cincinnati Commercial* reported on December 2, 1861, that there was only one "native abolitionist" in the Second Ohio Division commanded by Gen. Alexander M. McCook. Similar statements were made by a considerable number of the authors of regimental histories. Benjamin P. Thomas and Harold M. Hyman, *Stanton: The Life and Times of Lincoln's Secretary of War* (New York: Knopf, 1962), 230; Keil, *Thirty-fifth Ohio,* 3.   9. Mingo P. Murray to Parents, October 21, 1861, Mingo P. Murray Collection, Twentieth Ohio Regiment, USAMHRC.   10. Keil, *Thirty-fifth Ohio,* 4.
11. John Beatty, *The Citizen Soldier Or Memoirs of a Volunteer* (Cincinnati: Wilstach and Company, 1879), 84.   12. Judson L. Austin to Family, November 15, 1862, Judson L. Austin Civil War Letter, University of Michigan Historical Collection; Rev. Thomas M. Stevenson, *History of the Seventy-eighth Regiment, Ohio Veteran Volunteer Infantry* (Zanesville, Ohio: Hugh Dunne, 1865), 187; Henry Clemons to Wife, October 12, 1862, Henry Clemons Civil War Letters to His Wife, Wisconsin State Historical Society.   13. Eben P. Sturges, Battery B, First Ohio Artillery Regiment, Diary, October 1, 1862, to March 12, 1863, vol. 1, October 21, 1862, USAMHRC.   14. Diary of Alfred Glapin II, vol. 2, March 28, 1862, Alfred Glapin Family Papers, Wisconsin State Historical Library; Warren Gray Diary, November 11, 1862, Wisconsin State Historical Library.   15. Theodore C. Blegen, *The Civil War Letters of Colonel Hans Christian Heg* (Northfield, Minn.: Norwegian-American Historical Association, 1936), 79.
16. Abram Piatt Andrew III to A. P. Andrew, Jr., October 24, 1862, in Abram Piatt Andrew III, *Some Civil War Letters* (Gloucester, Mass.: Privately published, 1925), 27; John J. Hardin to John Hardin (Father), February 17, 1862, Civil War Letter of John J. Hardin, Indiana Historical Society.   17. Ralph E. Kiene, Jr., *The Journal of Francis A. Kiene, 1861-1864* (Kansas City, Mo.: Privately published, 1974), 36; Thomas E. Shepherd to Cousin Lessie, October 21, 1862, Thomas E. Shepherd Papers, Indiana Historical Society; Keil, *Thirty-fifth Ohio,* 3; Robinson, "Day of Jubilo," 375, 450; Josephine Covington to Father, March 2, 1862, Josephine Wells Covington Manuscripts, Filson Club Historical Society; Marion B. Butler, *My Story of the Civil War and the Underground Railroad* (Huntington, Ind.: United Brethren, 1914), 61-62; Alexander Smith to Andrew Johnson, June 27, August 18, 1862, Andrew Johnson Papers, University of Tennessee; Reed, "Personal Recollections," 218.   18. *National Anti-Slavery Standard,* January 18, 1862.   19. Basler, 5:329.   20. Braxton Bragg's decision to invade Kentucky was influenced by the intelligence that Kentucky was ripe for rebellion because of congressional measures and by Lincoln's proposal for border-state emancipation with compensation.
21. W. H. Bentley, *History of the Seventy-seventh Illinois Volunteer Infantry, September 2, 1862, to July 10, 1865* (Peoria: Edward Hine, 1883), 103.   22. Lysander Wheeler to Parents,

October 5, 1862, Lysander Wheeler Correspondence, Illinois State Historical Society; Charles A. Harper to W. G. Harper, May 24, 1864, Charles A. Harper Correspondence, Indiana Historical Library; Stevenson, *Seventy-eighth Ohio,* 186. 23. Frank McGregor to Susie, November 12, 1862, Frank McGregor Papers, Eighty-third Kentucky Infantry Regiment, USAMHRC. No Kentucky regiment became a haven for fugitive slaves. The Eighth and the Twenty-third Kentucky infantry regiments served in the state several months without taking slaves into their camps. In April 1862, while stationed in Tennessee, the Eighth Kentucky Infantry was in need of a cook but refrained from hiring one of the fugitive slaves who came into the camp, as suggested by the commander of the Ninth Michigan Infantry Regiment. See Thomas L. Wright, *History of the Eighth Regiment, Kentucky Volunteer Infantry, during Its Three Years of Campaigns* (St. Joseph, Mo.: St. Joseph Steam Press, 1880), 50. 24. *Louisville Democrat,* August 28, 1862. 25. George S. Bradley, *The Star Corps; or Notes of an Army Chaplain during Sherman's Famous "March to the Sea"* (Milwaukee: Jermain and Brightman, 1865), 66; Paul M. Angle, ed., *Three Years in the Army of the Cumberland: The Letters and Diary of Major James A. Connolly* (Bloomington: Indiana University Press, 1959), 27. Early in October 1862 a poll was taken in the 104th Illinois Infantry Regiment to determine how the soldiers viewed the president's Emancipation Proclamation. The proclamation was read to every company before the vote was taken. The troops supported the president's proclamation by more than 20 to 1; see *Ottawa* (Illinois) *Republican,* October 18, November 1, 1862.

26. G. Clay Smith to Moses Wisner, October 19, 1862, General Orders No. 2, William C. Russell, January 5, 1863, OR, 1, vol. 52, pt. 1, pp. 292, 319; Robert Steele to Wife, October 12, 1862, Civil War Correspondence of Robert Steele, Wisconsin State Historical Society: Marc Mundy to Abraham Lincoln, November 27, 1862, in NMSUS, 2:649; Collins and Collins, *History of Kentucky,* 1:117; Randolph C. Downes, ed., "The Civil War Diary of Fernando E. Pomeroy," *Northwest Ohio Quarterly,* vol. 19, no. 3 (July 1947), 135; Judson L. Austin to Family, November 15, 1862, Judson L. Austin Civil War Letters. 27. *Lexington Observer and Reporter,* December 17, 20, 24, 1862; *Cincinnati Enquirer,* December 24, 1862; *Louisville Journal,* December 19, 1862; H. G. Wright to Gordon Granger, December 14, 1862, *Cincinnati Commercial,* December 16, 29, 1862; D. C. Wickliffe, William Bryan, and John B. Johnson to Gordon Granger, December 11, 1862, RG 393, Ohio, NA, OR, 1, vol. 20, pt. 21, 177-78; *Louisville Democrat,* November 23, 1862. 28. H. G. Wright to H. W. Halleck, November 23, 1862; Halleck to Wright, November 24, 1862, in NMSUS, 2:647; OR, 1, vol. 20, pt. 2, p. 91. In his preliminary emancipation proclamation of September 22, 1862, Lincoln quoted from the articles of war of March 13 and the Confiscation Act of July 17, 1862, and ordered "all persons engaged in the military and naval service of the United States to observe, obey, and enforce, within their respective spheres of service" the laws cited. See Basler, 5:434-35. 29. Orders No. 5, October 15, 1862, in Levi Coffin, *Reminiscences of Levi Coffin* (New York: Arno Press, 1968), 611; Harvey Reid to Sister, October 16, 1862, in Frank Byrne, *The View from Headquarters: Civil War Letters of Harvey Reid* (Madison: State Historical Society of Wisconsin, 1965), 9-10; General Orders No. 9, Q. A. Gillmore, October 22, 1862, OR, 1, vol. 20, pt. 2, p. 162. 30. H. C. Wright to H. W. Halleck, December 12, 1862, in NMSUS, 2:694.

31. *Lexington Observer and Reporter,* October 29, 1862; "H.K." to Editor, *Chicago Tribune,* December 2, 1862; *Racine Advocate,* cited by *Boston Liberator,* December 5, 1862; *Cleveland Leader,* cited by *New York Tribune,* November 24, 1862; *Monroe Sentinel* and *Janesville Gazette and the Press,* cited by *National Anti-Slavery Standard,* November 15, December 16, 1862; Bradley, *The Star Corps,* 66, 76; *Lexington Observer and Reporter,* October 29, 1862.

32. William H. McIntosh, "History of the Twenty-second Wisconsin Volunteers," manuscript in Wisconsin State Historical Library, p. 9; James F. Robinson to Gordon Granger, November 22, 1862, Granger to Robinson, November 22, 1862, RG, 393, Ky., NA; Howard K. Beale, ed., *The Diary of Gideon Welles,* 3 vols. (New York: Norton, 1960), 1:1, 199

(December 20, 1862); *Louisville Journal,* December 11, 1862; Q. A. Gillmore to M. R. Keith, December 2, 1862, OR, 1, vol. 20, pt. 2, pp. 162-63.   33. George Robertson to A. Lincoln, November 19, 1862, RLP; Lincoln to Robertson, November 20, 1862, in Basler, 5:502; Col. William Utley to Abraham Lincoln, November 17, 1862, RLP; Diary of Charles H. Dickinson, October 23, 1862, Wisconsin State Historical Library; George Robertson to J. J. Crittenden, November 26, 1862, JCP; William L. Utley to Abraham Lincoln, November 19, 1862, RLP; Abraham Lincoln to George Robertson, November 26, 1862, in Basler, 5:512; John R. McBride, *History of the Thirty-third Indiana Veteran Volunteer Infantry* (Indianapolis: William R. Burford, 1900), 41-42, 69.   34. George Robertson to J. J. Crittenden, November 26, 1862, JCP. The trial was later canceled.   35. *Chicago Tribune,* November 12, 1862; "Union" to Editor, *Cincinnati Commercial,* November 17, 1862; "True Loyalty" to Editor, *Cincinnati Commercial,* November 26, 1862; *Ninety-second Illinois Volunteers* (Freeport, Ill.: Journal Steam, 1875), 38-40, 43.

36. *Louisville Democrat,* November 23, 1862.   37. John D. Brent to Alexander C. Semple, November 28, 1862, RG 393, Ohio, NA.   38. Daniel Wait Howe, *Civil War Times, 1861-1865* (Indianapolis: Bowen-Merrill, 1902), 73; *History of the Seventy-third Indiana Volunteers in the War of 1861-1865* (Washington, D.C.: Canahan Press, 1909), 105; Sanford A. Michael, "History of the 101st Regiment of Volunteer Infantry of Indiana by Levi P. Fodrea," typescript, Indiana State Library; Ormond Hupp, *My Diary* (New Albany, Ind.: Privately published, 18h3), 10, 19; O. H. Morgan and E. R. Murphy, *History of the Seventh Independent Battery, Indiana Light Artillery, War of the Rebellion, 1861 to 1865* (Indianapolis: Press of the Democrat, 1898), 11; D. D. Holm, *History of the Fifth Indiana Battery* (Indianapolis: Smith Cook, 1928), 19; William S. Dodge, *History of the Old Second Division, Army of the Cumberland* (Chicago: Church and Goodman, 1864), 335; William H. Doll, *History of the Sixth Regiment Indiana Volunteer Infantry in the Civil War* (Columbus, Ind.: Republican, 1903), 35-36; Civil War Diary of Robert Perry Hoge, October 3-4, 1862, Chicago Historical Society; Loren J. Morse, *Civil War Diaries of Bliss Morse* (Pittsburg, Kans. Pittcraft, 1964), 19.   39. Asa Walker Slayton Civil War Journal, November 30, 1862, Univesity of Michigan Historical Collection.   40. *Louisville Journal,* November 19, 20, 21, 1862; *Louisville Democrat,* November 21, 1862, cited by *Cincinnati Enquirer,* November 22, 1862; Robert Emmett McDowell, *City of Conflict: Louisville in the Civil War, 1861-1865* (Louisville: Civil War Round Table, 1942), 127.

41. *National Anti-Slavery Standard,* December 13, 1862; *Lexington Observer and Reporter,* December 6, 1862; *Louisville Journal,* December 3, 1862.   42. *Louisville Journal,* November 17, 19, 1862.   43. *Chicago Tribune,* February 9, 1863.   44. *National Anti-Slavery Standard,* December 13, 1862; Collins and Collins, *History of Kentucky,* 1:116; *New York Tribune,* November 29, 1862.   45. *Ninety-second Illinois Volunteers,* 65; Partridge, *History of the Ninety-sixth Regiment, Illinois Volunteer Infantry,* 91-92; Diary of Charles H. Dickerson, February 1, 2, 1863, Wisconsin State Historical Society; William H. McIntosh, p. 15; Harvey Reid to Sister, February 2, 1863, in Byrne, *The View from Headquarters,* 23-24; Bradley, *The Star Corps,* 77-78.

46. *Chicago Tribune,* February 9, 1863. Col. Lyman Guinnip, of the Seventy-ninth Illinois Volunteers, was indicted in October 1862 for aiding slaves to escape. Lincoln tried to intercede in his favor through civil channels in 1863, but the case was settled by a forfeiture of bond. See Abraham Lincoln to Joshua F. Speed, March 17, 1863, in Basler 6:140.   47. William L. Utley to Alexander W. Randall, November 17, 1862, RLP; William R. Hartpence, *History of the Fifty-first Indiana Infantry Regiment* (Cincinnati: Robert Clarke, 1894), 26-27; James S. Negley to Don Carlos Buell, March 9, 1862, James B. Fry to Gen. Lorenzo Thomas, December 22, 1861, OR, 1, vol. 7, p. 510; Thomas and Hyman, *Stanton,* 233.   48. Diary of Oliver Lyman Spaulding, November 4, 1862; Asa Walker Slayton Civil War Journal, December 5, 1862; Civil War Diary of William Boston, April 15, 1863, University of Michigan

Historical Collection; Downes, ed., "The Civil War Diary of Fernando E. Pomeroy," 144;
49. Nicolay and Hay, *Works of Lincoln*, 8:122.   50. Basler, 5:223, 318; James M. McPherson,
The Struggle for Equality: Abolitionists and the Negro in the Civil War and Reconstruction
(Princeton, N.J.: Princeton University Press, 1964), 82.

CHAPTER THREE

1. George Bancroft to Lincoln, November 15, 1861, RLP; Basler, 5:26.   2. John Jay to
Charles Sumner, July 4, 16, 1862, CSP; Jay to S. P. Chase, July 3, 1862, SPCP.   3. *Boston
Advertiser*, August 20, 1862; John Sherman to William T. Sherman, August 24, 1862, William
T. Sherman Papers, LC; Rachel Sherman Thorndike, *The Sherman Letters: Correspondence
between General Sherman and Senator Sherman from 1837 to 1891* (1894; reprinted., New York:
da Capo Press, 1969), 156   4. George W. Julian, *Political Recollections, 1840-1872* (1884;
reprint ed., New York: Negro Universities Press, 1970), 227; Basler 5:317-19, 336-37, *New
York Tribune*, July 19, 1862.   5. James Speed to Abraham Lincoln, July 28, 1862, RLP.

6. Julian, *Political Recollections*, 227. Joshua Speed was probably correct in recalling in 1866
that Lincoln foresaw the necessity of the proclamation "long before he issued it, but was still
anxious to avoid it, and came to it only when he saw that the measures would subtract from the
labor and add to the 'army quite a number of good fighting men' "; Joshua Speed to William
Herndon, February 6, 1866, HWC; Cassius M. Clay, *The Life of Cassius Marcellus Clay:
Memoirs, Writings, and Speeches* (Cincinnati: J. F. Brennon, 1886), p. 310.   7. Beale, ed., *Diary
of Gideon Welles*, 1:71.   8. Benjamin Quarles, *The Negro in the Civil War* (Boston: Little,
Brown, 1953), xi, 132. William E. B. Du Bois, *Black Reconstruction in America* (1935; reprint
ed., New York: by Atheneum, 1962), 62, 66-67, 121. Herman Belz, *A New Birth of Freedom*
(Westport, Conn.: Greenwood, 1976), 6; Basler, 5:329; Narrative of Mrs. Hattie Cash,
Muncie, Indiana (Indiana Narratives), in Federal Writers Project, *Slave Narratives: A Folk
History of Slavery in the United States: From Interviews with Former Slaves, 1936-1938*, 19 vols.
(Westport, Conn.: Greenwood, 1973), 6:99; see T. H. Jones to Father, March 16, 1863, for
an example of the John Brown marching songs; Tighlman H. Jones Correspondence, Uni-
versity of Illinois. *Chicago Tribune*, January 1, 1863; Francis B. Carpenter, *The Inner Life of
Abraham Lincoln: Six Months at the White House* (Boston: Houghton Mifflin, 1894), 20-21;
Basler, 5:531.   9. Blaine, *Twenty Years of Congress*, 1:369.   10. George Candee to Abraham
Lincoln, September 8, 1862, AMA Correspondence, Amistad Library.

11. John Fee to S. S. Jocelyn, October 3, 1862, AMA Correspondence; William Mobley to
Secretaries, December 1, 1862, *American Missionary*, vol. 8 (February 1863), 37.   12. By
January 1863 a newspaper to express the views and advocate the policy of the emancipationists
had been started by several Michigan regiments stationed at Lebanon, Kentucky. The paper
also argued for the enlistment of blacks. See *Washington Morning Chronicle*, January 21, 1863.
13. T. S. Bell to Joseph Holt, December 22, 1862, JHP; "Junius" to Editor, October 27,
1862, *New York Tribune*, October 30, 1862.   14. W. B. Campbell to Andrew Johnson,
November 2, 1862, Andrew Johnson Papers, LC.   15. *Louisville Journal*, October 3, 1862.

16. Anonymous to Editor, *New York Evening Post*, November 14, 1862, cited by *Chicago
Tribune*, November 19, 1862; *New York Tribune*, October 3, 30, November 24, 1862; Basler,
5:504.   17. Rerick, *The Forty-fourth Indiana Regiment*, 87; Joseph Scroggs Diary, 104 Ohio
Inf. Reg. October 1, 1862, USAMHRC.   18. R. H. Earnest to J. H. Earnest, November 17,
1862, R. H. Earnest Manuscripts, Kentucky Historical Society.   19. John W. Ford to Family,
December 14, 1862, Seventh Kentucky Infantry Regiment, 1862-63, USAMHRC.   20. Col.
W. F. Evans to Gen. C. W. Foster, RG 393, Ky., NA; Jac H. Stokes to Lyman Trumbull,
November 17, 1862, Lyman Trumbull Papers, Library of Congress; C. C. Gilbert to J. T.
Boyle, December 21, 1862, RG 393, Ohio, NA.

21. Basler, 5:435; James G. Randall, *Constitutional Problems under Lincoln* (Urbana:
University of Illinois Press, 1951), 357-64. *U.S. Statutes at Large*, vol. 13, 200.   22. *New York
Tribune*, November 14, 1862; General Orders No. 139, September 24, 1862 (a helpful index

of general orders is housed at USAMHRC). 23. *Louisville Journal,* December 18, 1862; *New York Tribune,* November 14, 1862; William B. Campbell to Andrew Johnson, November 2, 1862, Andrew Johnson Papers; Special Orders, John McHenry, Jr., October 27, 1862, Andrew Johnson Papers, University of Tennessee. 24. *Louisville Journal,* January 7, 1862; *Lexington Observer and Reporter,* December 13, 16, 18, 1862; *Frankfort Tri-Weekly Commonwealth,* December 15, 1863. 25. Collins and Collins, *History of Kentucky,* 1:116; *Louisville Journal,* November 19, 1862; *New York Tribune,* November 13, 1862; *Elyria Independent Democrat*(Ohio), February 18, 1863.

26. Felix G. Stidger, *Treason History of the Order and Sons of Liberty* (Chicago: By the author, 1903), 24-25; S. F. Horrall, *History of the Forty-second Indiana Volunteer Infantry* (Chicago: By the author, 1892), 183-84; Beatty, *The Citizen Soldier,* 223, 224-25, 184. 27. Narrative of Mrs. Mary Crane (Indiana narratives), in *Slave Narratives,* 6:10; *New York Tribune,* October 30, 1862; *Lexington Observer and Reporter,* November 26, 1862; *Louisville Journal,* December 1, 1862. 28. Josephus Lunette to Benjamin Yeager, December 8, 1862, Josephus Lunette Manuscripts, Filson Club Library; Anonymous to Editor, *New York Tribune,* cited by *National Anti-Slavery Standard,* November 29, 1862; M. U. Samuel to Thomas S. Page, RG 393, Ky., NA; *Louisville Journal,* cited by *National Anti-Slavery Standard,* December 27, 1862. 29. Basler, 5:527, 529-30. 30. *Danville Quarterly Review,* vol. 2 (December 1862), 671, 709; *Cincinnati Commercial,* February 5, 1863; Robert L. Stanton, *The Church and the Rebellion* (1864; reprint ed., Freeport, N.Y.: Books for Libraries Press, 1971), 358.

31. *Lexington Observer and Reporter,* December 6, 1862. 32. Diary of John Jones, January 31, 1863, JJP; Jesse Kincheloe to Joseph Holt, January 18, 1863, JHP; H. C. Wright to H. W. Halleck, December 30, 1862, OR, 1, vol. 20, pt. 2, p. 282; Halleck to Wright, January 5, 1863, "The Negro in the Military Service of U.S.," memorandum, NMSUS, 3, pt. 2:1896. 33. W. Davenport to Joseph Holt, January 8, 10, 1863, JHP; W. G. Brownlow to Montgomery Blair, January 9, 1863, BFP. 34. SJ (1861-63), January 8, 1863, pp. 723-724; HJ (1861-63), January 8, 1863, pp. 1123-24; *Washington National Intelligencer,* January 10, 1863. 35. Goodloe to Green Adams, January 25, 1863, G. M. Adams to Green Adams, February 12, 1863, RLP.

36. John W. Finnell to John J. Crittenden, January 26, February 3, 1863, JCP; *Cincinnati Gazette,* January 28, 29, 1863; *Cincinnati Commercial,* January 26, 1863. 37. *Cincinnati Commercial,* March 5, 1863; *Tri-Weekly Commonwealth,* January 24, 1863; *Kentucky Yeoman,* May 15, 1863. 38. *Louisville Journal,* April 6, 1863; *Acts of Kentucky* (1863), 391-93; *Cincinnati Gazette,* March 3, 1863; *Evansville Journal* March 2, 1863; *HJ* (1863), 1398, 1551, 1557; SJ (1863), 959-60. 39. Joseph C. Breckinridge to Robert J. Breckinridge, January 25, 1863, BP; T.S. Bell to Joseph Holt, March 16, 1863, JHP; R.H. Earnest to James H. Earnest, April 2, 1863, R. H. Earnest Manuscripts. 40. Special Orders No. 59, Brig. Gen. M. D. Manson, February 9, 1863, University of Michigan Historical Collection; Adj. C. Montgomery to Maj. Gen. William Roscans, February 19, 1863, Austin Blair Papers, Detroit Public Library; Chauncey Cook to Parents, March 10, 1863, "Letters of a Badger Boy in Blue," 324, 325, 327, 328; Diary of Oliver L. Spaulding, February 19, 1863, March 5, 7, 1863; "F" (James Fidler) to Editor, *Cincinnati Commercial,* April 22, 1863; Original Military Records Written by Colonel Orlando Hurley Moore, p. 6, U.S. Army, Twenty-Fifth Michigan Infantry, University of Michigan Historical Collection.

41. Edmund Kirke, *Down in Tennessee and Back by Way of Richmond* (New York: Carleton, 1864), 13-14; Stanley Matthews to Wife, January 23, 1863, Civil War Letters of Stanley Matthews, Cincinnati Historical Society; W. H. Ripley to M. E. Foley, July 9, 1864, M. E. Foley Letters, Indiana State Library. 42. Bell I. Wiley, *The Life of Billy Yank* (Indianapolis: Bobbs-Merrill, 1952), 40. Professor Wiley does not document his statement but refers the reader to a later chapter on slavery and the Negro which contains no discussion of emancipation. 43. *Frankfort Tri-Weekly Commonwealth,* February 21, 1863. The *Louisville Journal* agreed with the *Commonwealth.* 44. *Frankfort Tri-Weekly Commonwealth,* February 13, 1863.

45. Collins and Collins, *History of Kentucky,* 1:119; *Cincinnati Gazette,* February 18, 1863.

46. *Cincinnati Gazette,* February 18, 1863; Collins and Collins, *History of Kentucky,* 1:119. Before adjourning the convention, Gilbert spoke briefly and informed the delegates that he would not permit them to carry out their purpose of "opposing and disorganizing the plans of the administration for suppressing this rebellion." See Joseph J. Scroggs Diary, February 18, 1863. 47. Jesse W. Fell to F. Price, February 18, 1863, RLP; C. M. Clay to Editor, *New York Times,* February 26, 1863, p. 4; *New York Tribune,* February 26, 1863. 48. *Louisville Democrat,* February 27, March 8, 1863; *Louisville Journal,* March 3 to April 7, 1863. 49. John G. Fee to Editor, September 10, 1863, *American Missionary,* vol. 7 (1863), 253-54; William Mobley to S. S. Jocelyn, January 26, 1863, AMA Correspondence. 50. *Louisville Journal,* April 6, 1863; W. G. Brownlow to Montgomery Blair, March 25, 1865, BFP.

51. *Cincinnati Commercial,* July 7, 1863; *Frankfort Commonwealth,* July 7, 8, 1863; *Louisville Democrat* July 4, 7, 22, 25, 1863. 52. *Louisville Journal* April 9, 1863; *New York Times,* August 12, 1863; *Cincinnati Commercial,* April 18, 21, 1863. 53. McPherson, *History of the Rebellion,* 313; *New York Times,* May 16, 1863; *New York Tribune Almanac* (1864), 59; Collins and Collins, *History of Kentucky,* 1:128. For charges of interference in the election by the army, see *Louisville Democrat,* the organ of the Peace Democrats of Kentucky, for August 8 and 9, 1863. 54. "A Kentuckian" to Editor, *New York Times,* February 17, 1863; T. S. Bell to Joseph Holt, February 8, 1863, JHP; John W. Finnell to John J. Crittenden, January 26, 1863, JCP. 55. *Louisville Journal,* May 7, 1863; *SJ* (1863), 849. *HJ* (1863), 1009; *Acts of Kentucky* (1863), 362-64; J. T. Boyle to Selby Harney, December 9, 1862, RG 393, Ky., NA.

56. Joseph Holt to E. M. Stanton, April 24, 1863; Stanton to A. E. Burnside, April 29, 1863, H. W. Halleck to Burnside, April 29, 1863, Joseph Holt to E. M. Stanton, April 29, 1863, RG 94, Generals' Papers, NA; E. M. Stanton to A. E. Burnside, April 29, 1863, OR, 1 vol. 23, pt. 2, p. 291. 57. General Orders No. 53, Gen. A. E. Burnside, April 28, 1863, OR, 1, vol. 23, pt. 2, p. 287. External evidence seems to indicate that Burnside's orders may have been published after he received the orders from the War Department rather than the day before. 58. Pete Baily to A. E. Burnside, April 19, 1863, RG 94, Generals' Papers, NA; J. T. Boyle to Marc Murray, May 3, 1863, RG 393, Ohio, NA. 59. Testimony of Maj. D. C. Fitch and Capt. M. H. Jewett, Commissioners, American Freedmen's Inquiry Commission, File No. 7, Testimony Taken in Kentucky, Tennessee, and Missouri, 1863, pp. 20-22, RG 94, NA; *New York Tribune,* September 28, 1863.

CHAPTER FOUR

1. *U.S. Statutes at Large,* vol. 12, 592, 599; Mary Berry, *Military Necessity and Civil Rights Policy* (Port Washington, N.Y.: Kennikat, 1977), 41-42. 2. Charles S. Standiff to Major Selby Harney, January 8, 1862; C. C. Hare to Major Harney, March 3, 1862, RG 393, Ky., NA; Bruce Catton, *Grant Moves South* (Boston: Little, Brown, 1960), 294; J. C. Morton to W. H. Sidell, August 13, 1862, RG 393, Ohio, NA; "Mack" to Editor, *Cincinnati Commercial,* August 26, 1862. 3. *Evansville Journal,* August 29, 1862; *Cincinnati Gazette,* September 5, 1862; *Cincinnati Commercial,* September 15, 1862, cited by *Chicago Tribune,* September 16, 1862; *New York Tribune,* September 12, 26, 1862. 4. *New York Tribune,* September 3, 1862; H. G. Wright to J. T. Boyle, September 4, 1862, OR, 1, vol. 16, 480; *New York Times,* August 30, 1862. 5. John Brough to E. M. Stanton, August 8, 1862, NMSUS, 2:579; *New York Tribune,* December 13, 1862.

6. Provost Marshal Headquarters, Louisville, May 9, 1863, to PMGB, RG 110, Ky., NA. 7. James Guthrie to J. T. Boyle, March 2, 1863, RG 393, Ky., NA. 8. James Guthrie to J. T. Boyle, March 2, 1863, RG 393, A. C. Ky., NA; A.C. Simple to Henry Dent, March 3, 1863, RG 393, Ky., NA; J. K. Frick to Gen. Alexander Asboth, April 11, 1863, Asboth to Gen. S. A. Harlbut, April 12, 1863, RG 94, Ky., NA. 9. Collins and Collins, *History of Kentucky,* 1:95;

Diary of John Jones, March 25, June 20, July 31, 1863, JJP; Q. A. Gillmore to H. G. Wright, March 25, 1863, NMSUS, vol. 3, pt. 2, p. 1919; Diary of William M. Pratt, March 30, 1863, University of Kentucky Special Collections; *National Anti-Slavery Standard,* April 11, 1863. 10. *Congressional Globe,* 38th Cong., 1st sess., pt. 1, pp. 598-602, 677-78.

11. John Finnell to John J. Crittenden, January 26, 1863, JCP; *Congressional Globe,* 37th Cong., 3rd sess., pt. 2, appendix, pp. 73, 75; *Frankfort Commonwealth,* May 18, 1863; Allen E. Ragan, "John H. Crittenden, 1787-1863," *Filson Club Historical Quarterly,* vol. 18 (January 1944), p. 26. 12. *Chicago Tribune,* February 7, 1863. 13. *Congressional Globe,* 37th Cong., 3rd sess., pp. 282, 690, 695, 924; Dudley T. Cornish, *Sable Arm: Negro Troops in the Union Army, 1861-1865* (New York: Norton, 1966), 99. 14. John Boyle to John P. Usher, March 14, 1863, RLP; *National Anti-Slavery Standard,* June 6, 1863, Provost Marshal, Paducah, Kentucky, to Joseph M. James, June 16, 1863, Joseph M. James Papers, University of Kentucky; W. H. Sidell to District Provost Marshals, June 23, 1863, RG 110, Ky., NA.
15. J. T. Boyle to J. B. Fry, June 25, 1863, OR, 3, vol. 3, p. 416. The census of 1860 showed that Kentucky had 236,167 slaves. See U.S. Bureau of Census, *Negro Population, 1790-1915* (Washington, D.C.: U.S. Government Printing Office, 1915), 57. J. T. Boyle to Abraham Lincoln, June 26, 1863, RLP; J. B. Fry to J. T. Boyle, June 26, 1863, OR, 3, vol. 3, pp. 418-19; J. B. Fry to William H. Sidell, June 26, 1863, RG 393, Ky., NA.
16. A. E. Burnside to Abraham Lincoln, June 26, 1863, RLP; Abraham Lincoln to J. T. Boyle, June 28, 1863, Lincoln to A. E. Burnside, June 28, 1863, in Basler, 6:298-99.
17. A. E. Burnside to Abraham Lincoln, OR, 3, vol. 3, pp. 419-20; Lincoln to Edwin M. Stanton, June 28, 1863, in Basler, 6:299; vol. 3, pt. 1, (1863), 1350. 18. J. T. Boyle to James B. Fry, July 4, 1863, W. C. Grier to W. H. Sidell, July 30, 1863, Bland Ballard to Lincoln, July 8, 1863, RG 110, Ky., NA. 19. Collins and Collins, *History of Kentucky,* 1:126; *Frankfort Commonwealth,* July 8, 1863. 20. *Frankfort Commonwealth,* September 2, 1863; *National Anti-Slavery Standard,* August 1, 1863.
21. Lorenzo Thomas to A. E. Burnside, August 5, 1863, OR, 3, vol. 3, p. 630. 22. Henry Stone to W. H. Sidell, July 22, 1863, RG 110, Ky., NA; G. M. Sane to Sub-district, July 27, 1863, RG 110, Ky., NA; Diary of Frances D. Peter, October 19, 1863, EFP; Thomas E. Bramlette to Abraham Lincoln, October 19, 1863, RLP. 23. *Frankfort Commonwealth,* November 18, 1863. 24. E. M. Stanton to Lincoln, October 1, 1863, NMSUS, 5:1642-44; General Order No. 329, October 3, 1863, provided for recruiting of blacks. The order was listed as confidential and was not filed with the general series. *Louisville Journal,* October 27, 1863. 25. *U.S. Statutes,* (1863) vol. 12, p. 731; Jack Franklin Leach, *Conscription in the United States: Historical Background* (Rutland, Vt.: Charles E. Tuttle, 1952), 398; General Orders No. 41, August 10, 1863, RG 393, Ky., NA; *Louisville Journal,* August 13, 1863; Collins and Collins, *History of Kentucky,* 1:128; Diary of Frances D. Peter, October 10, 1863, EFP; Diary of John Jones, August 31, 1863, JJP.
26. *Louisville Journal,* September 17, October 3, 1863. 27. *Louisville Journal,* October 28, 29, 1863. 28. "Jalrey" to Editor, December 21, 1863, *Cincinnati Enquirer,* December 25, 1863. 29. Collins and Collins, *History of Kentucky,* 1:95; Louis DeFalaise, "General Stephen Gano Burbridge's Command in Kentucky," *Register of the Kentucky Historical Society,* vol. 69 (April 1971), 106-107; Diary of John Jones, August 31, 1863, JJP; *Cincinnati Enquirer,* February 4, 1864. 30. Thomas E. Bramlette to Capt. Edward Cahill, December 14, 1863; *Cincinnati Enquirer,* January 21, 1864.
31. Thomas E. Bramlette to J. T. Boyle, January 13, 1864, *Louisville Journal,* January 20, 1864; Collins and Collins, *History of Kentucky,* 1:130; Robert McBeath to T. R. McBeath, February 1, 1864, Thomas Robert McBeath Papers, University of Kentucky; *Cincinnati Commercial,* January 9, 1864. 32. *Louisville Journal,* February 1, 1864; *Lexington Observer and Reporter,* February 13, 1864. 33. "An Old Kentuckian" to Editor, December 17, 1863, *Louisville Journal,* December 22, 1863; B. H. Bristow, C. F. Burnam, and George H. Yeaman to E. M. Stanton, December 19, 1863, OR, 3, vol. 3, pp. 1174-75. 34. E. H. Hopper and

others to Thomas E. Bramlette, January 23, 1864, B. F. Bristow to T. E. Bramlette, January, 1864, Papers of Gov. Thomas E. Bramlette, Kentucky Historical Society. A letter to the *Nashville Times* reported that hundreds of slaves, both male and female, were fleeing from Southern Kentucky. In one neighborhood three farmers alone lost $100,000 worth of slave property. See *Nashville Times and True Union,* February 22, 1864.   35. "Loyal Citizen," January 23, February 1, 1864; "J.S.W." to Editor, February 1, 1864, *Louisville Journal,* February 1, 2, 1864.

36. *Frankfort Commonwealth,* December 8, 1863; HJ (1863-64), 23, 26.   37. *New York Tribune,* February 23, 1864; *National Anti-Slavery Standard,* March 5, 1864; T. S. Bell to Joseph Holt, February 8, 1863, JHP; *American Annual Cyclopedia and Register of Important Events,* 4 (1864): 447.   38. T. E. Bramlette to Abraham Lincoln, February 1, 1864, RLP.

39. John Vincent, Jr., "Slavery amidst Civil War in Tennessee: The Death of an Institution" (Ph.D. diss., Ohio State University, 1977), 77; Lorenzo Thomas to Edwin M. Stanton, February 1, 1864, NMSUS, 4:2345-46, RG 94, Ky., NA.   40. John Boyle to James B. Fry, April 5, 1864, RG 94, Ky., NA.

41. U. S. Grant to S. G. Burbridge, February 29, 1864, OR, 1, vol. 32, pt. 2, pp. 497-98; Collins and Collins, *History of Kentucky,* 1:132; H. E. Hobson to F. E. Hale, April 28, 1864, RG 393, Ky., NA.

CHAPTER FIVE

1. John G. Nicolay and John Hay, *Abraham Lincoln: A History* (New York: Century, 1886), 4:235.   2. Henry Wilson to Abraham Lincoln, October 25, 1863, RLP; James B. Fry to Edwin M. Stanton, December 25, 1863, OR, 3, vol. 3, p. 1191; John W. Blassingame, "The Recruitment of Colored Troops in Kentucky, Maryland, and Missouri, 1863-1865," *Historian,* vol. 29 (August 1967), 537.   3. Mary F. Berry, *Military Necessity and Civil Rights Policy* (Port Washington, N.Y.: Kennikat, 1977), 78-79; Leach, *Conscription,* 396-99.   4. *Louisville Journal,* March 1, 1864; Collins and Collins, *History of Kentucky,* 1:131; *Congressional Globe,* 38th. Cong., 1st sess., pt. 1, pp. 333-34, 338, 516, 768, 836; pt. 4, appendix, p. 102.   5. J. B. Fry to W. H. Sidell, March 7, 9, 1864, RG 110, Ky., NA.

6. W. H. Sidell to P. R. Shipman, March 7, 1864, Sidell to J. B. Fry, March 13, 1864, RG 110, Ky., NA. See *Louisville Democrat,* March 8, 1864, for the public notice of section 24 of the act of March 3, 1864, and *Louisville Democrat,* March 9, 1864, for publication of Circular No. 8. W. H. Sidell to J. B. Fry, August 3, 1865, RG 110, Ky., NA.   7. W. H. Sidell to H. F. Reid, March 12, 1864, PMGB, RG 110, Ky., NA; J. B. Fry to W. H. Sidell, March 21, 1864, PMGB, RG 110, Ky., NA; W. H. Sidell to J. B. Fry, March 24, 1864, PMGB, RG 110, Ky., NA.   8. W. H. Sidell to George M. Sang, March 7, 1864, PMGB, RG 110, Ky., NA. For progress reports, see: W. H. Sidell to J. B. Fry, March 14, 1864, NMSUS, 4:2424-27; W. H. Sidell to J. B. Fry, August 3, 1865, RG 110, Ky., NA; Edward H. Hobson to A. G. Hopkins, March 21, 1864, R. E. Jeter to E. H. Hobson, March 9, 1864, E. H. Hobson Papers, University of Kentucky; J. R. Grissom to W. H. Sidell, March 16, 1864, C. W. Foster to S. G. Burbridge, March 30, 1864, NMSUS, 4:2440-41.   9. *Lexington Observer and Reporter,* March 12, 1864; W. H. Sidell to J. B. Fry, March 13, 24, 1864, OR, 3, vol. 4, pp. 174-76, 201; W. H. Sidell to J. B. Fry, March 19, 1864, NMSUS, 4:2464; *Louisville Journal,* March 14, 16, 1864.   10. Diary of Frances D. Peter, March 10, 1864, EFP; General Orders No. 117, March 24, 1864, NMSUS, 4:2456; W. H. Sidell to J. B. Fry, March 13, 1864 (two letters), RG 110, Ky., NA; Diary of Elder Aylette Raines, March 1864, Lexington Theological Seminary; W. O. Goodloe to R. J. Breckinridge, March 14, 1864, BP; *Cincinnati Commercial,* March 30, 1864.

11. *Manitowoc Pilot* (Wisconsin), January 29, 1864; William Goodloe to T. E. Bramlette, March 10, 1864, T. E. Bramlette to William Goodloe, March 12, 1864, R. J. Breckinridge to

T. E. Bramlette, March 14, 1864, T. E. Bramlette to R. J. Breckinridge, March 14, 1864, BP; memorandum concerning Gov. T. E. Bramlette, April 1864, BP.   12. J. M. Kelley's Notarized Statement Concerning the Capitol Hotel Conference, April 1, 1864, from notes taken March 17, 1864, BP; S. G. Burbridge to Abraham Lincoln, March 16, 1864, OR, 3, vol. 4, pp. 188-89; R. J. Breckinridge to Brutus J. Clay, March 18, 1864, Brutus J. Clay Papers, University of Kentucky; T. S. Bell to R. J. Breckinridge, April 7, 1864, BP. In speeches in Danville and Perryville, Kentucky, Breckinridge explained the events that took place on the night of March 15 in the Capitol Hotel. When the substance of his account was published in the press, Bramlette insisted that "the parts omitted were not different in any principle from what was published" (*Cincinnati Commercial*, April 1, 4, 1864). T. E. Bramlette to R. J. Breckinridge, April 2, 7, 1864, BP. The editor of the *Louisville Journal*, Paul R. Shipman, had spent March 14 and 15 in Frankfort with Bramlette. On March 16, when the governor's proclamation appeared in the *Frankfort Commonwealth*, the *Louisville Journal* carried an editorial on the same day concerning the governor's proclamation, which reflected the sentiments of the original document rather than those of the revised proclamation. See *Chicago Tribune*, April 15, 1864. Bell's letter of April 7, 1864, agrees with Kelley's notorized statement. Wolford's references in his speeches urging the people to support and back the governor, Bramlette's order to the Danville provost marshal to stop black enrollment, the governor's letter to Lincoln warning that state laws would be enforced, and Lt. Gov. Jacob's letter to Lincoln on March 13, 1864, predicting armed resistance, OR, 3, vol. 4, pp. 175-76, present a chain of conclusive evidence that Bramlette intended to resist black enlistments.   13. *Louisville Journal*, March 17, 1864; *Cincinnati Commercial*, March 17, 1864.   14. W. H. Sidell to J. B. Fry, March 16, 1864, RG 110, Ky., NA; Diary of John Jones, March 17, 1864, JJP; Diary of Elder Aylette Raines, March 17, 1864, Lexington Theological Seminary.   15. Diary of William Moody Pratt, March 21, 1864, University of Kentucky.

16. *Cincinnati Gazette*, March 21, 1864, BP; Gov. John Brough to E. M. Stanton, June 11, 1864, OR, 3, vol. 4, p. 429.   17. M. M. Benton to S. P. Chase, March 16, 1864, RLP; *Frankfort Commonwealth*, April 4, 1864, cited by *Cincinnati Commercial*, April 5, 1864; Collins and Collins, *History of Kentucky*, 1:132; Howard K. Beale, ed., *The Diary of Edward Bates, 1859-1866* (1930; reprint ed., New York: Da Capo Press, 1971), 352; Lincoln to E. M. Stanton, March 28, 1864, in Basler 7:272; Abraham Lincoln to E. M. Stanton, March 28, 1864, RLP; Albert G. Hodges to Robert J. Breckinridge, March 31, 1864, BP.   18. *Chicago Tribune*, April 27, 1864.   19. *Chicago Tribune*, April 27, 1864; *Lexington Observer and Reporter*, June 8, 1864.   20. *National Unionist*, June 3, 1864; *Cincinnati Gazette*, March 16, 1864; *Lexington Observer and Reporter*, May 28, 1864, also July 2, September 20, 1864.

21. *Louisville Journal*, January 11, 1864; R. T. Jacob to Abraham Lincoln, March 13, 1864, OR, 3, vol. 4, pp. 175-76.   22. W. C. Goodloe to R. J. Breckinridge, April 3, 1864, BP; *Lexington Observer and Reporter*, April 6, 1864.   23. Ellis M. Coulter, *The Civil War and Readjustment in Kentucky* (Chapel Hill: University of North Carolina Press, 1926), 206; "Kentucky Politics", *Cincinnati Gazette*, cited by *National Unionist*, May 20, 1864.
24. William C. Goodloe to Green Clay Smith, May 29, 1864, M. L. McPherson to Abraham Lincoln, June 2, 1864, E. W. Hawkins and Others to Lincoln, June 5, 1864, RLP.
25. Statement of R. J. Breckinridge, Document No. 10691, June 2, 1864, BP.

26. John Boyle to W. H. Sidell, July 7, 1846, RG 110, Ky., NA.   27. T. E. Bramlette to Richard T. Jacob, July 11, 1863, *Louisville Democrat*, July 13, 1864; *Lexington Observer and Reporter*, July 16, 1864; Abraham Lincoln to Frank Wolford, July 17, 1864, in Basler, 7:447. Frank Wolford to Abraham Lincoln, July 30, 1864, RLP.   28. *Louisville Journal*, March 25, 1864; Collins and Collins, *History of Kentucky*, 1:133; *Draft in Kentucky during the Civil War*, 61st Cong., 1st. sess., 1864, S. Doc. 142, pp. 4, 5.   29. A. G. Hodges to Abraham Lincoln, July 19, 1864, RLP.   30. Coulter, *The Civil War and Readjustment in Kentucky*, 191; Collins and Collins, *History of Kentucky*, 1:133.

31. General Orders No. 34, Gen. S. G. Burbridge, April 18, 1864, OR, 3, vol. 4, pp.

233-34; NMSUS, 4:2490-2491; *National Unionist,* April 22, 1864. 32. Diary and Journal of David Millspaugh, January 3, 1863, University of Michigan Historical Collection; *Covington American,* cited by *National Anti-Slavery Standard,* June 25, 1864; Narrative of George Conrad, Jr., (Oklahoma Narratives), in *Slave Narratives,* 9:39-40. 33. Charles H. Brown and C. W. Foster to W. H. Sidell, May 16, 1864, NMSUS, 4:2589-90; John G. Fee to S. S. Jocelyn, April 28, June 6, 1864, AMA Correspondence. 34. Joseph Holt to E. M. Stanton, July 31, 1864, NMSUS 4:2731-32; James Fidler to W. H. Sidell, June 15, 1865, NMSUS, 6:3666-72; James Fidler to J. B. Fry, NMSUS, 4:2600; J. B. Dickson to S. G. Burbridge, June 2, 1864, RG 393, Ky., NA; W. H. Sidell to J. B. Fry, June 15, 1865, NMSUS, 4:3675; W. H. Sidell to G. W. Womack, June 9, 1864, PMGB, RG 110, Ky., NA; James Fidler to J. B. Fry, June 15, 1865, NMSUS, 6:3668-70. Even after the black troops were in camp, they continued to be annoyed by whites, especially at night. For example, the commander of the 118th U.S. Colored Infantry at Owensboro, Kentucky, arrested three citizens "for inciting and abetting the Rebellion" and sent them to Louisville. He sent a squad of men into the country to arrest two men accused of inciting rebellion and threatening to burn houses and murder Union citizens. See John C. Moore to J. H. Hammond, September 10, 18, 1864, RG 94, Ky., NA. 35. After the passage of the Enrollment Act of July 4, 1864, slaves who volunteered on their own initiative, rather than their owners, were to receive the bounty. See *U.S. Statutes at Large,* (1866) vol. 14, p. 357.

36. Abraham Lincoln to Lorenzo Thomas, June 13, 1864, in Basler, 7:390; Lorenzo Thomas to Lincoln, June 13, 1864, NMSUS, 4:2613; Matthew Howard to T. E. Bramlette, June 15, 1864, Papers of Gov. Thomas E. Bramlette; T. E. Bramlette to E. M. Stanton, June 20, 1864, NMSUS, 4:2638; S. B. McKinzie to Abraham Lincoln, June 14, 1864, RLP. 37. General Orders No. 20, Lorenzo Thomas, June 13, 1864, OR, 3, vol. 4, pp. 438-39; *National Anti-Slavery Standard,* July 2, 1864; Augustus Louis Chetlain, *Recollections of Seventy Years* (Galena, Ill.: Gazette, 1899), 104-105. 38. W. H. Sidell to J. B. Fry, June 1865, NMSUS, 6:3673-77. 39. S. G. Burbridge to Lorenzo Thomas, July 3, 1864, General Orders No. 24, Gen. Lorenzo Thomas, July 6, 1864, Thomas to E. D. Townsend, July 26, 1864, NMSUS, 4:2658, 2665, 2716; General Orders No. 2, Gen. S. G. Burbridge, September 10, 1864, RG 393, Ky., NA. 40. W. H. Sidell to J. B. Dickson, June 2, 1864, J. B. Fry to S. G. Burbridge, August 18, 1864, Rg 110, Ky., NA.

41. James Fidler to W. H. Sidell, June 9, 1864, RG 110, Ky., NA; S. Lusk to R. J. Breckinridge, July 12, 1864, BP. 42. Collins and Collins, *History of Kentucky,* 1:136. 43. R. D. Mussey to C. W. Foster, June 7, 1864, NMSUS, 4:2605; B. F. Bristow and Others to S. G. Burbridge, August 11, 1864, RG 393, Ky., NA; W. H. Sidell to R. D. Mussey, August 18, 1864, RG 110, Ky., NA; George M. Sane to W. S. Underwood, November 8, 1864, RG 110, Ky., NA. 44. *Chicago Tribune,* July 18, 1864; C. P. Buchanan, A. M. Bodley, Robert B. M'Crackin to W. H. Sidell, July 25, 1864, Letters Received, PMGB, RG 110, Ky., NA; W. C. Grier to W. H. Sidell, August 19, 1864, PMGB, RG 110, Ky., NA. 45. *New York Times,* July 6, 1964; *Chicago Tribune,* July 7, 1864.

46. S. G. Burbridge to N. P. Chapman, November 23, 1864, NMSUS, 4:2829; J. B. Dickson to N. C. McLean, OR, 1, vol. 39, pt. 3, p. 726. 47. Joseph Holt to E. M. Stanton, July 31, 1864, ESP; Lorenzo Thomas to E. M. Stanton, September 19, 1864, ESP; *Louisville Union Press,* August 26, 30, 1864; Collins and Collins *History of Kentucky,* 1:139. 48. W. H. Sidell to S. G. Burbridge, September 15, 1864, RG 110, Ky., NA; W. H. Sidell to J. B. Dickson, November 16, 1864, RG 110, Ky., NA. 49. Henry Wilson, *History of the Rise and Fall of the Slave Power in America,* 3 vols. (Boston: James R. Osgood, 1877), 3:399-402. 50. *Lexington Observer and Reporter,* October 1, 1864.

51. General Orders No. 25, Lorenzo Thomas, July 25, 1864, OR, 3, vol. 4, p. 543. 52. Collins and Collins, *History of Kentucky,* 1:133. 53. *Cincinnati Gazette,* February 11, 20, 1865. 54. Collins and Collins, *History of Kentucky,* 1:157. 55. J. M. Scofield to W. T. Sherman, October 3, 1864, OR, 1, vol. 39, pt. 3, p. 47.

56. *New York Tribune,* February 3, 1863, citing *Knoxville Register;* Document No. 10430,

BP; Collins and Collins, *History of Kentucky*, 1:202; *Evansville Journal*, March 23, 1863.
57. William Revere to J. H. Hammond, September 24, 1864, Hammond to Revere, September 1864, John Bishop to J. S. Churchill, July 30, 1864, RG 94, Ky., NA; W. H. Sidell to J. B. Dickson, December 15, 1864, RG 110, Ky., NA. 58. Meredith Martin to A. G. Hobson, March 20, 1864, Rg 393, Ky., NA; S. G. Burbridge to W. H. Sidell, March 24, 1864, RG 110, Ky., NA; E. M. Hobson to A. G. Hobson, March 28, 1864, RG 393, Ky., NA; W. H. Sidell to J. B. Fry, March 24, 1864, OR, 3, vol. 4, p. 201; James Fidler to J. B. Fry, NMSUS, 6:3670; S. G. Burbridge to E. H. Hobson, March 23, 1864, RG 110, Ky., NA; James Fidler to W. H. Sidell, June 17, 1864, RG 110, Ky., NA. 59. J. M. Fidler, to S. G. Burbridge, June 19, 1864, Fidler to J. B. Fry, June 20, 1864, RG 393, Ky., NA; J. M. Fidler to W. H. Sidell, June 19, 1864, RG 110, Ky., NA; S. G. Burbridge to W. H. Sidell, June 20, 1864, RG 393, Ky., NA; James Fidler to W. H. Sidell, June 21, 1864, RG110, Ky., NA; A. G. Hobson to W. H. Sidell, August 10, 1864, RG 110, Ky., NA. 60. Albert D. Kirwan, *John J. Crittenden: The Struggle for the Union* (Lexington: University of Kentucky Press, 1962), 464; *National Unionist*, April 26, 1864; *Evansville Journal*, May 2, 1864.
61. A. G. Hodges to Abraham Lincoln, September 29, 1864, RLP; *Nashville Union and True Press*, October 5, 1864. 62. *Liberator*, June 24, 1864. 63. R. Clay Crawford to Abraham Lincoln, March 18, 1864, NMSUS, 4:2442-43. 64. *Cincinnati Commercial*, March 11, 1864, Insp. Gen. E. H. Ludington, December 7, 1864, OR, 1, vol. 45, pt. 2, pp. 93-94; *Louisville Union Press*, April 11, 1865; Charles O. Alden to Abraham Lincoln, December 6, 1864, RLP. 65. Pease and Randall, *Diary of Browning*, 1:665; Abraham Lincoln to A. G. Hodges, April 4, 1864, in Basler, 7:282.
66. M. Sherely to Joseph Holt, October 4, 1864, JHP; S. P. Chase to E. M. Stanton, October 24, 1864, ESP; S. P. Chase to Zebina Eastman, October 24, 1864, Zebina Eastman Papers, Chicago Historical Society.

CHAPTER SIX

1. Abraham Lincoln to James C. Conkling, August 26, 1863, in Basler, 6:409. 2. By December 1863 Missouri and Maryland had taken steps which were to lead to emancipation. See Charles Wagandt, *The Mighty Revolution: Negro Emancipation in Maryland, 1862-1864* (Baltimore: Johns Hopkins University Press, 1964), 181. William E. Parrish, *Turbulent Partnership: Missouri and the Union, 1861-1865* (Columbia: University of Missouri Press, 1963), 200-201. 3. *Congressional Globe*, 38th Cong., 1st sess. pt. 2, p. 1004. 4. T. E. Bramlette to Abraham Lincoln, September 2, 1865, in *Cincinnati Enquirer*, January 9, 1865; *Cincinnati Commercial*, January 7, 1865. 5. General Orders No. 6, 1865, James Brisbin, February 5, 1865, WP.
6. A. F. Taylor to J. T. Foster, March 11, 1865, RG 393, Ky., NA; W. H. Sidell to S. G. Burbridge, February 18, 1865, RG 110, Ky., NA; W. H. Sidell to S. G. Burbridge, February 18, 19, 1865, J. B. Dickens to W. H. Sidell, February 21, 1865, RG 393, Ky., NA. 7. James Brisbin to B. F. Wade, February 21, 1865, WP. 8. T. E. Bramlette to Abraham Lincoln, November 14, 1864, *HJ* (1865), p. 49; C. Worley to Lincoln, February 11, 1865, D. L. Price to Lincoln, February 13, 1865, W. R. Kinney to Henry Wilson, February 23, 1865, RLP. 9. Wilson, *Rise and Fall of the Slave Power*, 3:438-39. 10. Wilson, *Rise and Fall of the Slave Power*, 3:440.
11. Robert J. Breckinridge to Reverdy Johnson, May 7, 1864, Reverdy Johnson Papers, LC. 12. Basler, 7:380. 13. Basler, 8:149. 14. T. S. Bell to Joseph Holt, January 18, 1864, JHP; J. R. Bailey to J. W. Irwin, January 7, 1864, RLP. 15. *New York Times*, December 26, 1864.
16. *Louisville Journal*, January 7, 1865; *Chicago Tribune*, January 8, 1865. 17. *Cincinnati Commercial*, January 5, 6, 1865. 18. *New York Times*, January 8, 15, 1865; *Liberator*, January 20, 1865. 19. *Congressional Globe*, 38th Cong., 2nd sess., pt. 1, pp. 170, 172. 20. *Con-*

gressional Globe,, 38th Cong., 2nd sess., pt. 1, pp. 179, 181; *Frankfort Commonwealth,* January 13, 1865; *Louisville Journal,* January 18, 1865; Wilson, *Rise and Fall of the Slave Power,* 3:450.

21. Isaac N. Arnold, *The History of Abraham Lincoln and the Over-Throw of Slavery* (Chicago: Clarke, 1866), 346-58; Hans L. Trefousse, *The Radical Republicans: Lincoln's Vanguard for Racial Justice* (New York: Knopf, 1969), 299; E. H. Lindington to E. M. Stanton, December 7, 1864, OR, 1, vol. 45, pt. 2, pp. 93-94.   22. A. G. Hodges to Lincoln, December 1, 1864, RLP; *National Unionist,* January 13, February 24, 28, 1865; A. G. Hodges to Lincoln, December 1, 1864, RLP. In December 1864 Lincoln asked James S. Rollins, congressman from Missouri, to talk to all the border-state delegations in Congress and to persuade them to vote for the Thirteenth Amendment. "The passage of this Amendment will clinch the whole subject," he said. See Isaac Arnold, *The Life of Abraham Lincoln* (Chicago: Jansen, McClurg, 1885), 358-59. When the amendment was adopted by Congress, Lincoln expressed the belief that it would be "the king's cure-all for all evils" (*Cincinnati Gazette,* February 2, 1865). In 1866, Leonard Swett, a close friend of the president's, described Lincoln as having resorted "to almost any means" to secure adoption and ratification of the Thirteenth Amendment. See Leonard Swett to W. H. Herndon, January 17, 1866, HWP.   23. W. R. Kenny to Henry Wilson, February 23, 1865, in RLP; Thomas Bramlette to Lincoln, March 2, 1865, RLP; *National Unionist,* January 3, February 24, 28, 1865.   24. George Morrison to R. J. Breckinridge, January 17, 1865, J. H. Bush to George Morrison, January 16, 1865, BP; W. R. Kinney to Henry Wilson, February 23, 1865, RLP.   25. John M. Palmer, *Personal Recollections: The Story of an Earnest Life* (Cincinnati: Clarke Press, 1901), 232-33; J. S. Brisbin to B. F. Wade, February 21, 1865, WP; John Palmer to E. M. Stanton, April 18, 1865, OR, 3 vol. 4, p. 1271; Stanton to Palmer, NMSUS, 6:3622; see Hambleton Tapp, "Three Decades of Politics, 1870-1900" (Ph.D. diss. University of Kentucky, 1960), p. 3, for an opinion that Palmer "used his office to free the slaves."

26. General Orders No. 7, John Palmer, March 4, 1865, *Louisville Democrat,* March 6, 1865; J. Palmer, *Personal Recollections,* 234-35; E. H. Meacheam to J. B. Dickson, March 8, 1865, RG 393, Ky., NA; J. B Dickson to E. P. Home, RG 393, Ky., NA. See J. M. Palmer to Thomas James, March 22, 1865, p. 4, Letter Book of John Palmer, Illinois Historical Society. 27. Edwin M. Stanton to Abraham Lincoln, March 3, 1865, NMSUS, 6:3589-90; John Fee to Editor, March 15, 16, 1865, *Louisville Press,* March 20, 1865.   28. *Lexington Observer and Reporter,* January 10, 1866; "Rural" to Editor, *Chicago Tribune,* January 20, 1865; "Howard" to Editor, May 18, 1865, *Chicago Tribune,* May 23, 1865; F. W. Houston to Editor, *Western Citizen,* February 24, 1865; T. S. Bell to Joseph Holt, June 2, 1865, JHP.   29. J. J. Talbott to John Palmer, April 9, 1865, RG 393, Ky., NA.   30. J. Palmer, *Personal Recollections,* 238; John Palmer to Philip Tomppert, May 11, 1865, RG 393, Ky., NA; J. M. Palmer to Philip Tomppert, May 11, 1865, Letter Book of J. M. Palmer, pp. 20-24.

31. *New York Times,* June 4, 1865; J. Palmer, *Personal Recollections,* 240; *Cincinnati Gazette,* June 9, 1865; T. S. Bell to Joseph Holt, June 2, 1865, JHP.   32. J. S. Brisbin to T. E. Bramlette, April 20, 1865, *New York Tribune,* May 1, 1865.   33. *Lexington Observer and Reporter,* April 29, 1865.   34. General Orders No. 6, Lorenzo Thomas, May 1, 1865, NMSUS, 6:3636, 3643-44; James B. Fry to W. H. Sidell, May 8, 1865, RG 110 Ky., NA. 35. *Free South,* May 31, 1865; W. H. Kinnairds and Twenty-five Others to John Palmer, May 25, 1865, M. L. Rice to Colonel Burbowen, May 29, 1865, RG 393, Ky., NA; *Cincinnati Gazette,* May 22, 31, 1865; Collins and Collins, *History of Kentucky,* 1:158-59; W. E. B. Du Bois, *Black Reconstruction in America,* (New York: Russell and Russell, 1935), 571.

36. J. B. Fry to John Palmer, June 1, 1865, James Fidler to J. B. Fry, June 10, 1865, RG 393, Ky., NA; *Cincinnati Gazette,* June 3, 1865.   37. James Brisbin to E. M. Stanton, May 30, 1865, ESP.   38. S. G. Burbridge to E. M. Stanton, July 20, 1865, ESP; *New York Tribune,* May 24, 1865. See Governor Bramlette's message, December 5, 1865, *HJ* (1865-66), 19; *Population of the United States in 1860* (Washington, D.C.: U.S. Government Printing Office, 1864), 598-605. Kentucky had 275,719 slaves in 1860. Of the 3,953,760 slaves in the United

States in 1860, Virginia had 490,865 and Georgia, Mississippi, Alabama, and South Carolina had more than 400,000; Benjamin Quarles, *Lincoln and the Negro* (New York: Oxford University Press, 1962), 166. Quarles listed 23,703 black Union troops for Kentucky and 24,052 for Louisiana. If Bramlette's figures from the Kentucky adjutant general's office are correct, Kentucky had more black troops in service than any other state.   39. J. Palmer, *Personal Recollections*, 240-42; John Palmer to Andrew Johnson, July 29, 1865, RG 393, Ky., NA; Diary of William H. Baker, synopsis, 1864-65, Wisconsin Historical Society; J. M. Palmer to Dave M. Payne, August 7, 1865, Letter Book of J. M. Palmer, p. 52. 40. Collins and Collins, *History of Kentucky*, 1:162; J. Palmer, *Personal Recollections*, p. 254; *Nashville Colored Tennessean*, August 12, 1865; *Cincinnati Gazette*, June 9, October 14, 1865.

41. *Louisville Union*, July 27, 1865; *Lexington Observer and Reporter*, August 2, 1865; *New York Times*, August 6, 1865; *Liberator*, August 11, 1865; J. Palmer, *Personal Recollections*, 253-54; John Palmer to Editor, *Louisville Press*, July 29, 1865, RG 393, Ky., NA.   42. J. Palmer, *Personal Recollections*, 242-43; General Orders No. 129, E. D. Townsend, July 25, 1865, *Index of General Orders, Adjutant General's Office, 1865* (Washington, D.C.: U.S. Government Printing Office, 1866).   43. John W. Lee to G. H. Thomas, July 26, 1865, RG 393, Ky., NA; John Palmer to Andrew Johnson, July 29, 1865, RG 393, Ky., NA.   44. G. W. Gwin to John Palmer, July 7, 1865, Palmer to Mayor of Paris, August 22, 1865, Palmer to J. L. Smedley, September 2, 1865, RG 393, Ky., NA; *Cincinnati Gazette*, August 14, October 23, 1865; Collins and Collins, *History of Kentucky*, 1:164.   45. *Louisville Democrat*, cited by *New York Times*, August 20, 1865; *Louisville Union*, August 12, 1865.

46. John Palmer to Joseph C. Fowler, September 4, 1865, RG 393, Ky., NA.

47. *Louisville Democrat*, cited by *Cincinnati Enquirer*, August 19, 1865.   48. *Cincinnati Gazette*, September 15, 1865.   49. G. C. Smith to E. M. Stanton, September 27, 1865, *Louisville Journal*, October 2, 17, 1865; *Union Standard*, October 17, 1865.   50. T. S. Bell to Joseph Holt, June 2, 1865, JHP; *Liberator*, November 3, 1865; *Louisville Journal*, October 17, 1865.

51. *Cincinnati Gazette*, cited by *Free South*, October 25, 1865; *New York Herald*, cited by *Chicago Tribune*, October 5, 1865.   52. *Free South*, October 25, 1865.   53. Collins and Collins; *History of Kentucky*, 1:164; E. D. Townsend to John Palmer, October 21, 1865, RG 393, Ky., NA; George Thomas Palmer, *A Conscientious Turncoat: The Story of John M. Palmer, 1817-1900 (New Haven: Yale University Press, 1941)*, 185-86. *Collins and Collins, History of Kentucky*, 1:164; *Union Standard*, October 17, 1865; John Palmer to Father, November 5, 1868, John Palmer Papers, Illinois Historical Society.   54. *Union Standard*, September 29, 1865; J. Palmer, *Personal Recollections*, 265-66; *Cincinnati Gazette*, October 21, 1865; Collins and Collins, *History of Kentucky*, 1:170.   55. *Cincinnati Commercial*, April 4, May 23, 1865.

56. *Frankfort Commonwealth*, May 26, 1865; *Cincinnati Commercial*, May 30, 1865.

57. *Frankfort Commonwealth*, August 1, 1865; *Free South*, July 12, August 2, 1865; *Lexington Observer and Reporter*, July 12, 1865.   58. *Louisville Journal*, May 9, 16, July 11, November 10, 1865; *Frankfort Commonwealth*, May 23, June 30, 1865; *Cincinnati Commercial*, July 17, 1865.   59. *Cincinnati Commercial*, June 6, 1865; *Maysville Eagle*, cited by *Lexington Observer and Reporter*, June 7, 1865; *Cincinnati Gazette*, June 22, July 28, 1865; *Louisville Journal*, July 3, 11, 1865.   60. *Cincinnati Commercial*, June 6, 9, 1865; *Maysville Eagle*, cited by *Lexington Observer and Reporter*, June 7, 12, 24, 1865; *Cincinnati Gazette*, June 22, July 28, 1865; *Cincinnati Commercial*, July 17, 1865; *Cincinnati Gazette*, June 22, July 19, 1865.

61. *Cincinnati Commercial*, May 24, 1865.   62. *Louisville Journal*, May 16, 1865; *Free South*, June 28, 1865.   63. *Cincinnati Gazette*, August 15, 30, 1865; *New York Tribune Almanac* (1866), 59-60, *American Annual Cyclopedia* 5 (1865): 465. The existence of viva voce, or oral, voting was much more important in shaping the results of the election than was the presence of the army. In 1862 and 1864 many Southern sympathizers stayed away from the polls rather than reveal their political views.   64. *New York Tribune*, December 11, 1865; Collins and Collins, *History of Kentucky*, 1:166.   65. *HJ* (December 5, 1865), 30-32; *Chicago*

Tribune, December 14, 1865; see "Memorandum of Arguments for the Adoption of the Thirteenth Amendment," Papers of Gov. Thomas E. Bramlette.
66. *Union Standard,* January 19, 1866. 67. *Cincinnati Commercial,* August 18, 1865; *Louisville Democrat,* cited by *Lexington Observer and Reporter,* September 6, 1865; *Frankfort Commonwealth,* August 29, 1865. 68. *Louisville Journal,* cited by *Liberator,* August 25, 1865; *Frankfort Commonwealth,* July 21, August 15, 1865; *Cincinnati Gazette,* July 22, August 15, 1865; *American Annual Cyclopedia* 5 (1865): 464-65. 69. *Cincinnati Gazette,* August 14, 1865. 70. John Palmer to C. A. Dana, July 31, 1865, RG 393, Ky., NA. 71. *New York Times,* January 13, 1863; Victor B. Howard, "The Kentucky Presbyterians in 1849: Slavery and the Kentucky Constitution," *Register of the Kentucky Historical Society,* vol. 73 (July 1975): 229-30, 238-40. 72. *New York Times,* January 13, 1865.

CHAPTER SEVEN

1. "Carleton" to Editor, *Boston Journal,* cited by *Waukesha Freeman* (Wisconsin), December 2, 1862. 2. Rev. J. E. Roy to Editor, *Chicago Tribune,* November 8, 1865. Peter Bruner, "A Slave's Adventures toward Freedom: Not Fiction, But the True Story of a Struggle," typescript, Miami University, Ohio, p. 41, 42; General Orders No. 9, Gen. Lorenzo Thomas, March 11, 1864, OR, 3, vol. 4, pp. 166-67. 3. Journal of Cora Hume (Owens), August 7, 1864, July 5, 18, 1865, Filson Club Historical Society. 4. *Louisville Journal,* December 8, 1864, May 4, 1865; *National Unionist,* May 23, 1865; *New York Times,* December 12, 1864. 5. J. S. Wheeler to Mattie Wheeler, January 13, 1865, Capt. and Mrs. Leland Hathaway Papers, University of Kentucky; "Pontiac" to Editor, August 3, 1865, *National Anti-Slavery Standard,* August 12, 1865.
6. James S. Brisbin to B. F. Wade, February 5, 1865, WP. 7. *Cincinnati Commercial,* July 17, 1865; *New York Times,* August 6, 1865. 8. *Cincinnati Gazette,* July 29, 1865; John Palmer to Philip Tompper, May 11, 1865, RG 393, Ky., NA. 9. *Union Standard,* October 24, 1865; Jesse W. Kincheloe to Joseph Holt, October 9, 1865, JHP; John D. Duckworth to E. M. Stanton, October 23, 1865, ESP. 10. *Louisville Journal,* May 16, July 23, 1865.
11. J. K. Grant to J. P. Flint, October 15, 1865, John Palmer to J. P. Flint, October 30, 1865, *Louisville Gazette,* November 8, 1865. 12. John G. Fee to Secretaries, *American Missionary,* vol. 10 (January 1866), 18; Richard B. Drake, "The American Missionary Association and the Southern Negro, 1861-1888" (Ph.D. diss. Emory University, 1957), p. 116; John G. Fee, *Autobiography* (Chicago: National Christian Association 1891), 182-83. 13. HJ (December 4, 1865), p. 33. 14. *Union Standard,* September 22, 1865; *Lexington Observer and Reporter,* December 6, 1865. 15. *Louisville Industrial and Commercial Gazette,* November 25, December 9, 22, 23, 30, 1865, January 13, 1866.
16. *Owensboro Monitor,* March 21, 1866. 17. *Louisville Democrat,* January 7, 1866; *Louisville Courier,* January 6, 1866. 18. *Louisville Journal,* January 13, 1866; *Louisville Courier,* January 13, 1866. 19. *HJ* (1865-66), pp. 446-47, 588-89; *Acts of Kentucky* (1865-66), 38-39, 43-44, 52, 66. 20. Circular No. 2, May 19, 1865, Circular No. 5, May 30, 1865, War Department; *Acts of Congress Relative to Refugees, Freedmen, and Abandoned Lands* (1866); *Annual Report of Commissioner Oliver Otis Howard,* 39th Cong., 1st sess., 1865, H. Doc. 11 Serial 1255), 11, 45, 49; John Ely to J. H. Donovan, June 25, 1866, BRFAL, RG 105, Ky., NA.
21. C. B. Fisk to O. O. Howard, October 6, 1865, BRFAL, RG 105, Ky., NA; Victoria M. Olds, "The Freedmen's Bureau as a Social Agency" (Ph.D. diss., Columbia University, 1966, 163; O. O. Howard to Assistant Commissioners, January 10, 1866, BRFAL, RG 105, Ky., NA. 22. 39th Cong., 1st sess., 1865, H. Doc. 70, p. 308; 39th Cong., 1st sess., 1865, S. Doc. 27, p. 23; J. R. Lewis to C. B. Fisk, May 12, 1866, BRFAL, RG 105, Ky., NA.
23. J. W. Kincholoe to Joseph Holt, January 17, 1866, JHP; L. F. Burnett to James Haggard,

May 22, 1866 BRFAL, RG 105, Ky., NA. 24. Ben Runkle to Sidney Burban, September 1866, BRFAL, RG 105, Ky., NA. 25. *Annual Report of Commissioner Oliver Otis Howard . . .*, 39th Cong., 2nd sess., 1866, H. Doc. 1 (Serial 1285), 748-49. John Ely to H. G. Brown, April 9, 1866, John Ely to J. C. Davis, August 15, 1866, John Ely to J. C. Davis October 8, November 5, December 13, 1866, J. C. Davis to O. O. Howard, November 5, 1866, BRFAL, RG 105, Ky., NA.

26. L. F. Burnett to A. W. Lawwill, October 3, 1866; G. W. Kingsberry to C. F. Johnson, December 18, 1866, BRFAL, RG 105, Ky., NA. 27. Circular No. 3, June 26, 1866, A. W. Lawwill to L. F. Burnett, December 15, 1866, BRFAL, RG 105 Ky., NA. 28. *True Kentuckian* (Paris), cited by *Louisville Courier,* January 4, 1867, C. J. True to R. E. Johnston, July 26, 1867, BRFAL, RG 105, Ky., NA. 29. R. E. Johnston to John Ely, July 4, 1867, R. E. Johnston to Ben Runkle, March 2, 1868, BRFAL, RG 105, Ky., NA. 30. R. E. Johnston to John Ely, August 31, 1867, John Ely to Sidney Burbank, September 10, 1867, BRFAL, RG 105, Ky., NA.

31. R. E. Johnston to B. P. Runkle, November 30, December 31, 1867, March 31, 1868, BRFAL, RG 105, Ky., NA. 32. R. E. Johnston to B. P. Runkle, December 31, 1867, March 2, 1868, BRFAL, RG 105, Ky., NA. 33. *Lexington Observer and Reporter,* cited by the *Louisville Journal,* January 7, 1868; R. E. Johnston to B. P. Runkle, November 30, December 31, 1867, March 2, May 31, 1868, BRFAL, RG 105, Ky., NA. 34. Collins and Collins, *History of Kentucky,* 1:188; *Lexington Observer and Reporter,* February 13, 1869; *HJ,* (1868-69) 1:559. 35. M. E. Billings to A. B. Brown, April 23, 1868, R. E. Johnston to Sidney Burbank, November 16, 1868, BRFAL, RG 105, Ky., NA; M. E. Billings to A. B. Brown, April 23, 1868, BRFAL, RG 105, Ky., NA.

36. *Kentucky Gazette,* September 17, 22, November 23, 1870. 37. *Louisville Courier,* March 22, 1867; *Lexington Observer and Reporter,* January 14, 21, 1871; *Cincinnati Gazette,* January 18, 1871. 38. *Acts of Kentucky* (1867), 2:2-3; *Lexington Observer and Reporter,* July 10, October 16, 1867; *Louisville Courier,* November 7, 1867. 39. SJ (1869), 21-23.

40. *Kentucky Yeoman,* January 8, 1869; *Lexington Observer and Reporter,* February 10, 1869.

41. *Kentucky Yeoman,* January 22, 1869; *Lexington Observer and Reporter,* February 10, 1869. 42. *Kentucky Gazette,* April 6, 1870; *Kentucky Statesman,* August 9, 1870; *Frankfort Yeoman,* cited by *Maysville Bulletin,* March 3, 1870. 43. *Lexington Observer and Reporter,* August 17, 1870; *Louisville Courier-Journal,* September 19, 1870. 44. *Georgetown Times,* August 10, 1870. 45. *Louisville Evening Sun,* cited by *Lexington Observer and Reporter,* August 24, 1870.

46. *Louisville Courier-Journal,* September 19, 1870. 47. *Lexington Press,* October 13, 1870. 48. SJ (1871), 14; Collins and Collins, *History of Kentucky,* 1:223. 49. *HJ* (1871), 52-53. 50. SJ (1872), 207-209, 385-87.

51. *HJ,* (1872), 1108. 52. *The Statistics of the Population of the United States, 1870,* 9th Census (Washington, 1872), 1:299. 53. *Lexington Observer and Reporter,* February 8, 1868; August 17, 1870. 54. *Lexington Observer and Reporter,* October 30, 1869. 55. *Cincinnati Gazette,* July 26, 1869.

56. *Lexington Observer and Reporter,* February 26, 1870. 57. J. C. Davis to O. O. Howard, November 5, 1866, BRFAL, RG 105, Ky., NA; *Senate Miscellaneous Documents,* 1871, 42nd. Cong., 1st sess., no. 49; *SJ, 1871,* 191-9; *Congressional Globe,* 42nd. Cong., 2nd. sess. (1872), 598-99. 58. *Lexington Observer and Reporter,* February 4, 15, 1871; *Kentucky Gazette,* January 28, February 15, 1871; Mary S. Donovan, "Kentucky Laws Regarding the Negro, 1865-1877," (Masters thesis, Univesity of Louisville, 1967), 68. 59. *Georgetown Times,* February 22, 1871; *Frankfort Commonwealth,* March 17, 1871; *HJ* (1872), 249, 282, 603; *SJ* (1872), 512-13; *Kentucky Yeoman,* February 17, 1871, December 3, 1872; *Acts of Kentucky* (1866), 52; (1872), 7-8, 12-14. 60. *HJ* (1872), 342-45; *SJ* (1872), 199-200; *Acts of Kentucky* (1873) 35-36.

61. Collins and Collins, *History of Kentucky,* 1:174, 198; B. P. Runkle to Elisha Whittlesey,

July 20, 1869, BRFAL, RG 105, Ky., NA. 62. Collins and Collins, *History of Kentucky,* 1:235. 63. *HJ* (1872), 24-25; (1873), 870; *Acts of Kentucky,* (1873), 35-36.

CHAPTER EIGHT

1. McGee, *Seventy-second Indiana,* 226; Lorenzo Thomas to W. S. Rosecrans, June 15, 1863, RG 393, Ohio, NA. 2. General Orders No. 37, I. F. Quimby, August 22, 1862, RG 393, Ky., NA. 3. H. M. Judah to J. T. Boyle, March 6, 1863, RG 393, Ky., NA; *National Anti-Slavery Standard,* March 28, 1863. 4. William Perkins to S. S. Jocelyn, January 19, 1863, S. G. Wright to S. S. Jocelyn, January 2, 20, 27, 31, February 4, 1863, AMA Correspondence. 5. General Orders No. 30, E. D. Townsend, January 25, 1864, OR, 3, vol. 4, pp. 44-45.

6. Western Freedmen's Aid Commission, Appeal in Behalf of the National Freedmen (Cincinnati, 1864), p. 5; Special Orders No. 28, Lorenzo Thomas, May 20, 1863, Special Orders No. 15, Lorenzo Thomas, March 28, 1864, RG 94, Generals' Papers, NA. 7. Ann Dicken Troutman to Mother, March 28, 1863, Dicken-Troutman-Balke Papers, University of Kentucky. 8. General Orders No. 4, Acting Adjutant J. B. Shaw, August 4, 1863, RG 94, NA. 9. George Parker to Commander, Department of Kentucky, November 20, 1864, RG 393, Ky., NA; W. H. Sidell to S. G. Burbridge, December 15, 1864, RG 110, Ky., NA. See Herbert Gutman, *The Black Family in Slavery and Freedom, 1750-1925* (New York: Pantheon, 1976), 383-84, for cases of cruelty by white masters to black soldiers' families. 10. William B. Sipes, *Seventh Pennsylvania Veteran Volunteer Cavalry* (Pottsville, Penn.: Miners Journal, 1905), 21; Thomas J. Morgan, *Reminiscences of Service with Colored Troops in the Army of the Cumberland, 1863-1865* (Providence, R.I., n.p., 1885), 12; Lorenzo Thomas to E. D. Townsend, May 20, 1863, RG 94, Ky., NA.

11. See, e.g., John Bishop to M. H. Kollock, August 1864, RG 94, NA. 12. Marrs, *Life of Marrs,* 23; John Fee to Secretaries, July 18, 1864, *American Missionary,* vol. 8 (September 1864), 222-23; J. S. Newberry, *The U.S. Sanitary Commission in the Valley of the Mississippi* (Cleveland: Fairbanks, Benedict, 1871), 225-26. 13. *U.S. Statutes,* vol. 13, 1864, pp. 144, 379. 14. "Humanitas" to Editor, *New York Tribune,* November 28, 1864, cited by *Louisville Democrat,* December 6, 1864; 38th Cong., 2nd sess. 1865, S. Doc. 28, pp. 10-11. 15. John Fee to S. S. Jocelyn, July 1864, AMA Correspondence.

16. *Liberator,* June 24, 1864. 17. J. B. Dickson to C. E. Hall, June 20, 1864, by Order of General Burbridge, J. B. Dickson to J. H. Johnson, June 25, 1864, S. G. Burbridge to Lorenzo Thomas, June 28, 1864, J. B. Dickson to C. D. Sedgwick, June 30, 1864, RG 393, Ky., NA. 18. Hugh Ewing to J. B. Dickson, June 29, 1864, D. A. Mims to S. G. Burbridge, September 3, 1864, RG 393, Ky., NA. 19. S. S. Fry to S. G. Burbridge, July 5, 1864, RG 393, Ky., NA; S. S. Fry to R. J. Breckinridge, November 28, 1864, BP; Collins and Collins, *History of Kentucky,* 1:139; Lorenzo Thomas to E. M. Stanton, July 6, 1864, General Orders No. 24, Lorenzo Thomas, 1864, OR, 3, vol. 4, pp. 467, 474. 20. Speed S. Fry to S. G. Burbridge, July 5, 1864, Endorsement by Burbridge and Lorenzo Thomas, July 6, 1864, RG 94, NA.

21. Lorenzo Thomas to E. M. Stanton, July 16, 1864, NMSUS, 4:2686-87, 2927; A. Scofield to William Goodell, November 30, 1864, AMA Correspondence, C. W. Foster to Lorenzo Thomas, July 28, 1864, RG 94, NA. 22. H. W. Barry to Gen. A. L. Chetlain, July 7, 1864, RG 94, NA. Lorenzo Thomas to E. M. Stanton, July 16, 1864, Lorenzo Thomas to S. C. Hicks, July 17, 1864, NMSUS, 4:2686-87, 2927; OR, 3, vol. 4, pp. 501-502. 23. Lorenzo Thomas to S. G. Hicks, July 25, 1864, NMSUS, 4:2715, RG 94, NA. 24. John Bishop to E. B. Harlan, August 10, 1864, Endorsement, E. B. Harlan, August 15, 1864, Endorsement, John Bishop, August 21, 1864, Endorsement, E. B. Harlan, August 27, 1864, RG 94, NA; *Revised Army Regulations,* 1863, sec. 3, p. 536. 25. J. B. Dickson to S. S. Fry, August 13, 1864, RG 393, Ky., NA; S. S. Fry to S. G. Burbridge, July 5, 1864, RG 393, Ky.,

NA; S. S. Fry to R. J. Breckinridge, November 28, 1864, BP; Collins and Collins, *History of Kentucky,* 1:139.

26. S. S. Fry to R. J. Breckinridge, November 28, 1864, BP; A. Scofield to M. E. Strieby, November 1, 14, 1864, AMA Correspondence; Thomas D. Sedgwick to Commander, Camp Nelson, November 14, 1864, RG 393, Ky., NA.   27. "Humanitas" to Editor, *New York Tribune,* November 28, 1864, cited in *Louisville Democrat,* December 9, 1864; Joseph C. Miller, "Affidavit of A Colored Soldier, Camp Nelson," in *Louisville Democrat,* December 9, 1864; *Liberator,* December 9, 1864; T. E. Hall to Eluthan Davis, December 14, 1864, AMA Correspondence.   28. J. B. Dickson to S. G. Burbridge, November 27, 1864; Dickson to T. E. Hall, November 28, 1864, Dickson to S. S. Fry, November 29, 1864, Dickson to Lorenzo Thomas, November 30, 1864, Dickson to S. S. Fry, December 1, 2, 4, 9, 12, 1864, RG 393, Ky., NA.; A. Scofield to William Goodell, November 30, 1864, Scofield to M. E. Strieby, December 1, 9, 1864, AMA Correspondence.   29. John Fee to M. E. Strieby, September 22, 1864, March 2, 1865, Fee to Lewis Tappan, February 21, 1865, Fee to George Whipple, February 21, 25, 1865, AMA Correspondence; John Fee to Editor, *Louisville Union Press,* March 22, 1865.   30. T. E. Hall to Eluthan Davis, December 14, 1864, AMA Correspondence.

31. Marrs, *Life of Marrs,* 61-62.   32. Special Orders No. 29, December 15, 1864, NMSUS, 4:2844; J. B. Dickson to T. E. Hall, December 17, 1864, RG 393, Ky., NA; S. G. Burbridge to E. M. Stanton, February 5, 1865, RG 393, Ky., NA.   33. Lorenzo Thomas to E. M. Stanton, December 27, 1864, OR, 3, vol. 4, p. 1018.   34. James Brisbin to John Fee, February 15, 1865, Fee to George Whipple, February 21, 25, 1865, AMA Correspondence; B. L. Kent to A. M. York, September 6, 1865, BRFAL, RG 105, Ky., NA.   35. John Fee to George Whipple, January 2, 1865, AMA Correspondence. See Miller, "Affidavit of a Colored Soldier"; "Humanitas" to Editor, *New York Tribune,* November 28, 1864; *Louisville Democrat,* December 9, 1864; *Liberator,* December 9, 1864; John Fee to Editor, *Louisville Union Press,* March 27, 1865; John Fee to Editor, *Louisville Journal,* May 27, 1865.

36. Marrs, *Life of Marrs,* 55-57. 37. Anonymous black soldier, Fifth U.S. Colored Cavalry, to E. M. Stanton, October 22, 1865, RG 94, NA.   38. Special Orders No. 26, D. A. Mims, August 31, 1864, O. A. Barthelomew to Charles Bentrick, August 31, 1864, D. A. Mims to J. B. Dickson, September 3, 1864, RG 393, Ohio, NA.   39. A. Scofield to William Goodell, November 30, 1864, AMA Correspondence; John Fee to George Whipple, January 2, 1865, AMA Correspondence.   40. W. H. Sidell to S. G. Burbridge, December 15, 1864, RG 110, Ky., NA.

41. *Congressional Globe,* 38th Cong., 2nd sess., pt. 1, pp. 160-62; anonymous correspondent to Henry Wilson, *Liberator,* June 24, 1864.   42. Wilson, *Rise and Fall of the Slave Power,* 3:403; E. M. Stanton to Abraham Lincoln, March 3, 1865, NMSUS, 6:3589-90.

43. General Orders No. 10, John M. Palmer, March 12, 1865, NMSUS, 6:3597; *Cincinnati Gazette,* March 18, 1865; J. Palmer, *Personal Recollections,* 232-33; G. T. Palmer, *A Conscientious Turncoat,* 173.   44. A. Harris to Richard S. Herndon, March 29, 1865, Herndon Family Papers, University of Kentucky.   45. Collins and Collins, *History of Kentucky,* 1:157; John Palmer to E. M. Stanton, RG 393, Ky., NA, John Palmer (endorsement) to Henry Plessner, March 24, 1865, RG 393, Ky., NA.

46. Collins and Collins, *History of Kentucky,* 1:164, 166; *Frankfort Semi-Weekly Commonwealth,* October 3, 1866.   47. Record of Contracts with Freedmen at Paducah, Kentucky, 1866 to 1868, vol. 183, BRFAL, RG 105, Ky., NA.   48. *Acts of Kentucky* (1865-66), 37. 49. O. O. Howard to Assistant Commissioners, March 2, 1866, BRFAL, RG 105, Ky., NA. 50. Circular No. 5, C. B. Fisk, February 26, 1866, BRFAL, RG 105, Ky. and Tenn., NA.

51. James Bolton to J. H. Donovan, June 26, 1866, BRFAL, RG 105, Ky., NA.   52. J. H. Smith to J. H. Donovan, July 12, 1866, J. H. Donovan to Assistant Commissioner, July 12, 1866, BRFAL, RG 105, Ky., NA.   53. T. F. Cheaney to J. C. Davis, July 13, 1866, BRFAL, RG 105, Ky., NA.   54. Henderson H. Donald, *The Negro Freedman* (New York: Henry

Schuman, 1952), 57. 55. C. J. True to R. E. Johnston, September 30, 1866, BRFAL, RG 105, Ky., NA.

56. H. C. Howard to R. W. Hutchcraft, October 16, 1866, A. W. Lawwill to John Ely, February 20, 1867, BRFAL, RG 105, Ky., NA. 57. A. W. Lawwill to John Ely, February 20, 1867, BRFAL, RG 105, Ky., NA. 58. "Complaint and Trial Ledger," vol. 152, pp. 92, 180, 183, vol. 153, pp. 43, 92, A. W. Lawwill to John Ely, June 19, 1867, extracts from I. S. Catlin's Report, in Sidney Burbank to O. O. Howard, November 16, 1867, BRFAL, RG 105, Ky., NA. 59. H. C. Howard to J. H. Rice, June 25, 1866, Howard to R. E. Johnston, July 13, 1866, BRFAL, RG 105, Ky., NA. 60. H. C. Howard to R. E. Johnston, February 25, 1868, March 26, 1868, BRFAL, RG 105, Ky., NA.

61. Estill v Rogers, 64 Ky. 62 (1866). 62. Lewis v Commonwealth, 66 Ky. 539 (1868). 63. Brown v McGee, 75 Ky. 428 (1874). 64. Robinson v Commonwealth, 69 Ky. 311 (1869). 65. James Fidler to John Palmer, October 25, 1865, RG 393, Ky., NA.

66. See, e.g., E. W. Stevens to John Palmer, July 18, 1865, RG 393, Ky., NA; C. P. Oyler to J. H. Rise, April 3, 1865, BRFAL, RG 105, Ky., NA; John F. Smith to F. Choise, July 2, 1866, James Dugsdale to John Roberts, December 18, 1866, BRFAL, RG 105, Ky., NA; James Brisbin to Jason Williams, Evansville Journal, November 1, 1865. 67. W. J. Kay to James McCleery, March 28, 1866, BRFAL, RG 105, Ky., NA; J. W. Kay to Assistant Commissioner, March 28, 1868, BRFAL, RG 105, Ky., NA; Narrative of Will Oats, George R. Rawick, in The American Slave: A Composite Autobiography, vol. 16, Kentucky (Westport, Conn.: Greenwood, 1972), 19. 68. Collins and Collins, History of Kentucky, 1:164; Evansville Journal, November 1, 1865; C. P. Oyler to J. H. Rice, April 3, 1866, BRFAL, RG 105, Ky., NA; J. F. Smith to J. H. Donovan, April 25, 1866, J. F. Smith to William Gore, September 27, 1866, BRFAL, RG 105, Ky., NA; C. F. Johnson to John Ely, November 23, 1866, BRFAL, RG 105, Ky., NA. 69. Louisville Democrat, February 20, 1866; O. O. Howard to Assistant Commissioners, October 4, 1865, BRFAL, RG 105, Ky., NA; Cincinnati Gazette, October 5, 1865. 70. John Ely to E. C. Ashcraft, August 9, 1866, BRFAL, RG 105, Ky., NA.

71. Acts of Kentucky (1865-66), 49. 72. John Ely to Sidney Burbank, February 1867, John Ely to Jeff C. Davis, February 13, 1867, BRFAL, RG 105, Ky., NA. 73. See, e.g., C. D. Smith to Mer Ary Elzell, April 18, 1867, BRFAL, RG 105, Ky., NA; affidavit of Linton Slaugher, January 4, 1867, affidavit of Patsy South, October 25, 1866, BRFAL, RG 105, Ky., NA. 74. C. J. True to J. M. Rogers, July 10, 1866, BRFAL, RG 105, Ky., NA; 40th Cong., 3rd sess., vol. 3, H. Doc. 1, pp. 1032, 1057; 40th Cong., 2nd sess., H. Doc. 1, p. 679; 39th Cong., 2nd sess., S. Doc. 6, p. 34. 75. True Kentuckian, January 17, 1867; Georgetown Times, January 23, 1867; Collins and Collins, History of Kentucky, 1:175, 178; H. C. Hastings to Assistant Commissioner of Kentucky, January 2, 4, 1867, BRFAL, RG 105, Ky., NA.

76. A. S. Bloom to John Ely, May 13, 14, 1867, John Ely to A. S. Bloom, May 15, 1867, BRFAL, RG 105, Ky., NA. 77. Collins and Collins, History of Kentucky, 1:178. 78. See Gutman, Black Family in Slavery, 363-431, for a study of the slave family during the Civil War. 79. John Fee to Editor, Louisville Union, July 7, 1865.

CHAPTER NINE

1. Kenneth M. Stampp, The Peculiar Institution: Slavery in the Ante-Bellum South (New York: Random House, 1956), 222-23. 2. Leon F. Litwack, North of Slavery: The Negro in the Free States, 1790-1860 (Chicago: University of Chicago Press, 1965), 93. 3. Robert S. Henry, The Story of Reconstruction (Indianapolis: Bobbs-Merrill, 1938), 91, 93, 96, 205; James E. Sefton, The United States Army and Reconstruction, 1865-1877 (Baton Rouge: Louisiana State University Press, 1967), 98. 4. Harold B. Hancock, "Reconstruction in Delaware," in Richard O. Curry, ed., Radicalism, Racism, and Party Realignment: The Border States during

Reconstruction (Baltimore: Johns Hopkins University Press, 1969), 211-12; W. A. Low, "The Freedmen's Bureau and Civil Rights in Maryland," *Journal of Negro History*, Vol. 37, no. 3 (July 1952), 239-40, 241; O. O. Howard, *Autobiography of Oliver Otis Howard, Major General, United States Army*, 2 vols. (New York: Baker and Taylor, 1907), 2:285. 5. "Circular No. 5, May 30, 1865," *Acts of Congress Relative to Refugees, Freedmen, Confiscate and Abandoned Lands* (Washington, D.C.: U.S. Government Printing Office, 1865), 2; *Annual Report of the Commissioner, Oliver Otis Howard*, 39th Cong., 1st sess., 1865, H. Doc. 11 (Serial 1255), 45.

6. Paul S. Pierce, *The Freedmen's Bureau* (New York: Haskell House, 1971), 53-54.

7. *Annual Report of Commissioner*, 39th Cong., 1st sess., 1865, H. Doc 11, p. 31. See circular in *Washington Morning Chronicle*, January 3, 1865. 8. See "Justice" to Editor, *Cincinnati Gazette*, December 30, 1865. 9. *Lexington Observer and Reporter*, December 13, 1865; *Cincinnati Gazette*, December 30, 1865. 10. *New York Tribune*, December 30, 1865; *Lexington Union Standard*, January 2, 1866.

11. *Chicago Tribune*, January 4, 1866; *Washington Morning Chronicle*, January 8, 1866.

12. *Frankfort Commonwealth*, January 2, 1866; *H. J., 1865-66*, 439. 13. *Acts of Kentucky* (1866), 38-39. 14. See, e.g., John Palmer to J. G. Hollingsworth, January 20, 1866, RG 393, Ky., NA. 15. John Fee to George Whipple, March 26, 1866, AMA Correspondence; *Louisville Courier*, March 28, 1866.

16. Peter Bonested to O. O. Howard, March 5, 1866, C. B. Fisk to O. O. Howard, March 12, 1866, BRFAL, RG 105, Ky., NA; *National Anti-Slavery Standard*, April 7, 1866.

17. *Washington Morning Chronicle*, February 20, May 21, 1866. 18. *Circulars, Reports of Assistant Commissioners*, 39th Cong., 1st sess., 1865, H. Doc. 70, pp. 230-31. 19. "A Farmer in Kentucky," *Washington Morning Chronicle*, April 6, May 21, 1866; Coulter, *The Civil War and Readjustment in Kentucky*, 270; Ross A. Webb, "Kentucky: 'Pariah' among the Elect," in Curry, ed., *Radicalism, Racism, and Party Realignment*, 118-19; C. B. Fisk to O. O. Howard, March 12, 1866, BRFAL, RG 105, Ky., NA; T. E. Bramlette to Andrew Johnson, February 12, 1866, Andrew Johnson Papers; A. M. York to C. B. Fisk, March 10, 1866, BRFAL, RG 105, Ky., NA; C. B. Fisk to O. O. Howard, February 21, March 17, 1866, Oliver O. Howard Correspondence, Bowdoin College. In 1871, Judge Bland Ballard remarked that Kentucky "exhibits an extraordinary degree of obstinacy. . . . All around us everywhere they [Negroes] have been granted this right. I don't know a country upon the face of the earth except Kentucky where freedmen are not allowed to testify" (*Louisville Courier-Journal*, October 5, 1871). 20. Wilson, *Rise and Fall of the Slave Power*, 3:687.

21. *U.S. Statutes* (1865-67), 27. 22. *Lexington Observer and Reporter*, April 25, 1866. 23. General Orders No. 44, July 3, 1866, RG 94, NA. 24. John Ely to J. C. Davis, August 15, 1866, Bland Ballard to C. H. Frederick, September 1, 1866, Thomas to B. P. Runkle, June 20, 1868, O. O. Howard to Sidney Burbank, February 29, 1868, James H. Rice to John Ely, October 22, 1866, BRFAL, RG 105 Ky., NA. 25. J. C. Davis to O. O. Howard, November 5, 1866, BRFAL, RG Ky., NA.

26. *Louisville Journal*, October 3, 1866. 27. Bland Ballard to Lyman Trumbull, March 30, 1866, Lyman Trumbull Papers. 28. Bland Ballard to S. P. Chase, August 16, 1866, SPCP; *Louisville Democrat*, September 26, 1866. 29. See the discussion of *United States v. Erasmus Breedem et al.* in *Louisville Journal*, October 11, 1866; also see *Louisville Courier*, October 15, 1866. 30. O. O. Howard to Thomas D. Elliott, April 8, 1866, Andrew Johnson Papers; *Louisville Journal*, February 15, 1866.

31. *Chicago Tribune*, January 5, 1867; *Cincinnati Gazette*, January 4, 1867. 32. *HJ* (1867), 373-75, 386; *SJ* (1867), 381. 33. For the final settlement of the Harrison case see: J. W. Read to C. B. Fisk, April 25, 1866, BRFAL, RG 105 Ky., NA. For the Livingston County case, see: Solomen Littlefield to John Ely, September 7, 1866, J. H. Donovan to John Ely, October 18, 1866, BRFAL, RG 105, Ky., NA. 34. See O. O. Howard to Wager Swayne, January 30, 1867, BRFAL, RG 105, Ky., NA; *True Kentuckian*, January 17, 1867. 35. *Louisville Courier*, February 15, 1867; *True Kentuckian*, July 29, 1868.

36. J. L. Graham to R. E. Johnston, May 20, 1867, C. J. True to R. E. Johnston, May 22, 1867, BRFAL, RG 105, Ky., NA.   37. *Bowlin* v. *Commonwealth*, 65 Ky. 5 (1865) at 7-32; *Century Edition of the American Digest,* 50 vols. (St. Paul: West Publishing, 1899), 10:39; R. E. Johnston to Assistant Commissioner of Kentucky, June 14, 1867, June 27, 1867, BRFAL, RG 105 Ky., NA.   38. Howard, *Autobiography,* 2:345.   39. Aug Ditson to Editor, *Cincinnati Gazette,* May 10, 1867; B. H. Bristow to Assistant Commissioner of Kentucky, June 11, 1866, Bland Ballard to Assistant Commissioner of Kentucky, September 1, 1861, Ballard to B. P. Runkle, July 9, 1869, BRFAL, RG 105 Ky., NA. "D.S." to Editor, *Cincinnati Gazette,* April 19, 1867. In July 1866, Bristow privately expressed doubts about the constitutionality of federal jurisdiction in black testimony cases. See Will P. Thomasson to Lyman Trumbull, July 5, 1866, Trumbull Papers. In January 1867, Bristow expressed strong reservations concerning federal jurisdiction but also a desire to have a new law passed which would give the federal government full authority. See Benjamin Bristow to Lyman Trumbull, January 7, 1867, Benjamin Bristow Papers (Library of Congress). One of the bureau agents felt that Bristow lacked confidence in himself. See Will P. Thomasson to Lyman Trumbull, July 5, 1866, Trumbull Papers. In October, 1866, Bristow wrote the U.S. commissioner in Lexington and asked him to issue no more warrants under the Civil Rights Act until the Rhodes case was settled. See *Cincinnati Commercial,* May 31, 1867. In 1869, Bristow considered it "a matter of first importance to the 225,000 colored people" of Kentucky that the Civil Rights Act "be maintained and enforced" (B. H. Bristow to E. R. Hoar, May 18, 1869, RG 60, NA). When Bristow retired at the end of 1869, he had prosecuted twenty-nine civil rights cases. See Ross A. Webb, *Benjamin Helm Bristow: Border State Politician* (Lexington: University Press of Kentucky, 1969), 70.   40. Collins and Collins, *History of Kentucky,* 1:182.

41. A. J. Ballard to Charles Sumner, February 23, 1869, E. D. Kennedy to Sumner, April 6, 1869, W. E. Riley to Sumner, March 6, 1869, CSP.   42. *Cincinnati Gazette,* May 10, 1867; *Lexington Observer and Reporter,* October 30, 1867. The attitudes of the assistant commissioner of Kentucky, Bristow, and Ballard were, no doubt, partially shaped by their superiors. Edwin Stanton and Howard were committed to equal rights for freedmen. Judge Noah H. Swayne, who presided over the Sixth Federal Circuit Court, interpreted the Civil Rights Act as remedial. See: *United States* v. *Rhodes,* 27 F. Cas. 785 (No. 16, 151) (C.C.D., Ky., 1867). Henry Stanbery, the attorney general of the United States, was an appointee of President Johnson and was completely in accord with him. According to Gideon Wells, Stanbery told the cabinet in 1867 that he had voted against Negro suffrage while a member of the Ohio legislature and would do so again were he in Ohio. See Beale, ed., *Diary of Gideon Welles,* 3:4. When E. R. Hoar became attorney general of the United States, the cooperative efforts of Ballard, Bristow, and Hoar effectively dealt with the problem of testimony in Kentucky; Ross A. Webb, "Benjamin H. Bristow: Civil Rights Champion, 1866-1872," *Civil War History,* vol. 15, no. 1 (March 1969), 39-53.   43. *Louisville Journal,* January 2, 7, 1867; *Louisville Democrat,* January 3, 6, 1867; *Louisville Courier,* January 4, 5, 7, 1867.   44. *Louisville Democrat,* October 10, November 21, 1867; *Louisville Journal,* October 12, 1867.   45. *United States* v. *Rhodes,* 27 F. Cas. 785 (No. 16, 151) (C.C.D., Ky., 1867).

46. B. P. Runkle to Sidney Burbank, November 15, 1867, Circular No. 8, BRFAL, RG 105 Ky., NA.   47. *Annual Report of the commissioner of the Freedmen's Bureau,* 40th Cong., 2nd sess., 1867, H. Doc. 1 (Serial 1324), 689.   48. C. J. True to R. E. Johnston, November 26, 1867, R. E. Johnston to B. P. Runkle, November 30, 1867, BRFAL, RG Ky., NA.   49. *Louisville Courier,* January 2, 1867.   50. *Louisville Courier,* March 11, 1867; *Chicago Tribune,* March 9, 1867.

51. *Elyria Independent Democrat,* May 1, 1867.   52. *Lexington Observer and Reporter,* June 29, 1867.   53. *Lebanon Clarion,* cited by *Louisville Courier,* June 12, 1867.   54. *Kentucky Statesman,* July 9, 1867.   55. *Louisville Courier,* August 2, 1867.

56. *New York Times,* October 26, 1867; *Frankfort Commonwealth,* October 25, 1867; *Louisville Courier,* October 26, 1867; *Glasgow Times,* November 21, 1867, cited by *Louisville*

Courier, November 25, 1867.   57. *Cincinnati Gazette,* November 27, 1867; *Chicago Tribune,* November 28, 1867.   58. *Louisville Courier,* January 2, 1868; *Address Delivered by Bvt. Lieutenant Colonel Isaac S. Catlin, U.S.A., State of Kentucky, to the Freedmen of Louisville, October, 1868* (Louisville: Calvert, Trippett, 1868), 9.   59. *Evening Star,* January 14, 1869. The federal courts could not handle all the civil rights cases that could qualify for state courts. In the November 1868 term of the Jefferson County criminal court, fifty-two cases of Negroes and sixty-one cases of whites were on the docket. See *Louisville Courier-Journal,* November 15, 1868.   60. *Chicago Tribune,* July 15, 16, 17, 1869; *Cincinnati Gazette,* July 15, 16, 1868.

61. *Louisville Democrat,* March 12, 1868; *Cincinnati Gazette,* November 11, 1868.

62. *Louisville Democrat,* April 10, 1867; *Louisville Courier,* February 5, 6, March 22, 23, 25, April 9, 10, 11, 1867.   63. James Fidler to Assistant Commissioner of Kentucky, July 15, 1867, BRFAL, RG 105 Ky., NA; *Louisville Courier,* November 1, 5, 1867.   64. A. W. Lawwill to Assistant Commissioner of Kentucky, October 17, 1866, John Ely to A. W. Lawwill, December 20, 1866, John Ely to Thomas Farleigh, February 18, 1867, BRFAL, RG 105 Ky., NA; *Owensboro Monitor,* October 17, December 19, 1866.   65. *Louisville Courier,* September 4, 5, 8, October 31, November 7, 1868; *Louisville Journal,* September 9, 17, 1868.

66. *Louisville Courier-Journal,* November 30, December 2, 3, 9, 1868.   67. *Louisville Courier-Journal,* January 19, 1869; Henry Hunter and others to Charles Sumner, February 6, 1869, G. B. Thomas to Charles Sumner, March 7, 1869, CSP.   68. *HJ* (1869), 431, 432; *SJ* (1869), 310-16.   69. *Lexington Observer and Reporter,* January 9, 1869; Bland Ballard to John Stevenson, December 5, 1868, John Stevenson Papers, LC.   70. Victor B. Howard, "The Breckinridge Family and the Negro Testimony Controversy in Kentucky," *Filson Club History Quarterly,* vol. 49, (January 1975), 54-56.

71. *Kentucky Statesman,* February 25, 1870; James S. Brisbin to James F. Wade, February 10, 1867, in *Louisville Courier,* February 16, 1867. For paternity cases see: "Complaint and Trial Ledger," vol. 152, pp. 180, 183, Vol. 153, p. 92, vol. 153, p. 43, A. W. Lawwill to John Ely, June 19, 1867, extract from I. S. Catlin's report, in Sidney Burbank to O. O. Howard, November 16, 1867, BRFAL, RG 105, Ky., NA. See *Kentucky Statesman,* May 18, 1869, for the editor's argument that the protection of the black female was one of the chief motives for the Negro's desire to testify against whites. When Rev. Frederick Braxton, John Breckinridge's former slave, was asked why he would not vote for the Democrats, he said that he could not vote for a party that enacted law "to protect white women from outrages, and refuse the same to Negro virtue." Also see *Kentucky Statesman,* July 7, 1868.   72. *Maysville Eagle,* March 2, 1870; *Louisville Commercial,* February 25, 1870; *Cynthiana News,* March 3, 1870.   73. *The American Annual Cyclopaedia and Register of Important Events,* vol. 10 (New York: Appleton, 1870), 427.   74. *Louisville Commercial,* May 24, June 11, 1870; *True Kentuckian,* May 25, 1870.   75. In January, 1871, a Democratic convention in McCracken County adopted a resolution in favor of admitting black testimony in state courts. See *Paducah Kentuckian,* cited by *Louisville Courier-Journal,* February 1, March 9, 1871. A Democratic convention in Spencer County adopted a similar resolution, and a nonpartisan convention in Hickman County called on the legislature to admit black testimony without discrimination. See *Hickman Courier,* February 11, 1871.

76. *The Louisville Courier-Journal,* January 21, 1871. Resolutions or laws were introduced to permit blacks to testify against whites in 1865, 1867, 1870, and 1871. See *HJ,* (1865-66), pp. 63-65; (1867), pp. 373-75; *HJ, Adjourned Session* (1869), pp. 431-32; *HJ* (1869-70), p. 373; *HJ, Adjourned Session* (1871), pp. 387-388.   77. See *Commonwealth v. Nathan Bibbs* in *Louisville Courier,* October 7, 1868, and that of *Commonwealth v. Andrew Downing,* in *Lexington Observer and Reporter,* June 13, 1868. The blacks of Lexington were especially active in the civil rights movement. In June 1871 they established the Fayette County Justice Association, which sought to aid blacks with legal problems, particularly helping them place their cases before the federal court. See *Kentucky Statesman,* June 16, 1871.   78. *Cincinnati Gazette,* June

10, 1870, W. A. Meriwether to B. H. Bristow, December 26, 1870, Benjamin Bristow Papers. 79. *Kentucky Yeoman,* February 24, 1871.   80. *Louisville Commercial,* April 8, 1871. 81. *Louisville Commercial,* May 16, 1871; *Lexington Observer and Reporter,* May 17, 1871. 82. *Louisville Ledger,* cited by *Lexington Observer and Reporter,* May 17, 1871.   83. *Louisville Commercial,* November 28, 1871; *Covington Journal,* December 2, 1871.   84. *Louisville Commercial,* September 24, 1871; *Cincinnati Gazette,* September 26, 1871. The U.S. commissioner wrote Benjamin Bristow that the representative of the Frankfort district in which the defendants resided had publicly stated that he would "move heaven and earth" to have a new law of evidence enacted. The commissioner added, "When you strike a Crittenden you strike the State." (One of the defendants was a Crittenden.) See W. A. Meriwether to Benjamin Bristow, November 8, 1871, Benjamin Bristow Papers.   85. *Louisville Courier-Journal,* August 12, 13, 21, 1871; weekly edition, August 16, 18, 1871.

86. *SJ* (1872), 190-200; *HJ* (1872), 389 *Louisville Courier-Journal,* February 2, 23, 1872, March 8, October 15, 1873.   87. John William Wallace, *Cases Argued and Adjudged in the Supreme Court of the United States, December Term. 1871,* vol. 13 (Washington: W. H. and O. H. Morrison, 1872), 581-99.   88. *Louisville Courier-Journal,* October 9, 1872. 89. Thomas D. Clark, *A History of Kentucky* (Lexington: Bradford, 1960), 351.   90. Webb, *Benjamin Bristow,* 55.

CHAPTER TEN

1. Arna Bontemps, ed., "Autobiography of James L. Smith," in *Five Black Lives* (Middletown, Conn.: Wesleyan University Press, 1971), 226-27.   2. *New York Tribune,* cited by *Lexington Observer and Reporter,* June 24, 1865.   3. *Liberator,* July 21, 1865; James Brisbin to Benjamin Wade, November 29, 1865, WP; J. S. Brisbin to Thaddeus Stevens, December 29, 1865, Thaddeus Stevens Papers, LC; John G. Fee to George Whipple, July 6, 1865, AMA Correspondence.   4. John Fee to George Whipple, July 15, 1865, Fee to M. E. Strieby, August 11, 1865, Fee to Whipple, November 30, 1865, Fee to Whipple, December 2, 1865, Fee to Whipple, January 29, 1866, Fee to Whipple, March 26, 1866, AMA Correspondence. 5. *Louisville Courier,* November 30, 1866; *Cincinnati Gazette,* August 2, 1866.

6. *Louisville Democrat,* January 3, 1866; *Louisville Journal,* January 4, 1866; *Frankfort Commonwealth,* January 2, 1866.   7. *Union Standard,* June 26, 1866.   8. *Union Standard,* January 23, 1866; *Louisville Courier,* January 25, 1866; John Fee to George Whipple, March 26, 1866, AMA Correspondence.   9. Coulter, *The Civil War and Readjustment in Kentucky,* 350. The bureau became the most significant force in Kentucky working for Negro suffrage. As early as August 1, 1865, Fisk felt that the political success of the Union party in Kentucky was essential for freedom. See C. B. Fisk to John Fee, August 4, 1865, AMA Correspondence. 10. *Cincinnati Gazette,* March 24, 26, 27, 1866; *Louisville Courier,* March 2, 1866; John Fee to George Whipple, March 26, 1866, AMA Correspondence; *Nashville Colored Tennessean,* July 18, 1866.

11. *Louisville Courier,* August 11, 1866.   12. *Union Standard,* January 19, 1866; *The American Annual Cyclopaedia and Register of Important Events* (New York: Appleton, 1870), 6:424.   13. *Louisville Courier,* January 2, 1867; *Louisville Democrat,* January 2, 1867. 14. James Speed, *James Speed, A Personality, by James Speed, His Grandson* (Louisville: Morton, 1905), 66-67; James Speed to Charles Sumner, November 28, 1866, CSP; James Speed to Edwin Stanton, August 4, 1866, ESP.   15. *Louisville Journal,* January 1, 1867; *Frankfort Commonwealth,* January 18, 1867.

16. Collins and Collins, *History of Kentucky,* 1:174; *Congressional Globe,* 39th Cong., 2nd sess., pt. 1, p. 79, 344.   17. *Cincinnati Commercial,* cited by *Owensboro Monitor,* March 20, 1867.   18. Tapp, "Three Decades of Kentucky Politics, 1870-1900," 27; *Cincinnati Gazette,* February 15, 1867.   19. See "Mack" to Editor, *Cincinnati Commercial,* April 4, 1867.

20. *Kentucky Statesman,* May 7, 1867; *Cincinnati Commercial,* October 2, 5, 1867; Coulter, *The Civil War and Readjustment in Kentucky,* 350.

21. "Toodles" to Editor, *Cincinnati Commercial,* May 13, 1867.   22. *Louisville Courier,* March 11, 1867.   23. *Cincinnati Gazette,* cited by *Elyria Independent Democrat,* May 1, 1867; *Louisville Courier,* August 2, 1867.   24. John Fee to W. E. Whiting, July 15, 1867, Fee to E. M. Cravath, September 3, 1867, AMA Correspondence; *Louisville Courier,* July 8, 1867.

25. *Lexington Observer and Reporter,* July 6, 10, 1867; *True Kentuckian,* July 16, 1867.

26. R. E. Johnston to W. R. Browne, May 30, 1867, C. J. True to Johnston, 158:67 BRFAL, RG 105, Ky., NA.   27. *Louisville Journal,* August 19, 1867.   28. *Georgetown Times,* August 21, 1867.   29. R. J. Breckinridge to E. M. Stanton, October 22, 1865, M. L. Rice to E. M. Stanton, October 23, 1865, James S. Brisbin to E. M. Stanton, November 5, 1865, ESP.   30. "Loyal Kentuckians" to Thaddeus Stevens, March 4, 1867, Thaddeus Stevens Papers.

31. Charles Sumner to James S. Brisbin, in *Cincinnati Commercial,* May 31, 1867.

32. "Publius" to Editor, *Cincinnati Commercial,* cited by *Louisville Journal,* May 29, 1867.

33. *Harper's Weekly,* cited by *Kentucky Statesman,* June 11, 1867.   34. C. J. True to R. E. Johnston, August 25, 1867, BRFAL, RG 105, Ky., NA.   35. *Georgetown Times,* August 21, 1867; *Cincinnati Gazette,* August 15, 1867.

36. James M. Ogden to Joseph Holt, August 17, October 22, 1867, JHP; *Georgetown Times,* August 21, October 16, 1867.   37. *Louisville Democrat,* October 3, 1867; *Georgetown Times,* August 21, 1867; "D.S." to Editor, *Cincinnati Commercial,* October 2, 1867.

38. *Cincinnati Commercial,* cited by the *Louisville Democrat,* October 3, 1867; *National Anti-Slavery Standard,* September 28, 1867; *Cincinnati Gazette,* August 15, 1867.

39. *Lexington Observer and Reporter,* August 31, 1867.   40. *Cincinnati Gazette,* August 31, 1867; *Georgetown Times,* September 4, 1867; *Louisville Democrat,* August 28, 1867.

41. *Cincinnati Commercial,* September 20, 1867.   42. *Maysville Republican,* October 11, 26, 1867.   43. *Louisville Journal,* October 23, 1867; *Louisville Democrat,* October 19, 1867; *New York Times,* October 26, 1867; *Frankfort Commonwealth,* October 25, 1867.

44. "Occasional" to Editor, *Louisville Journal,* October 28, 1867.   45. *Lexington Observer and Reporter,* November 6, 1867.

46. *Louisville Courier,* October 26, 29, 1867; *Glasgow Times,* November 21, 1867, cited by *Louisville Courier,* November 25, 1867; *Maysville Republican,* November 23, 1867.

47. *Kentucky Statesman,* November 8, 1867; *Maysville Republican,* November 9, 1867.

48. *Kentucky Statesman,* November 22, 1867.   49. *Kentucky Gazette,* November 2, 1867; *Kentucky Statesman,* November 26, 1867.   50. *Cincinnati Gazette,* November 27, 28, 29, 1867; *Louisville Journal,* December 3, 1867.

51. *Louisville Courier,* January 2, 1866.   52. Walter L. Fleming, *Documentary History of Reconstruction: Political Military, Social, Religious Educational and Industrial, 1865 to the Present Time,* 2 vols. (Cleveland: A. H. Clark, 1906-1907), 1:480; *Louisville Journal,* May 31, June 12, 1868.   53. Assistant Commissioner, Subdistrict, Henderson, Kentucky, to B. P. Runkle, April 1868, BRFAL, RG 105, Ky., NA; *Louisville Courier,* July 8, 1868.   54. *Cincinnati Commercial,* July 7, 1868.   55. Coulter, *The Civil War and Readjustment in Kentucky,* 351.

56. *Congressional Globe,* 39th Cong., 1st sess., 246, 40th Cong., 3rd sess., pt. 2, p. 712, pt. 3, pp. 1564, 1641.   57. *Louisville Courier-Journal,* January 3, 4, 1869.   58. *True Kentuckian,* July 7, 14, 1869; Collins and Collins, *History of Kentucky,* 1:197.   59. *Louisville Courier-Journal,* July 15, 1869.   60. *Cincinnati Gazette,* July 16, 1869.

61. H. H. Trumbo to Editor, *National Anti-Slavery Standard,* October 9, 1869.   62. J. W. Alvord to O. O. Howard, January 28, 1870, BRFAL, RG 105, Ky., NA.   63. *Frankfort Commonwealth,* February 4, 1870.   64. Few blacks attended the delegate meetings held in Estill and Owsley counties. See *Frankfort Commonwealth,* February 18, 1870; *Kentucky Statesman,* February 22, 1870.   65. *Kentucky Statesman,* February 18, 1870; *Louisville Commercial,* February 22, 1870.

66. *Shelby Sentinel,* March 2, 1870; *Louisville Commercial,* February 14, 17, 21, 23, 24, 1870.   67. *Louisville Commercial,* February 25, 1870.   68. *Kentucky Yeoman,* February 25, 1870; *New York Tribune,* February 28, 1870.   69. *Lexington Observer and Reporter,* March 9, 1870; *Louisville Commercial,* March 19, 25, 1870.   70. *Danville Advocate,* cited by *Maysville Eagle,* June 8, 1870; *Louisville Commercial,* March 24, 1870; *Lexington Observer and Reporter,* March 26, 1870.

71. W. E. Connelley and E. M. Coulter, *History of Kentucky,* 5 vols. (Chicago: American Historical Society, 1922), 2:91; *Kentucky Gazette,* February 12, 1870; *Shelby Sentinel* (Kentucky), March 30, 1870.   72. *Louisville Commercial,* March 23, 25, April 1, 1870.

73. *Cincinnati Evening Chronicle,* April 8, 1870; *Nashville Republican Banner,* April 9, 1870; *American Annual Cyclopedia and Register,* 10:427.   74. *Frankfort Commonwealth,* April 15, May 20, 1870; *Louisville Commercial,* April 30, May 13, 1870. Celebrations were held at Simpsonville, Munfordville, LaGrange, Cynthiana, Cadiz, Winchester, Carlisle, and Paris and in Garrard and Bullitt counties. See *Frankfort Commonwealth,* April 22, 23, May 7, 17, 24, 1870.   75. *Frankfort Commonwealth,* May 13, 1870; *Louisville Commercial,* June 15, 23, 24, 25, 29, 1870.

76. *Louisville Courier-Journal,* May 22, 1870; *Cincinnati Gazette,* June 3, 1870; *Kentucky Yeoman,* May 12, 1870; *Louisville Commercial,* May 7, 1870.   77. *Western Citizen* (Paris), June 7, 1870; "Avery" to Editor, *Cincinnati Commercial,* April 1, 1870.   78. *New York Tribune,* July 18, 1870; *Richmond Register* (Kentucky), cited in *Lexington Observer and Reporter,* July 6, 20, 1870.   79. *Flemingsburg Democrat,* July 28, 1870; *Louisville Commercial,* July 20, 1870; Marrs, *Life of Marrs,* 82-83, 86-87.   80. *Acts of Kentucky* (1871), 1:4; *Frankfort Commonwealth,* March 25, April 1, 1870.

81. *Madison Courier* (Indiana), February 25, 1870; *Louisville Commercial,* February 24, 1870; *Cincinnati Commercial,* February 1, 3, 10, 1870; *HJ* (1869), 3, 35, 429, 484, 900-901.   82. *Cincinnati Gazette,* August 5, 1870; *Cincinnati Commercial,* November 16, 1870.

83. *Louisville Commercial,* February 25, 1870; *Maysville Eagle,* March 2, 1870.   84. Edward A. Pollard, "The Negro in the South," *Lippincott's Magazine,* vol. 5 (April 1870), 383-84, 390-91; Horace Morris to Edward A. Pollard, *Washington Morning Chronicle,* April 12, 1870.

85. *Cincinnati Commercial,* November 16, 1870; *Kentucky Gazette,* May 6, 1871.

86. *Maysville Bulletin,* June 15, 1871; *Covington Journal,* August 10, 1871.   87. C. M. Clay to S. P. Chase, January 3, 1891, SPCP; *Lexington Statesman,* cited in *True Kentuckian,* January 11, 1871.   88. *Cincinnati Commercial,* April 1, 1871; *Covington Journal,* July 15, 1871. On May 23, 1871, the Negro supporters of Grant met in Covington and endorsed the general. See *Evening Star,* May 21, 1872.   89. *Louisville Commercial,* March 14, 1872.   90. *Covington Journal,* March 16, 1872, citing *Louisville Ledger.*

91. *Western Citizen,* October 1, 1872; *Maysville Bulletin,* October 10, 1872. *Covington Journal,* November 2, 1872; Collins and Collins, *History of Kentucky,* 1:231.   92. *Louisville Ledger,* February 20, 1873; *Louisville Courier-Journal,* February 20, 1873.   93. *Lexington Dollar Press,* December 3, 1873.   94. *Acts of Kentucky* (1873), 31; *HJ* (1873), 857-59; *U.S. Statutes* (1870), vol. 16, 140-46; *U.S. v. Reese,* 91 U.S. 563 (1875).   95. *Frankfort Yeoman,* cited by *Louisville Courier-Journal,* August 7, 1874.

96. In February 1882, speaker after speaker at a Negro citizens convention avowed that in the future the one question which would decide how the blacks would cast their votes would be whether the candidate was a friend of Negro education; blacks would support candidates who were, whether Democrat or Republican. See *Lexington Transcript,* February 27, 1882.

CHAPTER ELEVEN

1. *Preliminary and Final Report Touching the Condition and Management of Emancipated Refugees: Made to the Secretary of War, by the American Freedmen's Inquiry Commission, June 30, 1863, and May 14, 1864,* (New York: 1863-64) Senate Ex. Doc., No. 1, p. 7, and Doc. 53, p. 4,

38 Cong., 1 sess., serial 1176; OR 3, vol. 3, p. 432; *New York Times,* June 19, 1863.
2. *National Anti-Slavery Standard,* November 4, 1865.   3. *Cincinnati Gazette,* November 11, 1865; *Chicago Tribune,* March 21, 1866; John Ely to Anne Biddle, April 3, May 19, 1866, BRFAL, RG 105, Ky., NA.   4. "Justice" to Editor, *Cincinnati Gazette,* December 30, 1865; John Ely to H. G. Brown, April 9, 1866, BRFAL, RG 105, Ky., NA.   5. John Fee to Secretary of AMA, in *American Missionary,* vol. 9, no. 3, (March 1865), 57; no. 10 (October 1865), 230; W. H. Fourse, "Educational History of the Negroes of Lexington, Kentucky" (Master's thesis, University Cincinnati, 1937), 38.

6. Circular No. 2, May 19, 1865, *Acts of Congress Relative to Refugees, Freedmen and Confiscated and Abandoned Lands* (Washington, D.C.: U.S. Government Printing Office, 1866); Marjorie H. Parker, "Some Educational Activities of the Freedmen's Bureau," *Journal of Negro Education,* vol. 33 (winter 1954), 9; Victoria Marcus Olds, "The Freedmen's Bureau as a Social Agency" (Ph.D. diss., Columbia University, 1966), p. 148.   7. *Louisville Union Press,* December 29, 1865.   8. *Acts of Kentucky* (1865-66), 51; *Acts of Kentucky, the Adjourned Session* (1865-1866), p. 51.   9. *Cincinnati Gazette,* March 24, 27, 1866; John G. Fee to George Whipple, March 26, 1866, AMA Correspondence; W. E. B. Du Bois, *Black Reconstruction,* 568.   10. *Annual Report of the Superintendent of Public Instruction of Kentucky for the School Year Ending December 31, 1866* (Frankfort: Yeoman, 1867), 23; *Annual Report of the Auditor of the State of Kentucky For the Fiscal Year Ending October 10, 1866* (Frankfort: Yeoman, 1866), 7, 57, 275.

11. T. K. Noble to J. W. Alvord, February 11, 1867; R. E. Johnson to Assistant Commissioner of Kentucky, June 13, 1866, BRFAL, RG 105, Ky., NA; *HJ* (1867-68), 81; *Annual Report of the Superintendent of Public Instruction, 1866,* 22; (1867), 248.   12. John W. Alvord, *Fourth Semi-Annual Report on Schools and Finances of Freedmen, for July 1, 1867* (Washington, D.C.: U.S. Government Printing Office, 1868), 60.   13. Henry L. Swint, *The Northern Teacher in the South* (Nashville: Vanderbilt University Press, 1941), 3.   14. *American Freedmen,* vol. 1, no. 2, (May 1866), 26; no. 7, (October 1866), 110-112; *Report of the Bureau of Refugees, Freedmen and Abandoned Lands, November 1, 1866,* 39th Cong., 2nd sess., 1866, H. Doc. 1 (Serial 1285), 748. Tennessee received ten times as much private aid for black schools as Kentucky. See Alvord, *Fourth Semi-Annual Report,* 57.   15. John Ely to H. G. Brown, May 19, 1866, John Ely to Jeff C. Davis, August 15, 1866, Assistant Commissioner of Kentucky to O. O. Howard, November 5, 1866, BRFAL, RG 105, Ky., NA.

16. John Ely to Ann Biddle, April 3, 1866, BRFAL, RG 105, Ky., NA: report of Peter Bonestal, special inspector of the bureau, March 20, 1866, in *Chicago Tribune,* March 21, 1866.   17. Ben Runkle to Sidney Burbank, December 12, 1867, T. K. Noble to J. W. Alvord, April 16, 1867, BRFAL, RG 105, Ky., NA; John W. Alvord, *Third Semi-Annual Report on Schools and Finances of Freedmen for January, 1867* (Washington, D.C.: U.S. Government Printing Office, 1867), 30.   18. Monthly school reports received, 1868 to 1869, BRFAL, RG 105, Ky., NA; J. C. Davis to O. O. Howard, November 5, 1866, BRFAL, RG 105, Ky., NA; John W. Alvord, *Sixth Semi-Annual Report on Schools and Finances of Freedmen for July, 1868,* 50; P. C. Kimball, "Education for Negroes in Kentucky, 1865-1871 . . ." (Master's thesis, University of North Carolina, 1969); M. H. Parker, "The Education Activities of the Freedmen's Bureau" (Ph. D. dis., University of Chicago, 1951), 139.   19. T. K. Noble to J. W. Alvord, March 11, 1867, September 1, 1867, December 1, 1867, January 1, 1868; B. A. Brown to Assistant Commissioner of Kentucky, May 4, 1868, BRFAL, RG 105, Ky., NA.
20. Levi F. Burnett to Assistant Commissioner of Kentucky, April 17, 1866, BRFAL, RG 105, Ky., NA.

21. "XX" to Editor, the *Kentucky Statesman,* February 12, 1867; O. O. Howard to Assistant Commissioner of Kentucky, August 17, 1867, Black Citizens of Columbus, Kentucky, to O. O. Howard, August 13, 1867, BRFAL, RG 105, Ky., NA; *Annual Report of the Secretary of War, 1866* (Washington, D.C.: U.S. Government Printing Office, 1866), 26.
22. Martin Norton to R. E. Johnston, January 8, 1868, BRFAL, RG 105, Ky., NA.

23. Landers Abernathy and others to A. W. Lawwill, July 15, 1867, BRFAL, RG 105, Ky., NA.   24. *Acts of Kentucky* (1867), 1:96; *Annual Report of the Superintendent of Public Instruction of Kentucky, 1868*, pp. 248-49; John Ely to Sidney Burbank, October 4, 1867, T. K. Noble to J. W. Alvord, July 8, 1867, BRFAL, RG 105 Ky., NA.   25. *Acts of Kentucky*, (1868), 4; Ben Runkle to Sidney Burbank, December 12. 1867, BRFAL, RG 105, Ky., NA; *True Kentuckian*, March 10, 1868.

26. Ben Runkle to James Speed, November 1, 1867, Runkle to R. E. Johnston, January 4, 1868, Runkle to Speed, January 15, 1868, BRFAL, RG 105, Ky., NA. Ben Runkle continued to urge that the bureau challenge the Negro capitation law in federal courts, and he was eventually authorized to employ James Speed to take legal action against the law. See Ben Runkle to O. O. Howard, October 22, 1869, BRFAL, RG 105, Ky., NA.   27. *Annual Report of the Superintendent of Public Instruction of Kentucky for 1869*, p. 70; T. K. Noble to J. W. Alvord, October 30, 1868, BRFAL, RG 105, Ky., NA. James Speed was reluctant to resort to court action. Like other Republicans, he socialized with many of the leading Democrats in Frankfort and Louisville and did not relish taking extreme measures against officers in the state government under the Civil Rights Act of 1866. The U.S. district attorney and the federal district court commissioner was also reluctant to apply the Civil Rights Act and the Fourteenth Amendment in full force to secure the rights of blacks.   28. Ben Runkle to J. W. Alvord, 21:369, BRFAL, RG 105, Ky., NA; *Louisville Evening Express*, July 8, 1869.   29. *Chicago Tribune*, July 16, 1869.   30. *Louisville Courier-Journal*, July 17, 1869.

31. Horace Mann Bond, *The Education of the Negro in the American Social Order* (1934; reprint ed., New York: Octagon Books, 1966), 31.   32. *Louisville Democrat*, December 7, 1866; *Report of T. D. Eliot, March 10, 1868*, 40th Cong., 2nd sess., 1868, H. Doc. 30 (Serial 1357).   33. P. C. Kimball, "Freedom's Harvest: Freedmen's Schools in Kentucky after the Civil War," *Filson Club History Quarterly* (July 1980), 282.   34. John W. Alvord, *Second Semi-Annual Report on Schools and Finances of Freedmen, July 1866* (Washington, D.C.: U.S. Government Printing Office, 1866), 2.   35. Bond, *Education of the Negro*, 31.

36. Claude H. Nolan, "Aftermath of Slavery: Southern attitude Toward Negroes, 1865-1890," Ph. D. dissertation, University of Texas, Austin, 1963.   37. *Owensboro Monitor*, April 24, 1867. In November, 1868, seven meetings were held by the bureau in Negro churches in Louisville. Meetings of a similar type were held in Covington, Maysville, Danville, and other cities. The addresses also emphasized the necessity of continuing to work toward securing the right of suffrage and black testimony in the state courts against whites.   38. John G. Fee to Editor, May 15, 1867, in *Kentucky Statesman*, May 24, 1867.   39. T. K. Noble to J. W. Alvord, July 8, 1867, BRFAL, RG 105 Ky., NA.   40. Circular No. 8, Assistant Commissioner of Kentucky, July 16, 1868, RG 105 Ky., NA; *Address Delivered by Bvt. Lieutenant Colonel Catlin, to the Freedmen of Louisville*, 9.

41. *Cincinnati Gazette*, July 15, 16, 1868.   42. Assistant Superintendent of the Bureau of Schools of Kentucky to Ben Runkle, August 18, 1869, BRFAL, RG 105, Ky., NA.

43. Green Hardwick to Ben Runkle, October 17, 1869, BRFAL, RG 105, Ky., NA.

44. *Kentucky Statesman*, January 28, 1870.   45. *Washington Morning Chronicle*, April 6, 1870; *Annual Report of the Superintendent of Public Instruction of Kentucky for 1869*, 70-72; *Acts of Kentucky* 1869-70, 7, 8.

46. *Louisville Commercial*, August 17, 1870; *Cincinnati Gazette*, August 18, 1870.

47. *Acts of Kentucky* (1871), 1:18.   48. *Louisville Courier Journal*, December 13, 1872; Moses Edward Ligon, *A History of Public Education in Kentucky* (Lexington: University of Kentucky, 1942), 247-48; *Annual Report of the Auditor of the State of Kentucky for the Fiscal Year Ending October, 1873*, 43.   49. *Covington Journal*, February 22, June 14, 21, 1873; *Louisville Courier-Journal*, February 19, 1873.   50. *HJ* (1873), 930-31, 1148; *SJ* (1873), 920, 922.

51. *HJ* (1873), 715-17; *Acts of Kentucky* 1873), 205-06.   52. *New York Times,* November 27, 1873; *Lexington Dollar Press,* December 3, 1873. 53. *Kentucky Yeoman*, March 25, 1873; *Chase v. Stephenson*, 71 Illinois 383 (1874); *Dallas v. Fosdick*, 40 Howard Pr. 249 (New York,

1869), *Ward* v. *Flood,* 48 Calif. 36 (1874). See also: *Van Camp* v. *The Board,* 9 Ohio State 406. The *State* v. *McCann,* 21 Ohio State 198; *Acts of Kentucky* (1873-74), 63; Barksdale Hamlett, *History of Education in Kentucky* (Frankfort: Kentucky Department of Education, 1914), 137, 145; James A. Bond, "Negro Education in Kentucky" (Master's thesis, University of Cincinnati, 1930), 20. 54. *Louisville Courier-Journal,* May 18, 1874; *Marshal* v. *Donovan,* Kentucky, 10 (1873-1874), Bush, 681-95. 55. *Louisville Courier-Journal,* July 9, 1877, August 9, 1878; *Louisville Commercial,* August 11, 1880.

56. *Louisville Courier-Journal,* August 28, 1879, August 26, 1880; *Appleton's Annual Cyclopaedia and Register of Important Events,* (1879), New Series, 4:541; *Louisville Commercial,* December 12, 1881, August 11, 1882; *Paducah News,* February 25, March 13, May 13, 1882. 57. *Louisville Courier-Journal,* November 30, December 21, 1881; February 24, 26, 1882; *SJ* (1881-82), 494. 58. *Louisville Courier-Journal,* March 10, 1882, April 12, 22, 1882; *SJ* (1881-82), 1204, 1216; *Acts of Kentucky* (1881-82) 1: 130; *Louisville Commercial,* April 8, 1882. 59. *Louisville Commercial,* April 8, 11, 1882; *Lexington Transcript,* April 13, 1882; *United States* v. *Buntin,* 10 FED. REP. 730 (1882). 60. See *United States* v. *Buntin,* 10 FED. REP. 735 (1882); J. Q. Ward to Editor, *Louisville Courier-Journal,* August 4, 1881; See *Clark* v. *Board of Education, Iowa Reports,* 24 Stiles, 266-67 (1868); *Smith* v. *The Directors of the Independent School District of Keokuk, 40 Iowa* 40, 518-19 (1875).

61. *Louisville Commercial,* April 11, 20, June 9, 1882; *Louisville Courier-Journal,* April 12, 1882; *Commonwealth of Kentucky* v. *Ellis* originated in the summer of 1881 in the McCracken County Court. The state sought to compel the defendant to pay the Negro capitation tax of one dollar. Newspapers gave the case publicity in December. See *Louisville Commercial,* December 12, 1881. 62. *Louisville Courier-Journal,* April 12, 21, June 4, July 28, August 5, 1882; *Lexington Transcript,* April 13, 1882; *Louisville Commercial,* April 11, May 25, 1882. 63. See J. Morgan Kousser, "Making Separate Equal: Integration of Blacks and White School Funds in Kentucky," *Journal of Interdisciplinary History,* vol. 10, no. 3 (winter 1980), 399-428, for a different interpretation. Kousser does not note the significance of the law of 1882 as the forerunner of the principle elaborated in *Plessy* v. *Ferguson.* He is interested in classifying the various factions in the school controversy, but he chooses the wrong year for analysis. He should have chosen the year 1873 instead of 1882, as the votes during the session of 1882 reflected federal coercion rather than principle. In 1873, federal coercion was nonexistent. Kousser is under the impression that the school funds were equalized in 1882, but in fact they were not equalized until 1884, after *Claybrook* v. *Owensboro.* See Kousser, 422 and note 32. 64. *Paducah News,* cited by *Lexington Transcript,* July 24, 1882; *Louisville Courier-Journal,* April 21, August 2, 1881. 65. *Louisville Courier-Journal,* August 4, 1882; *Strauder* v. *West Virginia* 100 U.S. 303 (1880).

66. *Ex-Parte Virginia,* 100 U.S. 303 (1880). 67. *Louisville Courier-Journal,* June 14, 15, 1882; *Kentucky Yeoman,* June 15, 1882; *Lexington Transcript,* June 14, 1882. 68. *Lexington Transcript,* June 15, 1882. 69. *Lexington Transcript,* July 26, 1882; *Kentucky Yeoman,* July 29, 1882; *Louisville Courier-Journal,* August 4, 1882. The rural blacks and the Negro clergy were more inclined to accept the segregation clause in the school law of 1882 than were other blacks. 70. In many counties very few people knew that a race issue was involved before the referendum of August 1882. The legislature did not provide funds for advertising the law as usual in the newspapers. See *Henderson Reporter,* June 15, 1882; *St. Louis Globe-Democrat,* cited by *Owensboro Messenger,* May 4, 1883; *Louisville Commercial,* April 30, 1883.

71. *Claybrook* v. *City of Owensboro,* 16 Fed., 297-98, (1883). 72. The civic-minded citizens included such men as William Chenault, dean of the Louisville Law School, Dr. Basil Manly, Louisville Theology Seminary, and William C. P. Breckinridge. *Louisville Commercial,* February 1, 1883; *Owensboro Messenger,* April 13, 1883; *Louisville Courier-Journal,* September 20, 21, 1883. 73. *Louisville Courier-Journal,* March 23, 1883; *Louisville Commercial,* February 10, 1883. 74. *Louisville Courier-Journal,* April 12, May 1, September 20, 22, 1883; Resolutions of a black convention of July 13, which "hailed the harmony and progress with gladness,"

Louisville Courier-Journal, July 14, 1883.   75. *HJ* (1883-84), pp. 1734-35; *Acts of Kentucky* (1883-84), 1: 110.
   76. *Acts of Kentucky* (1883-84), 145; *Revised Statutes,* sec. 629, (2d ed., 1878), 16.
   77. Bond, *Education of the Negro,* 48; *Maddox et al* v. *Neal,* 11 Ark. 125 (1885); *Reid* v. *Town of Eatonton,* (Ga.). 9 S.E. Rep. 602 (1888); *Dawson,* v. *Lee,* 83 Ky. 49 citerd by *Plessy* v. *Ferguson,* 163 U.S. 558 (1896).   78. *Louisville Commercial,* June 16, 1882; *Louisville Courier-Journal,* June 15, 1882.   79. Henry Allen Bullock, *A History of Negro Education in the South from 1619 to the Present* (Cambridge, Mass.: Harvard University Press, 1967), 70, 168.

EPILOGUE

   1. Howard, "The Breckinridge Family", 16; Tapp, "Three Decades of Kentucky Politics, 1870-1890," Ph. D. dissertation, University of Kentucky, 1950, 464-65.   2. Allen W. Trelease, *White Terror: The Ku Klux Klan Conspiracy and the Southern Reconstruction* (New York: Harper and Row, 1971), 89; Coulter, *The Civil War and Readjustment in Kentucky,* 359-64.   3. *Senate Miscellaneous Documents* (1871), 42nd Cong., 1st. sess., no. 49.   4. *US Statutes at Large* (1871) vol. 17, 13-15.   5. Trelease, *White Terror,* 317.

Manuscript Sources and Government Documents

The records of the Bureau of Refugees, Freedmen, and Abandoned Lands, Record Group 105, National Archives, Washington, D.C., constituted the major manuscript source of this study. The proliferation of recent studies dealing with the Reconstruction period, and touching in different ways on the work of the Freedmen's Bureau, has brought into focus a wide range of aids in the use of the source materials. Valuable bibliographical aids to the bureau records are: *Preliminary Inventory of the Records of the Field Offices of the Bureau of Refugees, Freedmen, and Abandoned Lands,* in two parts, compiled by Elaine Everly and Willna Pacheli (National Archives and Records Service, General Service Administration, 1973); and *National Archives Microfilm Publications,* pamphlet accompanying microcopy no. 752 and other microcopies in RG105. The published reports of the commissioner, which incorporate the reports of the assistant commissioners of Kentucky, were a reliable source. The manuscript records of the bureau, especially the copies of letters sent from the commissioner's office over his signature, not only reflect the ways in which agency policies were applied, but reveal General Oliver O. Howard's administrative techniques, attitudes, and patterns of thinking. These letters are copied in manuscript in bound volumes, chronologically. The volumes also include the handwritten circulars and various reports issued by Howard. Registers and letters received by the commissioner, 1865-1872 (Microcopy No. 752), proved useful in locating letters that had been sent from the assistant commissioner of Kentucky.

The work of the various agents in Kentucky can be followed in the "Registers of Letters Received by the Assistant Commissioner of Kentucky." These volumes are abstracts of incoming communications. The detailed letters are found in "Letters Received by the Assistant Commissioner of Kentucky." The assistant commissioner's application of the bureau policy can be traced through "Letters Sent by the Assistant Commissioner of Kentucky."

The educational work of the Bureau can be found in "Letters Sent by the Superintendent of Education for Kentucky," and in the ten semiannual reports, *Schools for Freedmen,* of the general superintendent of education, John W. Alvord (Washington, D.C.: U.S. Government Printing Office, 1866-1870). Six volumes of press copies and two volumes of copies of letters sent by John W. Alvord to state superintendents of schools, aid society members, and other bureau officers are useful. The teachers of bureau schools also made monthly reports to the assistant commissioner. The register of marriages of freedmen in Kentucky and records of the Freedmen's Bureau Court are also available. Another important manuscript source for a background study of the freedmen is the American Freedmen's Inquiry Commission, 1863-1864, in "Letters Received by the Office of the Adjutant General, Main Series, 1861-1870," RG 94, National Archives.

The effect of the army on the slaves can be studied in detail through the records of the Military Department of Washington and the various departments that encompassed Kentucky: Department of Ohio, Department of the Cumberland, Department of Kentucky, Department of Tennessee. These documents are contained in RG393, National Archives. RG94 contains the adjutant general office records and general's papers. Valuable information concerning the enrollment and draft of blacks are found in RG110, Provost Marshall General Bureau.

The papers of the attorneys general, 1842-1870, RG60, National Archives, were very important in studying the civil right cases in the federal courts during Reconstruction.

A source that was extremely valuable for this study was "The Negro in the Military Service of the United States, a Compilation of Official Records, State Papers, Historical Extracts, Relating to His Military Status and Service, from the North American Colonies," RG94, NA, 7 volumes (nine chapters), 1888, prepared by Elon A. Woodward, chief of the Colored Troops Division of the adjutant general, under the direction of Brigadier General Richard C. Drum, Adjutant general of the army. Although the volumes contain information relating to Negroes in the colonial period and their service in the U.S. army prior to the Civil War, the major part of this work (chapters 4-9) pertains to the Civil War period. This source is available in microfilm (M858).

The record of what former slaves really experienced during the Civil War and Reconstruction is available in the Federal Writers' Project, *Slave Narratives: A Folk History of Slavery in the United States from Interviews With Former Slaves* (Washington, D.C.: Library of Congress, 1941). These have been published in nineteen volumes by Greenwood Press (Westport, Conn., 1973).

Published Government Documents

The War of the Rebellion: A Compilation of the Official Records of the Union and Confederate Armies, (130 volumes, Washington, D.C.: Government Printing Office, 1880-1901) is the most valuable published source relating to military affairs. This source is available in NARS Microfilm Publication MF62.

Most valuable for this study were the numerous documents and reports published by the two houses of Congress. The following were particularly useful:

Published Annual Reports of Commissioner Oliver Otis Howard: 1865 House Ex. Doc. No. 11, 39 Cong., 1 sess., serial 1255; 1866 House Ex. Doc. No. 1, 39 Cong., 2 sess., serial 1285; 1867 House Ex. Doc. No. 1, 40 Cong., 2 sess., serial 1324; 1867 House Ex. Doc. No. 1, 40 Cong., 3 sess., serial 1367.

Circulars, Reports of Assistant Commissioners, 1865 House Ex. Doc. No. 70, 39 Cong., 1 sess., serial 1256; 1865 Senate Ex. Doc. No. 6 39 Cong., 2 sess., serial 1276; 1867 House Ex. Doc. 329, 40 cong., 2 sess., serial 1346.

Preliminary and Final Reports of the American Freedmen's Inquiry Commission June 30, 1863, and May 14, 1864. Thomas Hood and S. W. Bostwick, *Report of the Commissioners of Investigation of Colored Refugees in Kentucky, Tennessee, and Alabama, December 28, 1864,* 1864 Senate Ex. Doc. No. 27, 39 Cong., 1 sess., serial 1238. *Report of T. D. Eliot, March 10, 1868, on the Freedmen's Bureau,* House Reports, 40 Cong., 2 sess., No. 30, serial 1357. *Senate Miscellaneous Documents, 1871,* Senate Ex. Doc. No. 49, 42 Cong. 1 sess., 1871.

For provisions of the laws passed during Reconstruction, the sources are *U.S. Statutes at Large, Containing the Laws and Concurrent Resolutions . . .and Proclamations, Treaties, and International Agreements,* 77 vols. (Washington, D.C.: Government Printing Office, 1789-1946), vols. 12, 14; *U.S. Congressional Globe,* 1833-1873, 36 Cong., 1 sess. to 41 Cong., 2 sess.

Manuscript Papers and Collected Correspondence

Amistad Library, New Orleans, American Missionary Association Correspondence.

Bowdoin College, Oliver Otis Howard Papers.

Chicago Historical Society Library: Zebina Eastman Papers; Robert Perry Hoge Civil War Diary; Frederick A. Starring Collection.

Cincinnati Historical Society, Stanley Matthews Letters.

Filson Club Library, Louisville: Benjamin Bristow Manuscripts; Josephine Wells Covington Manuscripts; Susan Preston Grigsby Collection; Josephus Lunett Manuscripts; Cora Hume Owens Journal; John W. Stevenson Manuscripts.

Harvard University (Houghton Library), Charles Sumner Papers.

Illinois State Historical Library: Roger Hannaford Diary; John M. Palmer Papers; Lysander Wheeler Correspondence; Ira Van Deusen Correspondence.

Indiana Historical Society Library: John J. Hardin, Civil War Letters; John J. Hardin Correspondence.

Indiana State Historical Library: Robert B. Hanna Family Papers; Ormand Hupp Diary; Thomas E. Shepherd Papers; Levi P. Fodrea, typescript, Sanford A. Michael, History of the 101st Regiment of Volunteer Infantry of Indiana; M. E. Foley Letters.

Kentucky Historical Society Library: Thomas E. Bramlette Papers; R.H. Earnest Manuscripts; Albert B. Fall Correspondence.

Library of Congress: Blair Family Papers; Robert J. Breckinridge Family Papers; Benjamin F. Bristow Papers; Salmon P. Chase Papers; John J. Crittenden Papers; William Herndon-Weik Collection; Joseph Holt Papers; Andrew Johnson Papers; Reverdy Johnson Papers; Robert Lincoln Papers; John Sherman Papers; William T. Sherman Papers; Edwin M. Stanton Papers; John Stevenson Papers; Thaddeus Stevens Papers; Lyman Trumbull Papers; Benjamin Wade Papers.

Miami University (Ohio), Peter Bruner, "A Slaves Adventures Toward Freedom: Not Fiction, But a True Story of a Struggle," typescript.

Michigan Historical Collection, University of Michigan: Judson L. Austin, Civil War Letters; William Boston Civil War Diary; Orlando Hurley Moore Manuscripts; Oliver Spaulding Diary; Asa Walker Civil War Journal.

U.S. Army Military Historical Collection, Carlisle Barracks, Pennsylvania: John

W. Ford Collection; John Love Letters; Frank McGregor Papers, Eighty-third Kentucky Infantry Regiment; David Millspaugh Diary; Joseph Scroggs Diary.

University of Illinois, Tighlman H. Jones Correspondence and Diary.

University of Kentucky, Special Collections: Benjamin F. Bristow Papers; Brutus J. Clay Papers; Dicken-Troutman-Balke Papers; John Fox Family Papers; Captain and Mrs. Leland Hathaway Papers; David Herndon Family Papers; Joseph M. James Papers; John Jones Diary; Kentucky Volunteers, Headquarters, Adjutant Generals Office, Papers; Thomas Robert McBeath Papers; John Means Family Papers; James M. Gill and Mary Gill Collection of Benjamin Bristow Papers; Frances D. Peter Diary; William Moody Pratt Diary; Elder Aylette Raines Diary.

University of Tennessee, Andrew Johnson Papers.

Wisconsin State Historical Library: William H. Baker Diary; William H. McIntosh, "History of the Twenty-second Wisconsin Volunteers," manuscript; Charles H. Dickinson Diary, Twenty-second Wisconsin Infantry; Alfred Glapin Family Papers; Warren Gray Diary 1862-1863, Twenty-third Wisconsin Infantry Regiment; Oliver L. Spaulding Diary.

Index